private property and the public interest

ALSO BY ANN L. STRONG

PLANNED URBAN ENVIRONMENTS: SWEDEN, FINLAND, ISRAEL, THE NETHERLANDS, FRANCE

OPEN SPACES FOR URBAN AMERICA

johns hopkins studies in urban affairs

**center for metropolitan planning and research
the johns hopkins university**

DAVID HARVEY, *SOCIAL JUSTICE AND THE CITY*

ANN L. STRONG, *PRIVATE PROPERTY AND THE
PUBLIC INTEREST: THE BRANDYWINE EXPERIENCE*

ANN L. STRONG

PRIVATE PROPERTY AND THE PUBLIC INTEREST:

the brandywine experience

THE JOHNS HOPKINS UNIVERSITY PRESS
BALTIMORE AND LONDON

The Johns Hopkins University Press, Baltimore, Maryland 21218
The Johns Hopkins University Press Ltd., London

Library of Congress Catalog Card Number 74-24390
ISBN 0-8018-1662-9

LIBRARY OF CONGRESS CATALOGING IN PUBLICATION DATA

Strong, Ann Louise.
    Private property and the public interest.
    (Johns Hopkins studies in urban affairs)
    Includes bibliographical references.
    1. Land—Pennsylvania—Brandywine Creek watershed. 2. Water resource development—Brandywine Creek watershed. 3. Regional planning—Brandywine Creek watershed. I. Title. II. Series.
HD211.P4S85   333.9'162'0974813   74-24390
ISBN 0-8018-1662-9

To the other members
of the Brandywine team,
and to William H. Whyte,
all of whom persisted
in fighting for an idea in
which they believe

contents

THE BRANDYWINE PLAN was an ambitious attempt to develop a politically acceptable way of protecting the water resources—and thus much of the natural character—of an urbanizing area while still providing for a normal amount of growth. To demonstrate the validity of its underlying concepts, it was essential that the plan actually be carried out. It differed from most other land use plans in that its adoption would have been a commitment to action.

This book is an account of the evolution of the plan, of the planners' aspirations and disappointments, and of the response of the people of the Brandywine to the challenges and uncertainties presented by the plan. Those of us who worked on the plan believe that there is a universality to this experience—that this is not just a story of the Brandywine but a story of planning for urban growth in the United States today.

The focus of the book is the six-year period from 1965, when development of the plan began, through 1968, when it was rejected, to 1971, when we returned to the Brandywine to talk to people about the plan and its impact. In addition, the book looks back to the major events prior to 1965 which led us to the Brandywine and speculates about the possible future directions of planning for urbanization of land.

We believed it possible to create a place for people to live at moderate densities without destroying the beauty and health of the natural environment. We chose water as the principal indicator of the character of the natural environment and sought to prove five related assumptions:

1. that through careful planning a normal amount of urbanization can occur without damaging the water resources of a watershed;

2. that people would prefer the land use pattern produced by such planning over conventional development;

3. that in adding up the costs and benefits—hydrologic, environmental, social, and economic—the Brandywine Plan would win by a significant margin when matched against conventional development;

4. that there are legally valid ways to turn the principles of the plan into land use realities; and

5. that political acceptance can be won for the planning principles and for a program for their implementation.

On paper, we proved all of the assumptions leading up to political acceptance of the implementation program. While useful, this was nowhere as valuable as success with an actual long-term experiment would have been. Political acceptance was the keystone of a successful plan. Three critical facts, common to the Brandywine and other urbanizing areas, shape what is politically acceptable.

First, the present residents are the decisionmakers; the future residents, for whom the area is being planned, are not there to participate in the planning and decision process, yet the present residents are a small, atypical minority of the future population.

Second, many of the present residents equate urbanization with deterioration. They are likely to accept, as lesser evils, plans which call for little change and which, as a result, are short-term in character. Incrementalism is less upsetting than long-term planning and seems to make possible delaying unpleasant decisions, although, in fact, such delay often forecloses potential choices.

Third, once urbanization comes, it is the personal profit to be made from land sales, not the overall benefits of one form of urbanization as compared to another, which counts most heavily with the present residents. The desire to avoid urbanization gives way to pressures for down-zoning to raise land values.

These observations lead to the question: what is the most democratic way of making decisions about the future use of urban fringe land? This question is linked inevitably and inseparably to another question: how should the profits from development of this land be distributed? Our experiences in the Brandywine have shaped my response to these questions. I think that the people of the entire urban area, through a representative council of elected officials, should make the major decisions about where and when urbanization shall occur and about what characteristics it shall have. Further, I see no reason why one landowner should be penalized and another landowner rewarded as a direct result of these decisions. The public at large should be the principal beneficiary of land use decisions.

I have chosen to write this book because, as one of the two lawyers on the planning staff, I was particularly concerned with carrying out the plan. The underlying questions about the politics of planning have absorbed my attention for many years. However, the Brandywine Plan was much more than an experiment in the planning process: it was an effort to measure public preferences and attitudes in advance of planning; it was an integration of water resource and urban development planning; it was a preliminary attempt to measure the values of various mixes of urbanization and open space.

Many people influenced the plan's final form; a few were involved from the beginning. Robert Coughlin, John Keene, Luna Leopold, and Benjamin Stevens shared with me all of the planning decisions as the other principals of the team. Robert Struble and Harold K. Wood, Jr., as staff of our client, the Chester County, Pennsylvania, Water Resources Authority, and as the local voice of the project, were key figures. Other participants—supporters and opponents from the Brandywine watershed, technical advisors, staff, politicians, and financial backers—will be introduced as the story of the plan unfolds.

scenes from the brandywine

I

introduction to a plan

Fateful evening in
East Brandywine

BY SEVEN-THIRTY on a suffocating July evening in 1968, a steady stream of cars was turning up the gravel drive to the old Guthriesville School and Lyceum Society, now the East Brandywine Township municipal building. Soon the small parking area was full, and the cars bumped slowly over the ground to the field beyond. In the still, humid air, dust rose slowly and hung suspended in the late, hot rays of the sun. People headed toward the old wooden schoolhouse, pausing to chat anxiously with a friend or neighbor. A few had gathered to caucus under a tree; their voices were loud and angry.

Inside, the single room was ready. Ranks of wooden chairs were split by a center aisle. Up front on the stage two chairs and a table awaited the arrival of the speakers. The strong, bare lights made the room even hotter than it was outside. Insects poured through the open windows, drawn by the heat and light.

Long before the eight o'clock starting time all of the chairs were taken, standees filled the back of the room and the entrance hall, and the windows framed others crowded together outside.

People had come to the meeting to say what they thought about a plan for their watershed. For some two years the Water Resources Authority of Chester County, Pennsylvania, had been working on a plan to protect the water resources of the Upper East Branch of Brandywine Creek. Now the Brandywine Plan was finished, and the residents of the eight townships which would be affected by it were being asked whether they approved of the plan and wanted to see it carried out. Long before the East Brandywine Township meeting, the Brandywine Plan had become highly controversial. The reasons why this was so and what the controversy says about the planning process will soon unfold.

The East Brandywine meeting was where the fate of the plan was likely to be settled. East Brandywine was the home of most of the violent opponents of the plan and of their leader, Harry Simms, a man with seemingly bottomless stores of energy and epithets to pour into the fight. It seemed unlikely that East Brandywine would endorse the plan, but, until the meeting ended, no one would know exactly how

Private property and the public interest

the scales were tipped. The supervisors of the other seven townships, each weighing a decision, might well see in the East Brandywine meeting some measure of the extent and character of objections to the plan. The Chester County commissioners, who would make the ultimate decision to adopt or reject the plan, were also watching East Brandywine. Their chairman, Theodore Rubino, was there that night to feel the local pulse.

Bob Struble, the director of the Water Resources Authority, would present the plan. He had arrived early to set up his slide projector and screen and to greet people. For everyone, friendly or hostile, he had a warm smile and firm handshake. It was going to be a long and stormy evening and Bob would be under fire for much of it, but he showed no sign of strain. However, Ken Wood, field man for the Brandywine project, was visibly concerned. He knew almost everyone in the room. He had been to see most of the landowners, some of them more than once. Now, anxiously, he was tallying those present who favored and who opposed the plan. He knew that the opposition leaders had organized a turnout for the meeting and had briefed their followers on who was to say what.

Promptly at eight, Carl Maenak, chairman of the Regional Planning Commission of the Upper Brandywine Watershed, took his place on the stage and called the meeting to order. The Regional Planning Commission had been formed in the spring of 1968 by opponents of the Brandywine Plan. Its first demands were that the county Water Resources Authority should cease all activity in the watershed and that it should cede to the new commission the role of organizing and running the hearings on the Brandywine Plan in the eight townships affected. The Authority agreed, except for hearings in two townships which had already been arranged between the Authority and the township supervisors.

Since this was the Regional Planning Commission's meeting, Carl Maenak set the ground rules. Bob Struble would have thirty minutes to present the plan. Next he, Maenak, would state the position of the Regional Planning Commission. There would be no rebuttal by Bob Struble. The floor would then be open for questions and comments from members of the audience who lived in the township. Ken Wood and the rest of us from the Authority and its planning consultants were not to be allowed to speak or answer questions. Bob would answer only those questions directed to him by Maenak.

Bob accepted these constraints and began his presentation. All landowners had received a copy of the plan in the mail, and he now reviewed it carefully. He showed slides of the mostly rural Upper East

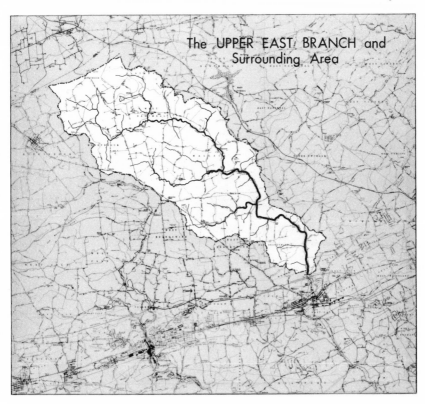

The UPPER EAST BRANCH and
Surrounding Area

Branch of Brandywine Creek: the fertile, well-cared-for farms; the springs where the river rises; the small tributaries bubbling through the woods; the rolling uplands; the broad meadows along the main stem; the handsome, dignified farmhouses and barns; the winding roads and stone bridges; horses and cows grazing and ducks on a pond; and a boy fishing.

Then he showed some of the changes which the population pressure from nearby Philadelphia already had brought to the Upper East Branch: a trailer camp, a new subdivision, a field filled with junked cars, a gash through the woods for a high tension line, industrial wastes dumped into the stream. He showed pictures of apartment complexes, shopping centers, and industrial parks being built just outside the Upper East Branch watershed.

Next he showed what development can do to a healthy watershed: how erosion from building, road, and utility sites can choke the

Private property and the public interest

streams; how both flooding and drought can increase after cutting of woods and paving and storm sewering; how building without proper sewage treatment leads to polluted wells and streams.

Bob then stated the aim of the Brandywine Plan: to make room for normal growth without impairing the flow, the quality, or the character of the Brandywine. To achieve this, development would be channeled into certain areas and excluded or limited in others, called the critical areas. The critical areas included the flood plains, buffers along all streams, steep slopes, and woods. On the flood plains and three hundred feet back from all streams, the plan recommended no further development. On the steep hillsides and in the woods, development at a density no greater than one house for every four acres could be allowed. Everywhere else, development of any type and denisty preferred by the township could take place, but the plan emphasized that it must be contingent on proper water supply, sewage disposal, and erosion and water runoff control, and proposed means of providing these facilities. Since this aspect of the plan had not aroused controversy, Bob did not include it in his presentation.

Until this point, Bob had been talking about how the land should be used in order to protect water resources. Now he reached the sensitive question: how to achieve such land use. Because denying landowners some or all of the right to develop their land would cause it to drop in value, the Water Resources Authority would offer to buy the right to build on land in critical areas. For these easements the authority would pay the difference between the current market value of the land and its value after some or all of the right to build had been removed. The owners would continue to hold fee title to the land and could sell or dispose of it as before—but not for any development prohibited under the easement.

He went on to say that the Authority members believed that the plan could not succeed in protecting the water resources of the Upper East Branch unless owners of almost all of the critical areas participated. For this reason, the Water Resources Authority initially had proposed to use its power of eminent domain in those instances in which landowners refused to sell easements voluntarily. However, during the course of developing the plan, it had become clear that the area residents were overwhelmingly opposed to use of eminent domain. Therefore, the Authority, if authorized to go ahead, would forgo eminent domain and would attempt to carry out the plan through voluntary agreements. Renouncing eminent domain had created a serious problem. The Ford Foundation, the state, and the federal government had all been ready to help pay for the easements because this was an innovative experiment in land use control, but they would participate only if the Authority used eminent domain.

Bob said that the Authority would try to find easement money without eminent domain strings attached and that the staff would then select a sub-watershed—one of the principal tributaries of the Upper East Branch—and talk with each owner of land lying within the critical areas. If, after appraisals and specific offers, people owning 80 percent of the land constituting the critical areas in that sub-watershed agreed voluntarily to sell development easements to the Authority, the plan would go into effect. The Authority would go on to another sub-watershed and contact the landowners there.

Tonight the citizens of East Brandywine were being asked to tell the supervisors what they thought of it. If the supervisors of most of the eight townships endorsed the idea, the Authority would ask the county commissioners for authorization to go ahead and pick a sub-watershed, make appraisals, and contact the owners of critical areas with offers for easements. With this explanation, Bob Struble concluded his presentation and sat down. There was moderate applause.

Several questions probably have struck the reader already. Why would people feel threatened by a plan which gave each landowner the choice of whether or not to participate? If the power of decision rested with each landowner, could the objectives of the plan possibly be realized? How much, per acre, would a landowner receive for easements prohibiting development or for easements limiting development to a density of one dwelling per four acres? How much would the easements cost? Who would pay for them? What would happen to land values in the areas open for development—would people there have a windfall? Why were some people in East Brandywine bitterly opposed to the plan?

Carl Maenak's presentation provided some of the answers, while raising further questions. He was there, he said, as chairman of the Regional Planning Commission of the Upper Brandywine Watershed, to represent the interests of the people of the Upper East Branch townships. While much work had gone into the plan and there was much in it that was good, it had, after all, been developed by outsiders —by the county Water Resources Authority and its professional consultants. The Regional Planning Commission had been organized in April 1968 by local people, not to "oppose outright" the Brandywine Plan but "to save local control" and to protect the watershed from the actions of "some companies." The commission had reviewed the plan and intended to come up with an advisory comprehensive plan for the township supervisors.

6
Private property and the public interest

Planning was properly a local function, Maenak said, not something to be carried out at a remote county seat to which the local people had little or no access. The people of the Upper East Branch already had had their fill of big government planning and didn't want any more; if they needed county, state, or federal advice they would ask for it. Nor did they want more outsiders coming in to take land by eminent domain. The Water Resources Authority already had shown itself to be untrustworthy, cooperating with the state in the use of eminent domain to acquire land at nearby Marsh Creek for a watter supply dam and state park, a project opposed by many residents of the Upper East Branch. Eminent domain had been used by a utility to acquire land for a 500-kV high tension line which now scarred the Upper East Branch hills and valleys. The local people had gone to court to keep out the high tension line but had lost that battle. The state had bought Upper East Branch land at public auction for a prison, and only the most valiant efforts of local legislators had turned aside that menace. Why should the local people trust anyone else to plan for them? Why should they believe that the Water Resources Authority would keep its word and not use eminent domain as it had at Marsh Creek? The local people didn't need anyone else to tell them how to manage their land. They had taken good care of it for the past two-hundred years, and they would continue to do so.

Maenak said that he had worked long and hard to get zoning enacted in his township, and he saw no reason why zoning would not prove entirely adequate to carry out plans for the Upper East Branch. Easements were forever. It would be unfair to people whose families had held on to their land for generations to take away their right to make money from their land. Zoning would be protection enough; it was local and involved no permanent sale of the right to develop.

Turning to his prepared remarks, approved by the Regional Planning Commission, he read the commission resolution calling upon the Water Resources Authority to cease all activity in the watershed, including its small watershed dam projects and the Brandywine Plan. He stated that the commission was in accord with the principles of the plan and that to oppose them would be something like opposing motherhood. However, it disagreed with the action program for the following reasons:

1. there was no assurance of its legality;
2. it wasn't known whether the Water Resources Authority or some state agency would enforce the plan;

3. an undue tax burden would fall on some owners;

4. what would happen if the plan failed?

5. the preliminary assessments were too low;

6. there was no assurance that the utilities would be kept out;

7. the easement might be superseded by state use of eminent domain;

8. local business interests would tend to benefit;

9. the Water Resources Authority had not established a satisfacroty liaison with the local people;

10. the Water Resources Authority had failed to take human considerations into account; and

11. it was doubtful whether there had been coordination between the Authority staff and consultants, the county planning commission, and the county sewer study.

Although the Regional Planning Commission had not yet had time to come up with specific counterproposals, Maenak promised that it would, recommended that East Brandywine and the other townships say no to the Brandywine Plan and produce their own plan through the Regional Planning Commission, and sat down to prolonged and enthusiastic applause.

Now was the time for the audience to speak its mind. Harry Simms led off with a prepared statement pleading for protection of the home against "Big Daddy" government and inveighing against the power grab and use of eminent domain by the state. Over the next couple of hours, as tempers rose to match the heat of the room, there would be several threats of physical violence addressed to the group at large, angry shouts, and general uproar.

It was soon easy to distinguish the opponents of the plan. Most of them were farmers or blue collar workers, burly and rough-spoken. Most had rural roots, if not in the Upper East Branch, then nearby. Their impotence to prevent government actions in the past had scarred and angered many of them. The plan's supporters were mostly business and professional people, quietly firm in their viewpoint and far more aware than the others of the urban pressures moving inexorably toward them. Many of them were comparative newcomers to the Upper East Branch, people who had fled the city and its suburbs in search of peace and quiet.

The basic interest of each of these groups was both identical and antithetical. Both groups wanted to protect their investment in the land, yet the meaning of protection differed. To the opponents, it

Private property and the public interest

meant protecting their right to make as much money as possible from the land at whatever time they might choose to sell. To the proponents, it meant preserving the present character of the countryside insofar as feasible and making a fair compromise with inevitable growth. Theirs was a rational, carefully weighed endorsement. To the opponents, compromise was a dirty word: they saw themselves as continual losers at the hands of government who were now being asked to give up the chance to make the maximum return from their only capital resource. Their rejection was highly emotional; they were unable to see how development in the area would affect them and unwilling to contemplate a partnership with government to carry out the plan.

The comments from the floor, occasionally interspersed with questions, were handled by Maenak. Some of the questions he chose to answer, some he passed on to Bob Struble. The atmosphere was one of mounting rage. Epithets ranged from "this thing stinks" and "you, Struble, and your bunch of louses, don't come near me" to "you pinkos." Each opponent's words roused in his sympathizers a greater sense of the injustices being meted out to them, of being pawns in the hands of government, industry, and other nameless outsiders. Faces purpled, veins throbbed, and voices rose, but Bob Struble refused to be a target for their anger. He remained polite, calm, and conciliatory even in the face of the charge that he was promoting the plan to get rich from real estate investments in the area. The supporters of the plan tried to reply logically to some of the wilder allegations, but it was no time for that sort of discourse. A few supporters charged the opponents with McCarthyism.

Finally Maenak called a halt and asked for a vote. Confusion reigned. There had been no discussion of a vote prior to the meeting. Only one of the three township supervisors was present. Who could vote? Some or all of those present? Any adult among the approximately 2,000 residents of East Brandywine township or among those 1,200 or so residents who lived in the Upper East Branch watershed? Or only people who owned land in the critical areas? Since only one-third of the township lay in the critical areas, and since not all of the residents there were landowners, limiting the vote to this group would further reduce eligibility. Maenak asked how many of the 85 or so people present were East Brandywine Township property owners; some 55 said that they were.

From this point on, the meeting became even more chaotic. Maenak asked that those owning land in the critical areas stand to be counted.

When a father and son, known to be strong supporters of the plan, stood up, the opponents shouted that they couldn't both vote. When they replied that they each owned land in their own name, Harry Simms demanded that each owner get a vote for each separate parcel that he owned. Maenak agreed, and began trying to tote up numbers of parcels per owner. A fence-sitter who had tried to stay on good terms with both groups demanded a secret, paper ballot, saying that open voting was undemocratic. A supporter of the plan suggested that the supervisors mail out a paper ballot, one for each owner of land in the critical areas, since only a small fraction of those owners were there at the meeting.

At this juncture, Maenak abruptly ended the squabbling by asking all who favored the principles of the plan to stand. Eleven people rose. Then he said, "Everybody who wants clean streams, stand." The same eleven rose again, joined by the fence-sitter. Next, Maenak asked all who wanted to go ahead with the easement program to stand. Eight responded. Supervisor McCausland then stood up and said that, on the basis of the count, East Brandywine rejected the plan.

Reasons for rejection

The East Brandywine Township meeting did prove a catalyst in the defeat of the plan. Two of the three prior township meetings had gone very well, and the third had been no worse than a draw. Even though somewhat less than 1 percent of the adult residents of East Brandywine came to the meeting, the virulence of those who came and were opposed to the plan had an impact that spread well beyond the boundaries of the township. Township and county politicians could anticipate the heat that they would feel if they endorsed it. Since those favoring it were not nearly as active or conspicuous as its opponents, rejection of the plan would carry fewer political costs. Further, most people apparently were either unaware of or indifferent to the plan.

By late summer, the supervisors of the eight townships had made their decision. Two townships voted in favor of the plan, and one of these endorsed eminent domain. Two townships endorsed the principles and urged the Authority to work with the Regional Planning Commission to come up with an acceptable means of implementation. The other four townships recommended that the county commissioners reject the plan. The county commissioners accepted the recommendation to reject the plan, and that was the end.

What were the reasons which underlay the rejection of the Brandywine Plan? Was there a basic antagonism to public control of land use? Was there a failure in the planning process which led to the misunderstandings and antagonisms? Or both? Whatever the reasons, was the Brandywine a microcosm of the urban fringe of the United States? Can one generalize from the experience there? My own answer to these questions is an unequivocal "yes."

Attitudes toward public control of land use were the principal issue in the second Battle of the Brandywine. The plan stressed public benefits—a clean and adequate supply of water and preservation of the countryside primarily for the enjoyment of present and future residents of the watershed but also, to a lesser extent, for those outside the watershed. There were important private benefits, too. A person wishing to live in or contiguous to open space could buy land knowing that the boundaries and future uses of the critical areas had been defined and fixed. Current owners of critical areas would receive cash for their easements; they could invest the money in development sites elsewhere if they chose and, at the same time, continue to use their land as before.

However, the opponents made a different calculation. To them, as landowners, the private costs of the land use controls outweighed the public and private benefits. What they considered anathema and thus unacceptable private costs emerged starkly that evening in East Brandywine: sharing ownership of land with government; forgoing the chance to speculate in the land market; and forgoing the chance to seek rezoning of their land for more lucrative uses.

Two beliefs underlay this calculation of costs. First, the opponents believed that government could not be trusted. They did not fear township government because they believed that they could control it. Second, they shared a passionate conviction that all Americans have a sacred right to own land and use it as they wish. To them, the Brandywine Plan was irredeemably flawed on several counts. It called for a partnership with county government, an entity in which they lacked confidence. It called for sale to the county of the right to develop private land at what was agreed to be less than maximum potential development value at some future time. They feared that public investment in easements would lead to greater public demand for control over the development areas. This, they believed, would be certain to lead to cheaper and denser development, flooded with "undesirable" people. They charged that downstream big business, well represented on the Water Resources Authority, would work with government to turn the whole area into a new T.V.A., with a giant reservoir to supply water to business and an equally giant park to supply recreation to busloads of city people.

By July 1968, many people in East Brandywine saw themselves battling to stave off the united forces of socialism and big business. Well and truly had Harry Simms convinced them to "stop the land grab" and to "fight Big Daddy government." Could it have been otherwise? Since Carl Maenak, speaking for the opponents, said that they endorsed the principles of the plan, would a different approach to planning have led either to endorsement of the plan or to a different and satisfactory way of carrying out principles of the plan? Possibly, but probably not.

We planners made many mistakes. For a start, our criteria for choosing an area to work with in developing a plan were faulty. The Upper East Branch, covering 37 square miles and with a population of 4,200, was much too big. We gave too much weight to the quality of the natural environment and paid too little attention to the necessity for strong local leadership supporting the plan. By choosing an area whose residents were a typical cross-section of the urban fringe, we burdened ourselves with an inevitable conflict between their dominant values and those underlying the plan. Later, we overinvested in the technical quality of the plan at the expense of field staff.

The fact that two municipalities did vote to go ahead with the plan suggests that a sounder planning process could have led to success in a sub-watershed of the Upper East Branch. However, the problem of raising money to pay for the easements would have remained. It is doubtful that a preponderance of landowners anywhere in the Upper East Branch would have accepted the original version of the plan calling for the county's use of eminent domain. It is equally doubtful that the county could have obtained funds for the easements without agreeing to use eminent domain. The plan, with eminent domain included, might have been acceptable in an atypical area where most of the landowners shared the values of those who supported the plan in the Upper East Branch.

We could and should have done a better job of involving local people in developing the plan. Could we have avoided conflict with those who became opponents of the plan? Working with them and others, could we have developed an alternative and acceptable way to carry out the plan? Some of the opponents were capable people with talent for leadership; in some cases we alienated them by not identifying them at an early stage and inviting them to participate in develop-

Private property and the public interest

ing the plan. Other opponents were typical rabblerousers who welcomed this chance to vent their spleen.

We planners did suggest alternatives for implementing the plan but failed to make the choices clear. The opportunities offered by a private local development corporation might have been an acceptable and feasible alternative.

The fact that the Regional Planning Commision has proposed a concept very similar to that of the Brandywine Plan but has eschewed recommending any means of implementation other than township regulatory ordinances suggests that a real commitment to realization of the Brandywine objectives is not yet at hand. Since one of the Upper East Branch townships had the dubious distinction, in 1970, of being the fastest-growing municipality in Pennsylvania, if such a commitment comes it is likely to be too late.

We believed that the mix of people living in the Upper East Branch was typical of the urban fringe. Assuming that we were right, it seems fair to conclude that any plan for urbanization which called for greater public benefits at the expense of reduced private benefits for some current residents would have encountered strong opposition.

how it all began

To UNDERSTAND why we were in the Brandywine Valley at all, one could look back some thirty years to Great Britain's Uthwatt and Barlow reports.[1] The fundamental issue raised and discussed so perceptively there was one of those which most concerned us in the Brandywine: to what extent should the public share in the gains or underwrite the losses in land values resulting from government actions? The greatly expanded role of government in planning and development has made the problem increasingly urgent in both Europe and the United States. American attitudes toward land add to the complexity of the issue in this country and, thus far, have led to a government response different from that in much of Europe. Between Barlow and the Brandywine there have been many efforts to shift to the general public some of the benefits accruing from development. Some of these experiences were in our minds as we formulated the ideas that underlie the Brandywine Plan.

The development value conundrum

If government intervenes to influence development, its action will raise or depress land values. In the abstract, most people would say that it is wrong for government to give a windfall to some landowners while stripping others of their investment. If there were in fact a public consensus that this is unfair, then government would be obligated to find a way to counterbalance the effects of its actions on land values. But opinions change when one shifts from an abstract statement to reality: people object vigorously to a government-created loss but cling tenaciously to a government-created gain. Recognizing this, planners long have sought to modify a strictly rational system of distribution of gains and losses to accommodate to some degree the human desire to profit from land speculation. One problem is how to develop a scheme which is politically palatable yet evens out inequities to some degree. A second and related problem is how to devise a method of distinguishing government-caused changes in development values from changes induced by private market actions. Both problems have proven thorny indeed.

Private property and the public interest

The initial approach by the British government to what it called "compensation and betterment"[2] was the nationalization of development values, subject to government compensation for accrued development value in properly established claims. People wishing to develop were then to buy development rights from the government while buying land from the private owner at its existing use value. Government income from sale of development rights was used to compensate landowners denied permission to develop. Between 1947 and 1971, when betterment taxes were abolished,[3] successive Labour and Conservative governments experimented with many variations on the theme set forth in the Barlow and Uthwatt reports.

These reports stimulated people in other countries to develop schemes, consonant with national values, to resolve the issue of government responsibility for the financial effects of intervention in the development process.[4] The widespread concern with this problem since World War II is a natural consequence of greatly increased public planning. The phenomenon of rapid urbanization is universal; recognition of the need for public planning has varied with the scale of the urbanization problem and with citizens' attitudes toward government intervention. Nevertheless, one can generalize and say that public intervention in the development process has been increasing virtually everywhere.

In the United States, acceptance of this increased public control has been slower than in most other developed countries, partly due to a deeply held belief in the sanctity of private property, particularly land. Also, many people have thought that our supply of land so greatly exceeded demands for it as to make public controls unnecessary. Yet, despite the wealth and size of the United States, our problems of urban growth are acute. Wealth encourages waste: we bulldoze and burn forests wholesale, we wash away millions of tons of topsoil, and we lay thousands of miles of roads, pipes, and cables to splatter single-family subdivisions across the countryside. We subdivide our most productive orange groves and truck gardens and then fertilize, grade, and irrigate poorer lands to replace them. During our vast postwar building boom we took for granted our reserves of land, air, and water. We saw no reason for government intervention. In Europe, where nations were worried about vanishing open land and diminishing natural resources, experiments were made, through public planning, with many types of public control of land use, including new towns programs, compensation and betterment, tax and investment incentives, and public assembly of land. Meanwhile, we built and sold, and built some more, urbanizing some million acres of land each year.

Gradually our profligacy caught up with us. We began to recognize that our resources are not boundless after all, and that squandering them has immediate as well as delayed costs. Europeans used to look to us and envy us the American dream house in the suburbs. We thought that Europeans were old-fashioned, inefficient, and non-market-oriented. Now, both they and we see that there are nightmarish aspects to the suburban dream. The cost of encouraging middle-class anarchy in the suburbs is social and fiscal bankruptcy there and in the cities.

The social costs include homes that are segregated by income and by race. Education is separate, unequal, and inadequate. The welfare rolls are huge. Communications are chaotic and deteriorating. The promise of the Congress in 1946 that every American family would be provided a decent home and suitable living environment now seems sheer hypocrisy to many. Our postwar development policy surely has contributed to today's bitter, divided society.

There are economic costs as well: the upward spiral of suburban real estate taxes to service inefficient, inadequately equipped development; the death throes of the center city as it loses its tax base and so provides ever poorer services; the bankruptcy of mass transit; the billions of dollars spent for dredging, flood control, and dams "needed" because of heedless development; and the untold billions to be spent in future to rid land, water, and air of our wastes. Now, to many, widespread planning and intervention by the federal government and the states seems inevitable and essential, if regrettable.

If these issues seem far removed from the Upper East Branch of Brandywine Creek, they are not. We planners went there believing that the public interest in the protection of natural resources for to-day's and tomorrow's citizens took priority over some of the rights of individuals. We thought that clean water, fresh air, quiet, and beauty belonged to the community, and that the community was entitled to preserve them. We thought that the definition of "community" should be broad enough to assure a voice to future residents. Our goals required joint public action for their fulfillment. When a Brandywine farmer said, "My grandfather didn't need government to tell him what to do with his land. What was good enough for him is good enough for me," he was voicing a sentiment traditionally American. On the other hand, when his neighbor, a corporation lawyer, said, "If we want to save this countryside we all love, we've got to be in this thing together. I'm for the plan only if the county will use eminent domain," he was

Private property and the public interest

recognizing a newer truth. What each owner does with his land inevitably affects the use and value of nearby land. If he develops his land without concern for wastes or flooding or his neighbors' view, he profits at the expense of others. Conversely, if he continues to farm the land, others benefit at his expense. If we value efficiency and beauty highly, achieving a fair plan for all demands some sacrifice of individual autonomy.

Government actions already are the principal influence on the distribution of land values and land use. For instance, suburban land rezoned from agriculture to apartments will rise in value even if the owner continues to farm it. At least temporarily, he is foregoing the gain from sale for apartment development, yet because the land has a development value, his tax assessment will rise. If others nearby develop their land, the farmer will face rising taxes for public services he does not need. Should he be charged? Alternatively, should others be entitled to public services whenever they choose to develop? Should those developing keep all the gains brought about by rezoning? Is the rezoning intended by government to pressure the farmer to develop? Should he be penalized for failing to develop? If government stacks the deck in favor of the developers, is this a direct reflection of public attitudes?

The Barlow and Uthwatt reports took the view that government planning did not alter the total value of all land for development (the global value) but did markedly alter the distribution of land values. They argued that government should pocket the gains and make up the losses occasioned by its planning and investment decisions. Roads and interchanges, water and sewer lines, defense contracts, dams and power projects all trigger changes in land values. The cost of these public investments is distributed among the public at large. Should the profits be skewed in the direction of a few lucky landowners? There is nothing in U.S. law that prohibits this, and it is, in fact, the normal outcome. Yet our law has a lack of symmetry; it does not allow government, by its actions, to depress land values substantially without compensating the landowner.

If government owned land in urban areas and sold the rights to use or develop it, the problem of who pays for and who benefits from the unequal distribution of development rights would disappear. In western Europe, public land ownership has been much more widely used than in the United States to capture for the public the increase in the value of land as it shifts from rural to urban uses. Public ownership of new town sites and of land on the urban fringe is common. In the

United States 40 percent of the land is publicly owned, but most of it is remote from urban areas. An attitude of national reverence for private land ownership has impeded new public acquisitions in urban areas. Only for urban renewal, where government subsidizes land costs, or for public facilities such as schools, municipal buildings, parks, or public housing, where there is no development profit, has the public accepted government ownership of urban land.

Tailoring land law to American values

Land use lawyers and planners in the United States have watched the British compensation and betterment experiments and the other European forays in urban land use controls with keen interest and not a little envy. Gradually, in this country, increasing numbers of people have acknowledged the need for some planned government intervention in the development process. Still, we remain more committed than the Europeans to permitting the individual to profit from development, even though this profit comes out of the pockets of the general public. Within this context lawyers and planners have come up with a sizable number of proposals which stop short of full public ownership of development land, yet achieve some redistribution of development gains from land or give some financial relief to the owner who is denied the possibility of development. Gradually some of these proposals have been enacted as law and put into practice. Experience with them during the early 1960s shaped our thinking in the Brandywine.

Charles Abrams[5] was one of the outstanding legal thinkers of this time. He advocated public land acquisition followed by resale to private investors for development subject to public plans. He long sought, unsuccessfully, to persuade the federal government to use the existing urban renewal law to acquire undeveloped urban fringe lands, to plan their development, and then to sell the lands for development in accord with the plans. This would have made it possible to relocate many people living in city slums and to achieve large-scale planned development on the urban fringe. He also proposed state legislation which would have allowed public development corporations, or private developers acting in accord with public plans, to use the power of eminent domain to assemble land for new towns and other large-scale development and then to resell it. The innovative and significant New York State Urban Development Corporation law, as initially worded, followed Abrams' ideas closely.

Private property and the public interest

Most U.S. planners have concentrated on the "compensation" side of the compensation and betterment problem. Quite naturally, much of their work has focused on open space, since it is controls limiting land use to open space which impose the severest losses on landowners. William H. Whyte[6] has been, since the late 1950s, the leading proponent of conservation easements. Easements are legal rights to the use of land. The purpose of conservation easements is to protect specified natural values of the land. Such an easement, often owned by a public agency, prohibits the owner of the underlying land from developing it. The landowner retains the right to sell the land, to use it as before, and frequently to use it for many other purposes compatible with the conservation objectives. So long as easement rights are split away from the fee, or underlying ownership of the land, the owner cannot develop it. Therefore, the land, quite properly, is taxed at its open space rather than its development value.

Prior to development of the Brandywine Plan, a number of states had passed laws authorizing public purchase of conservation easements. Many of these laws permit use of eminent domain. The purposes for which easements might be purchased varied from state to state but included protection of water resources, forests, scenic areas, and prime farmland and provision of areas for public fishing, hunting, hiking, and horseback riding. These laws were not just on the books; they were being used. By 1965 the state of California had acquired easements for over a thousand miles of a planned three-thousand-mile hiking and riding trail. In 1952 Wisconsin began to buy scenic easements to limit development and protect the view along the Mississippi River and the highway bordering it. Where development values are not too high, there was evidence accumulating that easements are an economical way to preserve open space not needed for intensive public recreation.[7]

In addition to counseling many states on the wording of their conservation easement laws, Whyte pioneered in the development of preferential tax assessment laws for land committed to open space uses. These laws establish the structure within which landowners and the taxing authorities can strike a bargain. The landowner makes a commitment not to develop his land for a stated number of years. In return, the assessor is bound to assess the land at its open space rather than its development value. Early experience with these laws showed that the land speculator was benefiting as much as the farmer, so provisions were added to penalize the landowner who withdrew from his commitment. Whatever their form, the preferential assessment laws are an inducement to follow government preferences for use of land.

Whyte also deserves much credit for the growing acceptance of cluster development and planned unit development, forms of zoning which permit the government and the developer to negotiate development plans which make the best use of each site while meeting overall specifications for density, types of uses of land, and open space. While no overt compensation is offered the developer, the greater efficiency in construction and ready marketability of such units offers a bonus which has been quickly recognized.

Jacob Beuscher[8] was the prime force behind Wisconsin's long leadership in environmental legislation. He wrote, and shepherded through the Wisconsin legislature, scores of bills granting the state or counties the right to intervene in the private use of land, timber, and mineral resources. Among the rights given the public was that of buying or condemning easements. In addition to the scenic easement program, the state has acquired extensive hunting and fishing easements at very modest prices.

Beuscher, along with Daniel Mandelker,[9] also urged expansion of the use of an uncommon legal technique called "inverse condemnation." A public agency regulates the use of the land, paying no compensation for any loss in land value. Landowners so regulated can demand compensation for the regulation. If a court finds that the government regulation is unconstitutionally onerous, it may hold that the government has in fact condemned part of the rights to use of the land and must pay for these rights. Under some circumstances the government may choose to abandon its regulations rather than pay their cost. Inverse condemnation places the initiative with the landowner to go to court and demand payment for public limitations on his right to develop. Beuscher's and Mandelker's approach gained great currency in 1962, when the United States Supreme Court relied on this theory in holding that Allegheny County had condemned easements near the Pittsburgh airport by its regulations permitting noisy low-altitude approaches and takeoffs.[10] While we were planning in the Brandywine, several states were drafting inverse condemnation provisions for their coastal wetlands bills.

In 1960, Penjerdel (Pennsylvania-New Jersey-Delaware Metropolitan Project, Inc.) made its first research grant to the Institute of Legal Research of the University of Pennsylvania Law School to develop new legal approaches for preserving open space. The Ford Foundation provided Penjerdel's initial funding and thus was involved from an early date in development of some of the ideas later proposed for implementation in the Brandywine. The narrative must now become personal, since it was at this point that I first thought intensively about the problem of open space retention within the American ethos of private property. As the recipient of the Penjerdel grant, I spent almost a year reviewing and evaluating other people's proposals and then working, with Jan Krasnowiecki and James C. N. Paul,[11] to develop a system for retaining private open space and compensating the owner for loss of development opportunities.

Our proposal, called "compensable regulations," assured owners of land planned and regulated as open space that they would be paid for any loss in value suffered as a result of the regulations. Compensable regulations differ from conservation easements in that payment is not made at the time that the regulations are enacted. Instead, a public agency guarantees that, whenever an owner chooses to sell, he will receive a price at least equal to the value of his land prior to the open space regulation, corrected to reflect changes in the value of the dollar. If the sale price on the open market is less than this guaranteed price, the government which enacted the regulations pays the difference to the seller.[12] Just as with land subject to conservation easements, the land remains in private ownership and continues on the tax rolls with no public maintenance cost.

Penjerdel publicized this idea and others through pamphlets, conferences, and committees. The open space constituency in the Philadelphia region began to grow and to coalesce. Penjerdel's Open Space Committee, consisting of representatives of conservation, park, watershed, and other such organizations throughout the region became such a useful means of communication that it remains active today, years after Penjerdel's demise.

Maurice Goddard, four-term secretary of Environmental Resources for the State of Pennsylvania,[13] early recognized that use of easements and other land use controls giving the public less than fee title could stretch public funds to preserve more land in open space uses while also compensating the landowners for loss of development value. In 1960, speaking for the Pennsylvania State Planning Board, he asked me to draft a bill which would authorize the state to acquire easements and other less than fee title rights in land for open space purposes. Although we anticipated some resistance to a bill creating further options for government control of land, we did not expect that it would take until 1968 to secure passage of the legislation in a much revised form. Our experience, matched in many of the other urban states which now have comparable legislation, shows that hostility to public ownership, even of easements, and to the use by public bodies of the power of eminent domain is widespread, particularly among farm groups and their legislative representatives. Underestimation of the depth and extent of this hostility was later to prove a prime error in the Brandywine project.

Another puzzle:
Calculating the value
of open space

Part of the land value puzzle is the lack of a satisfactory system for measuring the monetary value of land to be kept as open space. Open space has both a market and a public value. If it is not easy to determine the former, determining the latter is many times more difficult. Measurement of both values is vital: market value makes possible an accurate calculation of the loss of development value when land is restricted to open space use, and public value helps governments decide how much to invest in preservation of a particular site as open space.

The market value of development land is established by determining the range of prices at which land similarly situated and with similar development expectations has traded hands recently and then making an estimate based on the characteristics of the particular tract of land in question. If land is to be bought in fee for public open space instead of for development, this system works adequately; if land is to remain in open space either by government regulation or by purchase of limited rights, valuation may be difficult. The limitation on the right to develop will probably result in a loss in market value. If the land is kept open by some government regulation, such as wetland zoning, will the law require compensation for this loss? Under what circumstances? How can it be measured? If government has decided that its restrictions on development are compensable and proceeds to acquire an easement, how can the market value of the land as restricted by the easement be calculated?

The principal legal yardstick for determining whether compensation must be paid is given in a phrase which rolls smoothly off the tongue: payment must be made if the private burden of the restriction outweighs the public benefit gained from it. But what is the measure of the burden and benefit? The dollar loss to the private landowner is hardly likely to be greater than the dollar benefit to the public unless one employs an exceedingly narrow definition of public value. Not surprisingly, given the quixotic nature of the principles, judicial decisions are variable, pragmatic, and unpredictable. They provide only limited guidance to governments trying to decide how to proceed to preserve open space and to landowners considering a court suit for compensation.

Would it not be far simpler and fairer if the law were to establish for all land a percentage loss in value which could be imposed by government over a given number of years? Much regulation already causes a loss; what has never been clarified is how great that loss may be. After all, if people wish to retain some right to gain from speculation, should they not accept some limited chance of loss? The loss might occur through zoning, through acquisition of a utility right-of-way, or through taking some land for a street or park. Beyond this percentage loss—perhaps 25 percent—the government would be required to compensate the landowner. Beyond some higher percentage loss—perhaps 75 percent—the government would be required to offer to buy the fee title to the land.[14]

Under current procedures, if compensation is payable the problem is to calculate how much is owed, a process complicated by the uncertainty of what the market value would have been had development been allowed. If the land has been shown on a plan as remaining in some open space use, this knowledge may well have depressed past sale prices, making them unreliable evidence of development value. If the land is not being sold, and if there have been few sales of land similarly restricted, there are further difficulties. Also, what sort of development use should be considered in approximating the market price? The price for industrial land might be ten times that for low density residential land, yet a tract of land might be appropriate for either use. Further, if the land is marketable for industrial use, this may be because government has built an expressway and installed utilities nearby. Should calculation of the loss in development value payable to the owner include these publicly created values? After the estimate of market value has been fixed, it is necessary to determine the value of the land as restricted to open space and then subtract this figure from the market value.

Even these perplexing questions of market value are relatively easy to answer in comparison with that of establishing the public value of open space. Governments need this valuation in order to decide how much money they should invest in open space. Do you value picnic pleasure in number of picnickers per acre? Or fishing value in fishermen per mile of stream? Any such formulation is patently ridiculous, since it ignores the quality of the experience, yet systems of this sort are now in use for putting a price tag on public recreation. There are complex formulas to fix recreation or resource protection values. Flood damage avoided through maintenance of flood plain storage is one such yardstick. The possibility of an increase in real property tax revenues from adjacent development land benefited by the flood plain open space may be considered, in addition to any direct public recreation permitted on the flood plain. Then there are public development costs forgone or diverted elsewhere by continuance of open space uses. For instance, sewers may not be needed because the land can handle the few wastes generated by the open space uses. Other costs may be decreased because of more efficient distribution of open space and development land. Some of these open space values carry price tags in cost-benefit studies; however, the accuracy of the values assigned often is highly questionable because the methods of measurement still are primitive.

The invention of legal techniques for controlling land development and compensating for nondevelopment is constrained by the weight of public opinion and court decisions. Public sentiment might alter considerably, however, if the costs and benefits of development and open space were better understood. If the owner of open space could see that the value of his land as open space plus the money offered to him not to develop equaled the price for which his neighbor could sell for development, his willingness to accept open space controls would increase significantly.

People who own land are determined to get the full value from their investment. They are skeptical about new public controls of open space because they do not know how much money they will receive and whether what they get will be a fair price. This uncertainty has reinforced a natural reluctance to try something new. Lack of experimentation with new controls means lack of data on the market and public values of various types of open space. As a result, governments are reluctant to invest public funds in programs other than traditional ones, such as park acquisition or dam construction. Often we talk about preserving farms and marshes, about the need for open space to define and form a boundary for urban development, and about the restoration of our stream valleys. Seldom do we act. Action was our goal in the Brandywine.

Setting up an experiment

Work on the compensable regulation proposal brought me a theoretical awareness of the legal and economic issues discussed here. It was only later, in the course of writing a pamphlet,[15] that I became aware of how far experience lagged behind theory. That was written, at the request of the Housing and Home Finance Agency (now the Department of Housing and Urban Development), to broaden public understanding of open space needs and of action possibilities under existing or proposed programs. I found a proliferation of imaginatively written, recently enacted enabling legislation providing for protection of open space through a wide range of land use controls. However, very little use was being made of any provisions save those for conventional regulation or public purchase. Between the ill-defined point at which a court will say that an open space regulation is unconstitutional because it fails to compensate the owner for the loss in value which he has suffered due to the regulation, and the point at which the proposed use clearly calls for public land acquisition, lie scores of open space uses which legally can be provided for by some combination of compensation and control short of full public ownership. In most urban states the enabling laws have been passed, and during the 1960s a number of the highest courts upheld them. The right to condemn scenic easements and the right to authorize cluster development, the use of inverse condemnation and the use of compensatory zoning—all have been affirmed.[16] What governments had not yet done, I found, was to experiment with these partial payment, partial control laws in order to gather sound and sufficient information on the value of land restricted indefinitely to open space.

By 1964 I had concluded that the most vital next step for the compensation side of urban land use controls was to test a number of the new legal approaches to preservation of open space in order to learn which worked best in terms of cost, public acceptability, simplicity, and ease of administration. Since many of the most difficult unanswered questions were in the field of land economics rather than law, specialists in that field would be needed from the start to participate in designing an experiment. Fortunately, two very able men were concerned with the problem and eager to participate. Robert E. Coughlin, a planner-economist and a principal of the Regional Science Research Institute, and I had been discussing these issues informally for some time. Soon we were joined by Benjamin H. Stevens, president of the Regional Science Research Institute and then professor of regional science at the University of Pennsylvania.[17]

By the autumn of 1964, Bob, Ben, and I had developed the skeleton of our proposal, which became the Brandywine Plan almost four years later. It was first presented at the annual conference of the National

Municipal League in November. At that time we suggested testing five land use controls:

1. public fee purchase of open space, followed by resale of the land to a private buyer, subject to public easements to prevent future development;

2. public fee purchase of open space, followed by lease of the land for private open space uses;

3. compensable regulations;

4. conservation easements; and

5. installment purchase by the public over a period of years.

We suggested use of public purchase and resale, compensable regulations, or conservation easements for land planned primarily for private open space use over an indefinite time. Either public purchase followed by a lease for open space uses or installment purchase would be suitable for land planned for short-term private open space use, to be succeeded by public open space. The purchase and lease arrangement would provide the public with some income until the land was needed for public use, while installment purchase would permit a public body to postpone payment of part of the cost. Regardless of which control was used, the land use restrictions would be the same: at least ten acres per dwelling, plus stringent regulation of changes in the natural topography.

Because there had been little or no experience with land use controls such as these, each of the five suggested raised a number of questions:

1. What public costs would be incurred for compensation and administration, and when?

2. How would each control affect the private real estate market? What would be the patterns of gain or loss for parcels of varying size, topography, use, and ripeness for development?

3. What would be the tax consequences of each control? What changes in local real property assessments would occur? What federal income and estate tax treatment would be accorded to land subject to these controls and to the transfer of interests in land pursuant to them?

4. What management problems would arise in conjunction with policing use restrictions?

5. How would these partially compensated controls tie in with uncompensated regulations under the police power like zoning or those

covering subdivisions? What criteria could be developed to indicate when the full fee title should be purchased, when these intermediate compensated controls should be used, or when straight regulation would suffice?

6. How could the controls be drafted to make adequate provision for the problems of divided and successive interests of mortgagees, trustees, and lien holders?

Turning to a choice of a site, we proposed that land included in the experiment "be chosen for its natural beauty as well as for its value for flood prevention and water supply protection. Any sample area chosen would be large enough so that it has visual integrity; in general, an area would consist of land on either side of a stream extending away from the stream to the nearest ridge lines. Most of the land would have at least one of the following characteristics: marsh, 50-year flood plain, aquifer recharge, forest, or slope in excess of 15 percent."[18] We knew that we would need the help of an unusually skilled hydrologist to refine this rough concept into a precise prescription for land use that would represent wise water resource management.

We wanted an area small enough to work with, yet large enough to yield adequate information and decided that two thousand acres would be the optimal size. We hoped to place four hundred acres under each type of land use control. Half of the land chosen would have little current development value, selling for less than $500 per acre, while the other thousand acres would have a market value of from $500 to $2,000 per acre. We estimated the cost of the experiment at $1,500,000—$1,150,000 for compensation to landowners and $350,000 for planning and continued research. I had worked previously on open space costs with William Grigsby[19] and David A. Wallace in Baltimore County, Maryland,[20] and in the Philadelphia metropolitan area.[21] This work helped us to arrive at the estimate of compensation costs. Unless the benefits outweighed the land cost of approximately $500 per acre, the public investment would not be warranted. We wished to measure increases in nearby land values which could be attributed to the continued existence of the open space, benefits to the general public from preservation of the open space, benefits from more efficient land use patterns, and natural resource benefits. The objectives of the experiment were "(1) development of the means to measure and evaluate benefits to the public of maintaining private open space; (2) evaluation of each control as to costs and benefits and acceptability to landowners and administering agencies; and (3) assessment of the range of use for each control and recommendations for modification of the form of each."[22]

The idea was greeted with an encouraging display of interest and enthusiasm. A number of local officials expressed their conviction that it was essential to preserve large tracts of private open space and that the political deterrent to such action was lack of convincing evidence of either the public or market value of such open space. Arthur Davis, then deputy assistant secretary for metropolitan development of the Department of Housing and Urban Development and in charge of HUD's open space program, voiced his interest in federal participation in such an experiment. He too saw lack of knowledge about open space values as the major obstacle to use of public monies to preserve open space having a substantial component of private benefit. Maurice Goddard had already endorsed the concept; it was the logical next step toward the open space legislation which he had been advocating since 1960.

Cheered by the interest of these officials, we decided to seek funds to prepare a much more detailed, specific proposal and to look for a public agency eager, and legally able, to join with us in the experiment. It was fortunate that Gordon Harrison, program officer at the Division of National Affairs, Resources and Environment of the Ford Foundation, and I heard of each other at this time, and, from August 1965 forward, we had his participation in our endeavor and the financial backing of the Ford Foundation.

III

the choice of the brandywine

THE PURPOSE of the Ford Foundation grant of $9,660 was to enable us to prepare a detailed proposal for the water resource protection-land use control demonstration and to seek a public agency ready to work with us on planning and implementation. Ford gave us from the summer of 1965 to the spring of 1966 to work out a fundable proposal, to include:

1. choice of a site, with information about its water resources, land values, ownership patterns, and current planning and land use controls;

2. preliminary recommendations on types of land use for the site;

3. preliminary recommendations for land use controls;

4. a description of water resource and open space benefits which would be achieved by the plan and a research program for measuring these benefits;

5. a timetable, budget, and administrative framework for both planning and implementation of the demonstration;

6. endorsement by a public agency empowered to carry out the plan; and

7. tentative financial commitments from public and private agencies to support the demonstration.

While the initial grant did not cover our costs in developing the proposal, it was evidence of the Ford Foundation's interest. Bob, Ben, and I stepped up our own work, hired others to work with us, and talked seriously with public officials in the region about a site. By April of 1966 we had met most of Ford's conditions and had submitted a proposal, endorsed by the Chester County commissioners and the supervisors of seven townships, that we and the county engage in the planning phase of the demonstration. The proposal further provided for funding of planning and research by a number of public and private agencies.

Gordon Harrison did express concern about investing Ford funds in planning without some assurance that the resulting plan would be accepted and carried out. However, the county and township officials believed that, at such an early stage, they could not commit themselves to supporting implementation of the plan. Thus the proposal submit-

28

ted covered the planning stage only, with an understanding that another proposal would be prepared if the plan was approved.

The choice of the Brandywine as the locus for planning was our most critical decision. I have described the people and agencies involved in some detail because an understanding of personalities and relationships is central to all planning case histories. Very early in our conversations, Gordon Harrison told us to keep complete daily diaries because he and members of his advisory committee, particularly William H. Whyte and the late Jacob Beuscher, believed that the political story might well be the most important outcome of the Brandywine project. We followed his advice, and what is recounted here is drawn from voluminous files of memos, clippings, and correspondence. The interpretation is mine but incorporates the thoughts and recollections of the entire team—Bob Coughlin, John Keene, Luna Leopold, Ben Stevens, Bob Struble, and Ken Wood.

The criteria

By the close of 1965 we had articulated our thoughts about the several areas which we were considering as potential sites for the demonstration. Initially Bob Coughlin, Ben Stevens, and I had decided that the principal criteria were the area itself—it should be beautiful land with clean streams; its potential for growth; the enthusiasm of public agencies and private organizations for the demonstration; and the adequacy of government power to carry out the type of plan we contemplated. We then began to look around the outlying fringes of the Philadelphia metropolitan area. Initially we concentrated on the Pennsylvania side, where we all lived and knew people; later we expanded the search to New Jersey.

EXPANDING THE PLANNING TEAM. As soon as we received the Ford money, we hired two young landscape architects, Carol Levy and David Streatfield, to map characteristics of the three major river basins of Bucks, Chester, and Montgomery counties. Some months earlier, before the initial grant from Ford, we had talked with planning officials in the three counties, as well as with Maurice Goddard, about our ideas and possible sites for the plan. Some part of the Neshaminy, Brandywine, or Perkiomen river basins seemed likely to prove most promising, so these were the ones which we elected to study in some detail. If we had an early preference, it was for the Brandywine: we knew the most about it and had the most contacts there.

Private property and the public interest

The basins are large; for instance, the Brandywine covers 330 square miles. At this stage we wanted an overall impression, so we asked Carol and David to map three land types: flood plains, steep slopes, and plateaus. These maps gave us a sense of the topography of each basin and sub-basin and later helped Luna Leopold to arrive at some preliminary impressions about the hydrology of the basins.

Two other people joined us in the summer of 1965. John Keene,[1] who had been practicing law in Philadelphia for five years, had come back to school to study city and regional planning. After completing half of the master's program at the University of Pennsylvania he elected to work with me for the summer. By fall he was so interested in what we were trying to do and we were so favorably impressed with him that we invited him to become one of the principals of the planning team. Bill Matuszeski[2] had finished his second year at Harvard Law School and had worked for several of us at Penn for the previous three summers on planning research jobs. In 1965, I asked him to try to find out what effect open space easements had on market value. Grants from the America the Beautiful Fund and the Institute of Legal Research of the University of Pennsylvania supported Bill's work.

Of the land use controls which we were advocating, only easements had been used widely enough or long enough for evidence as to their impact to accumulate. This was key information. Landowners would want to know two things: what they would be paid to keep their land undeveloped, and whether this would be a fair price given the effect of the land use controls on market value. Bill provided detailed evidence about controls which limited development of land subject to development pressures.[3] He studied four programs, in two of which—Great River Road in Wisconsin and Mill Creek Valley in Lower Merion Township, Pennsylvania—there were enough sales data to warrant analysis. The Great River Road scenic easement program was launched in 1952; the Mill Creek covenant program has been in effect since 1942. Although samples were too small to draw statistically valid conclusions, study of both programs indicated that restrictions severely limiting development had no effect on market value in many situations, while in other cases, particularly where parcels are small, the sales price had been moderately depressed. Bill's report concluded:

there may be a modest depressing effect where the restrictions prevent residential development, and there already is speculation in land for such purposes. Indications are, however, that once this period of speculation passes and the surrounding area has become fully developed with housing, the opposite may be the case. The natural beauty preserved may provide its own assets and raise the value of the properties which share in the preservation. Although our limited data does not show such a trend, interviews with public officials and landowners in Concord and Lower Merion Township indicate that this increment is a very real possibility.

The continued satisfaction of the Mill Creek property owners with their voluntary, uncompensated covenants and the expansion by the state of Wisconsin of its open space easement program were further persuasive evidence that open space land use controls of the sort we were contemplating could work.

Our planning team still had one gaping hole. We were proposing to develop a land use plan based on sound water resource management, yet not one of us had had any training in hydrology. We had come to believe that, if we started by setting high standards for the water resources of an area, we could create the framework for a desirable and efficient pattern of development and open space. We also knew that conventional urbanization had disastrous and costly consequences for water resources: flooding, low flow, erosion, and pollution.

Our early leads in the search for a hydrologist all were dead ends. We grew discouraged, for it seemed that no hydrologist of standing had any interest in problems of urbanization. A few even said that they didn't believe urbanization had any serious impact on water resources. (Today it is hard to imagine that someone would hold such an opinion, but, in 1965 urban hydrology was a field of study whose time had not come.) Finally we decided, with some hesitancy, to write to Luna Leopold, one of the world's outstanding hydrologists. We were pessimistic about his being able to help, for he was then chief hydrologist of the United States Geological Survey, with all of the administrative and research responsibilities that the position entailed. To our delight, he responded at once, with great enthusiasm, that he had been thinking along similar lines and wondering where he would find urban planners and lawyers who shared his concerns. After we met with him and discussed our proposal in some detail, he agreed to become the fifth principal of the planning team.[4] With the addition of Luna, we were ready to refine our criteria for site selection and to look at the land and talk with local people.

WATER RESOURCES. Luna agreed emphatically with our assumption that the water resources of the site chosen should be capable of supporting the projected amount of urbanization without importing water, ex-

Private property and the public interest

porting sewage, or causing deterioration in stream quality. Since we planned to measure, over at least a decade, the hydrologic changes as urbanization increased, this dictated two decisions: the area chosen was to be in good hydrologic shape, unaltered by large engineering works such as reservoirs or channelization, and largely unurbanized at the start of the demonstration; and there was to be a control area, comparable in all respects at the outset, which could be expected to undergo typical urbanization in the near future. In neither area should major engineering works be imminent.

Building a land use control plan around water resource protection suggested two other site requirements. First, the headwaters of a basin should be chosen in order to control land use upstream, since changes there could negate our effort to protect downstream water resources. For example, sewage could come bubbling downstream, consuming the oxygen and killing the fish; eroded soils could cut the stream banks, muddy the water, and smother hatching fish; construction in the flood plains could lead to downstream flooding. Second, the site should be defined by watershed rather than political boundaries, since this was how the changes we hoped to monitor would be measured.

This second constraint was correct hydrologically but probably was a mistake politically. Most people do not think of their land as being located in a particular watershed; they think in terms of their municipality. Later, in planning, our use of watershed boundaries confused many people. Why only some properties and only some parts of other properties were included in the plan was never clear to all those affected. Since decisions about the plan were made by municipalities, it might well have been wiser to include all the land within the municipal boundary in the planning and land use control proposals. Hydrologic research could have been limited to that part of the municipality within the chosen basin's headwaters.

Luna introduced one further requirement: the size of the basin. He said that it would be virtually impossible to demonstrate the hydrologic impact of the plan on a watershed of less than twenty-five square miles. Since we had been thinking of an area of two thousand acres, or a bit over three square miles, this was a dismaying piece of information. If one increased the number of property owners, the cost of land use controls, and the number of local governments involved approximately eight times, the problems multiplied at a dizzying rate. The prospect of working with such a large area seriously troubled the rest of us, yet we felt that we must accept Luna's recommendation. We were, after all, seeking to prove that the costs of the plan were warranted in large part by the water resource benefits to be gained. Therefore, it seemed essential to pick an area large enough for adequate measurement of these benefits.

Looking back, I think we were wrong to do so. I think that we should have asked Luna to estimate what could be measured successfully given watersheds of different sizes—say five, ten, and twenty square miles—and then balance the hydrologic research potential of each against its communications, political, and financial handicaps.

AMENITY. All of us agreed that the area chosen should meet our admittedly subjective standards of beauty.[5] Since the plan would propose keeping substantial amounts of land in open space, the land should be lovely to look at. We favored well-kept farmland, wooded hillsides, and farmhouses and barns typical of this part of Pennsylvania. Also, since the streams would be the focus of the plan, they should be inviting. Most of the open space in the plan would be private. Therefore, much of the amenity benefit would come from being able to see the open space rather than from having access to it. As our mapping became more refined, we indicated where choice views could be seen from public roads. We also noted the locations of junkyards, smokestacks, and weed-choked streams.

GROWTH PROSPECTS. A normal rate and type of suburban growth, starting soon, was what we sought for both the demonstration and control areas. Since changes in land values would be one important variable, we did not want these changes to be attributable to factors other than response to our plan as compared to a conventional plan. Therefore, we excluded any area in which a major new highway, highway interchange, or regional shopping center was to be built and inquired about any other unusual factors which might lead to atypical growth. It was important that urbanization already be on the horizon in the area chosen so that, in a decade, there would be enough change for us to develop valid hydrologic, social, and economic comparisons between demonstration and control areas.

LOCAL SUPPORT. For the demonstration to succeed, enthusiastic local support was needed. John Keene emphasized this point early in our work:

The proposed project will make its impact in two ways: first, a new cultural attitude toward a relationship with a particular geographical area will be created, and second, the natural physical processes in an area will be protected or restored to some desired level. It seems to me that most of the thinking has been directed toward the latter and that the former, which is at least as important, has not received adequate attention. Obviously, it is just as important that enabling legislation be enacted and local municipalities, landowners and residents—or at the least, government officials at some relevant level of government—be convinced of the desirability of the project as it is that the relevant natural resources be developed or conserved. The proposed project requires, in effect, that the values of the present population be changed in order that natural areas may be protected.

Thus, I suggest that a significant part of the proposal and study be devoted to developing, testing and evaluating different strategies for winning citizen approval of stream development and protection. This goes beyond finding the relative costs and benefits of the five land use controls. It involves politics, public relations, and persuasion.[6]

Determining in advance which group of citizens would be most receptive was a chancy business and one to which we did not devote sufficient attention. We were looking at areas totaling thousands of square miles and trying to make a judgment about several factors, local support only one among them. Since the specifics of the proposal had yet to be developed, we saw no direct way of presenting the concept and then taking the public pulse in each of many areas. Instead, we chose to meet with state, regional, and county officials—some elected and some appointed—with watershed organization directors and boards, and with civic leaders where we could identify them. We told these people what we hoped to do, asked how their jurisdiction was currently involved in land use and water resource planning, and sought their advice as to any areas that would be likely candidates for our proposal—and receptive to it.

In Pennsylvania we assumed that we would work primarily with an agency of county government and secondarily with the state: in New Jersey it would be the reverse. The distribution of power is quite different between the two states, with local government stronger in Pennsylvania and state government stronger in New Jersey. Local government power in Pennsylvania is centered at the municipal rather than the county level. However, we thought county government the best locus for our project, for two reasons: first, any watershed we chose, given Luna's twenty-five-square-mile minimum, would include parts of a number of municipalities, and intermunicipal cooperation has been limited at best; second, we were looking for a public agency with large enough jurisdiction to represent potential future residents of the project watershed as well as present residents. This, we thought, would give the agency a broader perspective as to the types of land use for which the plan should provide.

We chose to eliminate some areas from consideration because of the characteristics of the local population—a very difficult decision. We decided to look only for a typical farming transitional area and to reject any area peopled predominantly by gentlemen farmers with country estates. We recognized that these were just the people most likely to welcome our proposal. Their land was not their only nestegg, and they had chosen to move to the country because they valued highly those amenities which the plan would preserve. However, we were committed to picking urban fringe land where experiences in planning and plan implementation would be prototypical. We all concurred in this decision and in fact were strongly convinced that it was correct, even though we recognized that we were markedly increasing the difficulty of our undertaking. Even if we had felt differently, it is hard to believe that the Ford Foundation or federal and state agencies would have agreed to take on the planning and implementation costs of a demonstration whose direct benefits would be enjoyed primarily by the rich and the very rich.

We might have hedged a bit, and chosen an area somewhat above average in income and educational level, yet not an enclave of the wealthy. Picking a population mix slightly biased toward a group which, we thought, would support our ideas could have been a prudent and sensible move. We may have been guided too much by our desire for a demonstration which would be widely applicable, and too little by practicality.

THE LAW. A precondition to choice of any site was that some level of government be empowered to acquire property interests in land for open space purposes. We believed it to be essential that the power not be limited to voluntary purchase but include eminent domain.

APPLYING THE CRITERIA. With all of these factors agreed upon, we began studying our maps, growth projections, and land value data, crisscrossed the countryside in the company of county and state planners, and launched a series of meetings and conversations to spread our ideas and get the public reaction. This process went on for some months. We concentrated on the three Pennsylvania basins—the Neshaminy, Brandywine, and Perkiomen—but in mid-fall we extended our consideration to four New Jersey watersheds and to the area of Tocks Island, a planned National Recreation Area along the upper Delaware River.

Private property and the public interest

We were invited to New Jersey by Robert Roe, then commissioner of the Department of Conservation and Economic Development, and Paul Van Wegen, founder and then president of the Stony Brook-Millstone Watersheds Association.[77] The watersheds which we considered there were the Stony Brook and Millstone, near Princeton, and the Paulins Kill, Pequest, and Musconetcong, all tributaries of the Delaware in the Tocks Island vicinity. The staff of the Delaware River Basin Commission suggested consideration of land adjacent to the planned federal holdings at Tocks Island, and we discussed this idea with Frank Dressler, then director of the Tocks Island Regional Advisory Council.

What were the pros and cons of each area? How did we apply our criteria to reach a decision? Several areas failed to meet one or more of our conditions and so were eliminated. Portions of other watersheds met all of the conditions, some more fully than others. For these areas, each of us filled in a personal evaluation, ranking each factor on a score of 1 to 5. We weighted each factor equally, which I now think was a serious error. Facing the same choice today, I would weight local support equally with the *sum* of all of the other factors.

Tocks Island was the least likely prospect. Ten million visitor days per year were forecast, which meant that the area outside of the National Recreation Area would be subject to tremendous development pressures; many local people so resented the federal presence that any additional outside intervention to control land use could be expected to meet with much hostility; land values would be affected by many factors other than our plan. Further, since the timing of construction of Tocks Island dam was uncertain even then, it was not clear when growth would occur. Of particular importance, Tocks Island was so far from Philadelphia that none of us had any direct acquaintance with local people and their views. The same disadvantages held for the Paulins Kill, Pequest, and Musconetcong. In addition, portions of both the Pequest and Musconetcong rivers already were heavily polluted. The Paulins Kill was a beautiful watershed, but its moderate growth potential was in part tied to the unpredictable fate of Tocks Island.

The political climate at the state level, however, was highly favorable. New Jersey already had a strong law enabling the state to acquire open space property rights of the sort we were proposing. Equally important, there were many capable, vigorous officials from the top down who already had been involved in innovative state-wide open space planning and acquisition programs. I knew and had much respect for Secretary of Agriculture Philip Alampi, an outspoken proponent of state acquisition of interests in prime agricultural land to keep farming alive in the nation's most urbanized state. Thus, there was much in favor of choosing a New Jersey watershed. However, the Paulins Kill seemed too remote, we were unclear about development pressures, we did not know the local people, and it was a long way from our home base in Philadelphia.

The Stony Brook and Millstone watersheds suffered from none of these handicaps and were highly attractive prospects in all respects save one: the beautifully manicured properties were visible proof that this was an atypical, affluent area. This, of course, also meant that land values already were high. Paul Van Wegen lived there and had long worked with other residents to build a local commitment to water resource protection. Going beyond an initial survey to meet with residents of a sub-basin there, such as the Upper Millstone, was tempting, yet we could not overcome our belief that it would be wrong to choose an area in which the majority of landowners were wealthy.

This then left us with the prospect of finding an appropriate sub-basin of the Neshaminy, Perkiomen, or Brandywine, and it was for these watersheds that we filled in our evaluations and added up the score. Luna was not present but agreed with our unanimous choice of the Brandywine. All three watersheds offered beautiful stretches of stream valley, portions of all three were under development pressure already, all were easily accessible to us, and all had good people working at the county level and participating in watershed associations. The major problem we perceived was Pennsylvania law, which was unclear as to eminent domain power for open space purposes. This was a matter which troubled us then and to which we subsequently devoted much effort.

Of the three watersheds, we thought the Perkiomen least desirable. Its more beautiful sub-basins were also those more removed from development pressures. Some streams in areas under considerable development pressure were suffering from algal blooms. Another factor was that the site for a major state park and reservoir was being staked out on the lower Perkiomen. Local animosity toward the state for proposing a recreation facility which would attract "outsiders" from Philadelphia was running high. Pressures on local and county officials to oppose the reservoir were strong and mounting (the assistant director of the Planning Commission later was fired for saying that opposition to the reservoir on environmental grounds was "a smokescreen to keep blacks out of the county"[8]).

Private property and the public interest

Arthur Loeben, the able and astute planning director of Montgomery County, had reviewed drafts of our proposal to the Ford Foundation and had discussed possible sites with us at length. Now he suggested that, given the park fight and other changing factors in the Perkiomen, the county might not be able to help us there but that it probably could in another watershed, the Wissahickon. The Wissahickon presented about the same mix of advantages and the same outstanding disadvantage, from our perspective, as did the Stony Brook and Millstone watersheds, and so we did not give it much consideration.

Choosing between the Neshaminy and Brandywine might well have been a toss-up but for one event which occurred just as we were reaching a decision. The Neshaminy's greatest attraction was the quality of the county leadership, especially in its planning and water resource programs. The Bucks County Planning Department has long had a reputation for excellence which reaches well beyond the Philadelphia area. There was an existing county comprehensive plan with an open space component highly compatible with our ideas. Furthermore, Bucks was the only county we considered with a Division of Natural Resources, staffed with people working principally on water management programs, including flood plain protection, small dam construction, and sewage disposal. Its director, John Carson, is a biologist who, before coming to the job, was president of the Neshaminy Valley Watershed Association. By 1965 he had given ample evidence of an extraordinary ability to get things done through a combination of tenacity, reasoned argument, and innate decency. However, the day after one of our visits with him to discuss likely areas in the Neshaminy, he suffered a major heart attack, and for quite a time it was doubtful that he would return to his job. It was this event which tipped the scales in favor of the Brandywine.

What did we perceive as the advantages of the Brandywine? Were our perceptions accurate? If not, to what extent could further research have corrected them? I believe that we reached two fundamental erroneous conclusions, namely, that the attitude of the people of the Upper East Branch toward the Brandywine Valley Association was positive and that the B.V.A. had many members from the area. Further investigation could have shown the true situation. Otherwise, those factors which we perceived as advantages were so in fact at that time.

Obviously there is a large element of unpredictability which shapes the outcome of planning, and we should therefore have weighted our evaluation heavily toward local support and made an effort to evaluate the political longevity and strength of those holding power. We knew that planning in Chester County lagged considerably behind that in the other suburban counties, and we knew that this was a reflection of the county's political conservatism. In my own Chester County township I had seen the conflict between advocates of planning and zoning and those who believed they were the first step on the road to communism and who fought bitterly against them. Yet much had changed in the early 1960s. Along with my township, most others in the county had adopted zoning and had established planning commissions, usually in that order. Rapidly increasing urbanization convinced many people that regulation of land use was essential. Thus, while we ranked the Brandywine below the Neshaminy and Perkiomen in this respect, we concluded that it was changing fast and in a direction which we thought was favorable to our project. Further, we had considerable confidence in all three of the county commissioners.

The most apparent advantage of the Brandywine watershed is its exceptional beauty. The soil is rich, and the wooded hills, contour-plowed fields, farm ponds, and bottom land pastures are visible evidence of respect for the land's capabilities. Substantial credit for this often is given to the Brandywine Valley Association. Founded in 1945, the B.V.A. is one of the older watershed associations in the country. Through Clayton Hoff, its first director, and Bob Struble, long-time staff member and director since 1963, the B.V.A. has worked for wise use of land and water. It has a large membership, and its staff is known for its efforts to promote soil conservation, minimize flooding, and improve water quality. Bob Struble's many enjoyable and persuasive slide talks to farmers, school children, and civic groups, the field trips he led, and his work with individual farmers to plan use of their land had made him familiar and popular throughout much of Chester County. It was our awareness of the reputation of the B.V.A., and of Clayton Hoff and Bob Struble personally, that led us to a major mistake in evaluating the Upper East Branch watershed.

There were a number of sub-watersheds of the Brandywine which would have been suitable but less desirable: some had streams which were overfertilized from intensive cattle grazing; some were farther from development pressures; some already were undergoing moderate development, with accompanying rises in land prices; and some were held in large estates, including one cattle ranch of ten thousand acres! What it simply did not occur to us to ask Bob was whether the B.V.A. was active in the Upper East Branch and whether many of its ordinary members and at least some of its board members lived there. We assumed this, and therefore assumed that the B.V.A. would be a major help to the project no matter what section of the Brandywine we might pick. Even when we met with the B.V.A. projects committee and then with the board to obtain endorsement of our proposal, we did not inquire further into the geographic reach of the organization. Much later, when we were committed to the Upper East Branch, we learned that our assumptions were wrong.

We did look with reasonable care at other aspects of the Upper East Branch. Field visits showed the stream to be in excellent condition almost everywhere. The only plans for altering its flow were for two small dams, Supplee and Barneston, one designed for fishing and flood control and the other for flood control only. Land acquisition was under way for a large water supply and flood control reservoir and state park on Marsh Creek, a tributary of the Upper East Branch. This had no hydrologic implications for us, since Marsh Creek joins the Upper East Branch below the area we had picked out. However, part of the park surrounding the reservoir would be in the Upper East Branch basin. The presence of Marsh Creek did have political implications. The project is a joint venture of the state, specifically, of the department headed by Maurice Goddard, and of the Chester County Water Resources Authority. Bob Struble, in his capacity as executive director of the Water Resources Authority, had handled land purchase and condemnation at Marsh Creek. He told us that there was a residue of antagonism among local residents toward both the county and the state for coming there to build both a dam and a park and for taking land either by condemnation or the threat of it.

Land values in the Upper East Branch varied widely, from $50 to $4,000 per acre, with an average of $550. This gap reflected the great disparity in development pressures within the basin, which was ideal for our test of land use controls under different land value conditions. While growth was imminent, the lack of an expressway or major highway made it unlikely that any regional shopping centers or large industrial parks would be built. One non-rural intrusion had occurred. Eight gas pipelines had been laid across the watershed, and a right of way for a 500-kV high tension line was being acquired. Local groups recently had lost court battles to keep out the high tension line and one of the gas pipelines. We recognized that the feelings engendered by these utility fights and by opposition to the nearby Marsh Creek project would handicap our efforts, yet there seemed to be no watershed on the fringe of development in which comparable or greater struggles with the forces of change had not occurred.

Meetings which our group held with the Chester County commissioners, the county Water Resources Authority members, the county planning commissioners, and their staffs and solicitors concluded with a request from all three groups that we choose the Upper East Branch or another site in Chester County. Some individuals expressed reservations about the potential use of eminent domain or about the political heat that the project would generate. Jospeh Munshower, long-time executive secretary of the County Planning Commission, was one person who spoke out frankly. He said that he agreed that the demonstration should be tried somewhere, but why couldn't we find a place other than Chester County? For the most part, however, response from county officials was encouraging. Thus we decided that the Upper East Branch, along with the adjacent Pickering Creek as a control area, was our first choice.

Adequacy of the law

While evaluating prospective sites, John and I had been reviewing the enabling laws which empowered various public agencies to carry out a program of acquisition of rights in land such as we were proposing. As already mentioned, New Jersey law was altogether satisfactory.

Pennsylvania law was not as explicit as we thought desirable. While it could be said that the law was broad enough to cover what we contemplated, there was no precedent to reassure us. We decided to work hard for passage of revised versions of the open space bills I had previously written for Maurice Goddard and the State Planning Board. By the time it became clear that we would have only a partial success with this legislation, we were rather firmly committed to the Upper East Branch. We had felt under pressure to make a site decision before some of the key facts were known. Our commitment to Gordon Harrison to present a proposal to Ford by spring of 1966 was a continuing goad to us.

Still uneasy about Pennsylvania law, we explored the possibility that the Delaware River Basin Commission could act as the public agency for planning and implementation. This suited the D.R.B.C. but not Chester County officials, so we elected to stick with the site and the group of public officials already chosen.

PENNSYLVANIA LAW 1965. When we looked at the Pennsylvania laws, John and I found two ways in which the county could acquire interests in land for water resource protection. The County Code and the Municipal Authorities Act enabled the Water Resources Authority to acquire any type of interest in land, by eminent domain or otherwise, for purposes consistent with those for which it was created. The statutory language is very broad, but to our knowledge no authority had used it to buy rights to keep land in open space in order to prevent erosion, siltation, and pollution. All of the court decisions spoke of sewage or water treatment plants, sewage collection and water distribution systems, flood control works, and the like.

John and I consulted with Ted Rogers and Jim O'Neill, county solicitor and solicitor to the Water Resources Authority, respectively, and they agreed with us that while it covered what we hoped the Authority would do, such action by the Authority was highly likely to be challenged because it would deviate so greatly from usual uses of the law. They advised the county commissioners and the Authority that they would be able to go ahead under existing law but concurred with us that the county would be in a far stronger position if more specific legislation were passed.

Unpredictability has been mentioned as a hazard to all planning. Here was another instance. Ted Rogers and Jim O'Neill both were exceptionally able lawyers. In addition, they may well have been the most capable people in Chester County government at that time. Their judgment was widely respected in the county. Having them favor our planning effort was a considerable advantage. Yet when the fate of the plan was decided, Ted Rogers had been appointed to the state Commonwealth Court, and Jim O'Neill, still a young man, had died suddenly.

THE NEW BILLS. In the spring of 1965 I started to revise the open space bill that had previously passed only one house of the Pennsylvania legislature. A number of us, including State Representative R. Lawrence Coughlin,[9] the chief sponsor, decided that I should draft three bills. One (House Bill 1633) was very similar to the bills previously introduced. It authorized the state to acquire fee or less than fee interests in land "to help curb urban sprawl, and to meet needs of urban residents for recreation, amenity, and conservation of natural resources, including farm land, forests, and a pure and adequate water supply." Eminent domain was authorized. If fee title was purchased, the state was required to resell the fee, subject to an open space restrictive covenant, within two years of acquisition. The second bill (House Bill 1634) authorized counties to enter into five-year covenants with landowners to keep their land in farm, forest, water supply, or open space uses in return for assessment of the land at its use rather than its development value. It included a penalty provision for breach by the landowner: all taxes which would have been payable without the covenant, plus compound interest at 5 percent per year, became payable to the county. The third bill authorized use of compensable regulations. It was not introduced because Larry Coughlin sensed that the sailing would be rough enough for the first two bills.

Bills 1633 and 1634 were introduced in the House on July 20, and Bob Coughlin, John, and I began a six-month struggle on their behalf. We talked with legislators, state officials, including the attorney general, reporters, civic groups, national and state representatives of the homebuilders, grange leaders, conservation groups, planners. We researched legal points raised by various opponents. Different groups opposed different aspects of the bills. The homebuilders didn't want legislation which would lead to less land available for development. The farmers didn't want any penalty for breaching a covenant with a county, and they didn't want the state to have increased eminent domain powers. The utilities wanted assurance that they could continue to condemn rights of way across the open space. We drafted revisions to overcome these objections.

By mid-October, after a statewide show of support by conservation organizations including the Brandywine, Neshaminy, and Perkiomen Valley Watershed Associations, the House passed both bills and they went to the Senate. There they encountered the opposition of the majority leader, a rural Republican. Cabinet members, key legislators, and members of the governor's staff spoke with him and with other senators. The bills were on the governor's "want list." The farm bloc, a strong group in Pennsylvania, said they favored the bills but were reputed to be working behind the scenes to scuttle them. I wrote a memorandum to the many supporters of the bills pointing out that H.B. 1633 did not give the state greater powers, since it could already buy fee interests for the same purposes, that puchase of less than fee interests had been urged in a recent opinion of the state Supreme Court which outlawed four-acre zoning, and, further, that the Senate had passed a similar bill in 1961. All to no avail. The majority leader refused to have the bill reported out of committee, and there it died. We fared better with H.B. 1634. Amended in response to a grange request to limit its use to urbanized areas, it passed in January of 1966.[10]

THE DELAWARE RIVER BASIN COMMISSION. In mid-December, when we concluded that the fight for H.B. 1633 was lost, we began to explore an alternative. If the state would not work with Chester County on acquisition of less than fee interests, could the Delaware River Basin Commission do so? A federal-state agency whose members—Delaware, New Jersey, New York, Pennsylvania, and the United States—all have an equal voice, the commission's compact gave it power to acquire interests in land to protect water resources. We talked with Bob Struble, Maurice Goddard, and Gordon Harrison about this possibility, then went to see the director and the secretary of the commission, James Wright and W. Brinton Whitall. Their response was tentatively favorable so long as we did not ask the commission to assume part of the cost. They suggested that Maurice Goddard, in his role as commission alternate for Pennsylvania, propose at the next commission meeting that the comprehensive plan be amended to add the Brandywine as a project. In the interim we were to meet with the other alternates to solicit their endorsement. All went smoothly. Maurice Goddard offered the proposal at the December meeting, and the commission scheduled a decision for the January meeting. With Maurice Goddard we met several top officials at the Department of the Interior and obtained the backing of the U.S. commissioner, who stated that "the Geological Survey and the Secretary were deeply interested in this pilot study and its possible implications regarding controls over land use in connection with water resource development programs."[11]

The commission then adopted a general statement of support, which its staff viewed as authorization to participate in planning the project. It said that the proposal was "a promising and desirable undertaking. The Commission agrees to join with other Federal, state, and local agencies in sponsoring this project and to lend appropriate assistance to it." The staff concluded that a specific commitment to acquire and hold open space property interests, should a court hold Chester County unauthorized to do so, was premature, and could follow later if needed. We were elated with the commission's interest and support and felt fortunate, after the failure of H.B. 1633, to have found an alternate agency with sufficient powers to back up a county program to acquire development rights.

The Chester County commissioners, however, viewed it differently. Bob Struble had discussed with them our request for Delaware River Basin Commission endorsement and the reasons for it. However, when we met with them in February they had decided that they favored Chester County's going it alone even though there were legal uncertainties. They did not want to risk letting a regional agency gain control of what clearly was going to be a controversial project. We feared that neither Ford nor a federal agency would commit acquisition funds if they were not convinced of the legal capacity of one of the participating public agencies to buy the rights in land. The county commissioners recognized the validity of our argument but valued county autonomy more. Our confidence in their personal interest in and commitment to the project somewhat allayed our disappointment. In any event, it seemed too late to reopen the question of a site.

A proposal for the
Upper East Branch

By February of 1966, the conclusion of this first stage of evaluation, we knew that county-level officials and watershed association people were supportive of our preliminary plans and in agreement with our choice of a site. We did not yet know how township officials and local landowners would respond. While we assumed that county government would be our main collaborator—it was the government which would adopt plans, acquire interests in land, and manage the demonstration over the years—county government in Pennsylvania is not so strong that it would act if there were widespread township opposition. Therefore, the next key task was discussion with officials and civic leaders in the Upper East Branch. At the same time, we had to put together commitments to finance the project. The Ford Foundation had requested that a preliminary budget be submitted in January, and February 1 was the deadline for requesting research support from the U.S. Public Health Service. The lead time between a proposal and receipt of government funding is so long that we were anxious not to delay until the next application date many months later. We applied to the Public Health Service in February of 1966 but did not receive formal notice of approval until July of 1968, although we were then allowed to budget funds retroactive to January of that year.

As for publicity, we thought it best to invite the usual news coverage of meetings but not to seek special articles, interviews, radio spots, and the like until we had met with people in the Upper East Branch. The chairman of the county commissioners and the chairman of the executive committee of the county Republican party were of the same opinion.

LOCAL ENDORSEMENT. The first meeting of county officials at which formal action on the proposal was scheduled for consideration was held on February 21. The three county commissioners called the meet-

Private property and the public interest

ing and invited the County Planning Commission, the Water Resources Authority, their staffs and solicitors, and the chairman of the county Republican party. There was press coverage. Copies of the current version of the proposal were mailed out in advance, and Luna, Ben, and I presented it at the meeting and responded to extensive questioning. In brief, the proposal was that we develop a plan for the 37-square-mile (or 23,500-acre) Upper East Branch basin of Brandywine Creek which would permit normal growth with a minimum of damage to the water resources and natural amenities of the area. Our stated estimate was that development should be limited or prohibited on approximately half of the land in the basin—the flood plains, lands adjacent to streams, steep hillsides, and forests. A preliminary calculation suggested that acquiring public development rights on this land might cost $4 million.

Three days later, after receiving formal notice of support from the Planning Commission and the Water Resources Authority, the commissioners unanimously adopted a resolution in favor of the proposal if they received letters of endorsement from the townships affected. The commissioners also voted to provide money to publish an informational leaflet for distribution throughout the Upper East Branch.

The meeting had a very positive tone, but there were three negative repercussions. The chairman of the County Park and Recreation Board, Everett Henderson, complained to the commissioners that his board was not invited and that the demonstration was not carried out under its aegis. The chairman of the county commissioners, C. Gilbert Hazlett, told him that the board had not been included because the plan did not include any proposal for public recreation areas. Getting off on the wrong foot with Everett Henderson was unfortunate because he lived near the Upper East Branch and was a prominent realtor. His initial annoyance ripened into antagonism to the project, which he frequently expressed in comments at public meetings.

The second negative reaction took the form of an editorial in the *West Chester Daily Local News*. David Yaeck,[12] the columnist, voiced the opinion that we should have approached the residents before the county officials and complained that we were outsiders. My reply was as follows:

[I]t has been difficult to know with what group of county residents one should first discuss the proposal, since we felt that no matter where we started someone would feel offended that he had not been the first to be approached. . . . Since it is the county which we are asking to undertake the demonstration, we concluded that it was proper to begin our discussions with the county officials. This we did, meeting first in August, 1965 with the three county commissioners, the chairman and a board member of the Water Resources Authority, and Bob Struble. At that time it was the opinion of everyone that no publicity should be given to the matter until the proposal had been further refined and until we were in a position to say that there seemed a good likelihood of obtaining funds. It would not then have been possible to state which landowners would be affected; even now this cannot be fixed with any precision since the plan would require much further refinement by all local planning groups. . . . As to your comment that we are people "far removed from this area," I would say that one of our reasons for selecting Chester County and the Brandywine is that, since I am a Chester County resident who has been active in the county (chairman of the Housing Authority, former board member of the Housing Advisory Board to the County Commissioners, former vice chairman of the Citizens Committee for Better Housing, former president, now vice president, of the Devon Citizens Association, occasional advisor to the West Chester Regional Planning Commission), I have had considerable opportunity to observe the quality of county government and the calibre of the officials . . . and had concluded that these were strong recommendations in favor of this area. In addition, Dr. Leopold has carried out a good bit of work on the Brandywine in years past and was not only knowledgeable about it in particular but also was enthusiastic about its potential for the project proposed.

The points Dave Yaeck raised proved sore spots with some residents of the Upper East Branch and bear upon a question central to planning: how can ideas formed elsewhere be accepted in a community? We were sensitive to this question from the start. It was one reason for choosing a county where one of us lived and was active in civic affairs. Our main hope, however, was that the plan would come, in fact and in the residents' perception of it, to be the plan of the Water Resources Authority. The commitment and leadership of the Authority members and staff could, we believed, reduce the onus attaching to the plan because outsiders had initiated it. We thought that it would be particularly helpful that two Upper East Branch farmowners were members of the nine-man Water Resources Authority board.

The third negative event was that we planners were contacted privately by two officials who expressed considerable doubt about the capacity of the Authority to undertake a project of this magnitude. The Authority had been created in 1961 to be a sponsor and prime mover in implementing the small watershed work program for the Brandywine. Its first major task was Marsh Creek and, these officials reported, the Marsh Creek project was way behind schedule and in disarray. They pointed out that Bob Struble had two other jobs—he was director of the Red Clay Valley Watershed Association as well as of the B.V.A.—and that the Authority had no other professional staff. The tenor as much as the content of the comments was disquieting, particularly since Bob Struble and we would need the support and help of both of these officials. Further, if they were right, and the time of the Authority board and of Bob Struble was already overcommitted, would they give the plan the active, local support it required? These new doubts confirmed our belief that it would be essential to have someone outstanding work for Bob on this project alone.

The next major event at the county level was a meeting on March 4th with the county commissioners, their solicitor, Ted Rogers, the executive secretary of the County Planning Commission, Joe Munshower, Gordon Harrison, Ben Stevens, and me. Now that the resolution in support of the project had been passed, the commissioners were ready to consider exactly how we should proceed. The question of use of eminent domain was explored. Chairman Hazlett was worried that people would not distinguish its use here from its use by the utility companies. Leo McDermott, the minority Democratic commissioner, disagreed; the arbitrary manner of the utilities and their refusal to submit plans to the County Planning Commission for approval, he said, were what had generated such overwhelming opposition. Russell Jones, the third commissioner, expressed personal reservations about eminent domain.

Ted Rogers brought up the problem of judicial interpretation of the law upon which we would be relying. He recommended that a friendly suit be encouraged as soon as the Authority began buying rights in land so that its powers to acquire less than fee interests by eminent domain could be tested promptly.

Gordon Harrison sought and received a promise that the county would commit a modest sum of money to the project as well as staff services. Joe Munshower could not see the need for this, observing wryly that it would be sufficient responsiblity for the county to be saddled with perpetual responsibility for the property rights whether or not the project was a success. Leo McDermott, a realtor as well as a county commissioner, backed Joe Munshower's argument that the county should not commit funds, but for a very different reason. He argued that the area would surely go up in value and the Ford Foundation would have a success of national significance, thanks to Chester County's participation. However, he was persuaded to go along with the other two commissioners and vote to contribute county funds. We also talked about the need to find someone at once to work for Bob Struble exclusively on this project, and all agreed that the presence of such a person would be crucial to success.

The key decision was that the project should be undertaken in two stages: first, planning, and second, implementation. Because we needed and wanted to develop the specifics of the plan together with the county and the townships, we were in no position to ask public officials for a commitment to implement whatever plan might take shape. No one, including us, knew what restrictions would be proposed for which properties or approximately what a particular landowner might be paid for his right to develop. We agreed that the townships should be asked to endorse the planning phase with the understanding that the commissioners would seek their reaction to the finished plan before deciding whether or not to proceed with the implementation stage.

We were now ready for the meetings with the townships. They all followed the same format. We talked in advance with the professional planners who were consultants to the townships. Then Bob Struble, Joe Munshower, and one or two of us met with the township supervisors and planning commission members. In some townships the supervisors also invited certain residents, such as a realtor, a large landowner, or a member of some county board. Sometimes the planning consultant was invited.

Joe Munshower's presence at these meetings was no accident. He was there as the eyes and ears of the county commissioners. Two people told us that the commissioners wanted him to evaluate the political risk the project was likely to entail. His political sense and his loyalty to the commissioners and to the Republican party made him perhaps the most trusted of county employees. He had long been county engineer, and when it came time to create a county planning commission he was the natural choice to run that as well. His conservative outlook and his commitment to the right of the individual property-owner to use his land as he wished were in accord with the views of those behind the scenes who were in political control of the county and, perhaps, of a majority of the residents. I had known Joe Munshower for a decade and liked and respected him for his fairness, candor, and consistency, even though we disagreed wholeheartedly on fundamental planning issues. Bob Coughlin, too, had known him for many years. We hoped that his love for rural Chester County and his appreciation of the speed at which it was changing would lead him to reevaluate his opposition to the land use controls we proposed.

At each township meeting one of the planning staff presented the proposal and then engaged in lengthy discussion. Some of the comments and questions about the plan recurred frequently. People wanted to know exactly where the boundaries of the land to be kept open would be drawn. We responded that we did not know yet, that this was one of the major planning tasks in which we wanted their help. Bob Struble repeatedly suggested choosing a farm, taking people out on it, and actually staking out the areas where development would be restricted. We agreed that it would make the plan come alive for people but said that it was premature. We very much wanted to avoid giving a public definition of open space areas which we might later have to change. Bob, on the other hand, wanted to be able to give specific answers when asked about the plan. Also, he said that he suspected that we had more land in mind than he did.

Township officials agreed that a leaflet to all residents describing the project would be a good idea as a start. They recommended telling people who was putting up the planning money and who would pay for the development rights in order to dispel any air of mystery.

People who owned flood plain land were upset by the notion that no further building should occur there. This was one type of land about which we were ready to make a specific statement, so it is not surprising that this recommendation drew the most specific and negative questions. Several people offered the opinion that they could get more money for their flood plain land as a building site than any appraiser ever would award them.

Some people were concerned that there would be no way to protect the open space from later condemnation by the utilities or the state highway department. Recalling our struggles with the utility lobbyists in the fall over the proposed open space legislation, we agreed that this was a serious problem.

Another concern expressed was that the townships would lose tax revenues once the open space rights were acquired because assessments on that land would drop. We pointed out that, since farmland in Chester County was assessed at farm rather than development value, there should be no change in those assessments. This, we were to learn, was a statement that few landowners would believe. They were convinced that their taxes were too high and that it was because they were being assessed at development value.

Joe Munshower urged at these meetings that we keep the best farmland as open space and put the development on the hilly, wooded, or boggy lands. His preference gave voice to a real dilemma. We all wanted farming to continue, yet the plateaus which were best for farming were also the areas where development would be least hazardous to water resource protection. They were also the areas of highest development value. Acting through the Water Resources Authority under the existing legislation, water resource protection was the only justification we could advance for purchase of development rights.

Furthermore, we were committed to allowing a normal amount of growth. If we were to propose keeping open both prime agricultural land and land most critical to water resource protection, where would all the new people live? Since we knew that, wherever it had been proposed, people in the county had reacted very negatively to cluster zoning or planned unit development, that did not seem to offer a solution.

A few people asked whether accepting federal funds for this project would give the federal government a foot in the door for other programs, especially dams and subsidized housing. We said no.

Some people asked what would happen if the Water Resources Authority failed to enforce the development restrictions or tried to sell off the property rights it had acquired. We answered that the Ford Foundation and the public agencies which put up acquisition money would have the right to prevent this and could be counted on to assert that right to protect their investment.

Zoning was a frequent topic. Most people said that they wanted to keep land in farming, and many thought that large-lot zoning was the way to do this. We predicted that the courts would not uphold such zoning. Bob Struble was worried about this statement because several of the townships either had just adopted zoning or were about to do so. In some townships there had been much opposition to zoning as a socialistic interference with property rights. The major motivation for enacting zoning had been to keep land open, and so most of the land was zoned for large lots. Bob cautioned us against criticizing zoning because a number of the supervisors and planning commission members had had to overcome tenacious opposition to get it passed.

In sum, the township reactions were cautiously favorable. Naturally, people wanted to know more than we were yet in a position to tell them. There was, however, a general concern about protection of the countryside and a receptive attitude toward our proposals. Several large landowners called or wrote to Bob Struble or me expressing their strong support. All townships wrote to Bob supporting the objectives we had put forth and endorsing the planning stage. Several letters added the caveat that the supervisors would need considerably more information before they would know whether or not they favored implementation of the plan.

BACK TO THE COUNTY. Bob Struble presented the letters to the Water Resources Authority, which unanimously passed the following resolution: "Be it hereby resolved that the Water Resources Authority recommends that the County proceed with the necessary applications to obtain funds from the federal government and the Ford Foundation for planning the open space project, and that the County expend an amount up to $20,000 as their share of the planning stage of approximately 15 months." The question of the duration of the planning phase was one on which we differed. Gordon Harrison initially wanted to limit it to nine months, while most of us believed that more time was needed to establish working relationships with people in the Upper East Branch and then to agree on the details of the plan. At this point in the negotiations we compromised on twelve months. Later, after a detailed review of the work to be done, it was extended to eighteen months.

The Authority members concurred with us that it was time to hire someone to work for Bob. We said that we would try to find candidates but that the hiring decision would be his. We thought that the ideal person would have a background of success in conservation and in rural community organization and would also be someone known and trusted in the Upper East Branch. We suggested two people, both men with degrees in the natural resources field and considerable practical experience. Both had roots in the Philadelphia area but not in Chester County or the Upper East Branch. One had spent years working, successfully, to establish conservation commissions, and we recommended him enthusiastically. Bob was cool to the idea, and we concluded that it was because of our backing rather than the man's qualifications. Though he was too polite ever to say so, we were responsible for putting Bob in a precarious position. If the county commissioners and Joe Munshower now realized that there could be political reefs ahead, it was Bob who would bear prime responsiblity for whatever happened. His reputation and his job were on the line. His principal interest was in protecting the lands and waters of the Brandywine; ours was in demonstrating as conclusively as possible that urbanization under this plan was better than conventional urbanization—that people liked it better, that it was more efficient, and that it better protected water resources. In view of all this, we decided that Bob was right to want to hire someone certain to have his perspective, not ours and that we should make no further suggestions.

In mid-April, soon after the Water Resources Authority meeting, the county commissioners voted to authorize an expenditure of twenty thousand dollars on the planning phase and directed Bob to work with us to obtain outside funds. They also directed the County Planning Commission to prepare and file an application for federal assistance for county planning under the "701" program of the U.S.

Department of Housing and Urban Development (HUD). Chester County was the only county in the metropolitan area which had not applied for and received such funds. Concern over the influence that such aid might give the federal government in local affairs had previously deterred the County Planning Commission, but now an application was essential to the future of the Brandywine project.

Officials at HUD had expressed keen interest, and there was a strong possibility that they would provide half of the acquisition funds for the project from the HUD open space program. However, they pointed out that Chester County would be ineligible for the funds unless it was carrying out planning under the "701" program. Bob Coughlin agreed to work with the County Planning Commission staff on the application. He, John Keene, and Joe Munshower met with federal officials and with the state officials who first had to pass on the application. While Joe Munshower was most reluctant to proceed, the state people were enthusiastic and helpful. One commented that he and people in his office found the project "particularly interesting and worthwhile."

At this same time, under Luna's leadership, we began the long process of determining exactly which lands and how much land would need development restrictions in order to preserve stream health. John and I began to develop a questionnaire so that we could survey the Upper East Branch residents to learn how they felt about their environment and community.

Bob Struble initiated meetings with the press to outline the project. He was quoted as calling it "one of the best grass roots approaches to the preservation of a water supply area anywhere in the United States."[13] However, a description of the project in the *Daily Local News*, the paper perhaps most widely read in the Upper East Branch, ended with the following statement: "Park Board Chairman Everett G. Henderson said it was his view that the same plan had been rejected by New Jersey, Bucks County, and Montgomery County."[14] John Carson of Bucks County responded in a letter to the editor: "I can state categorically that the Open Space Proposal was never 'rejected by Bucks County.' In fact, many of us in Bucks County were disappointed when we learned that Chester County had been picked for its initiation. . . . To allow people to continue to own and utilize the land, while preserving the basic resources, is one of the soundest open space programs yet devised."[15]

THE PLANNING BUDGET. The most immediate task was to revise the budget so that it would cover the planning period only and to obtain

Table III-1. Open space demonstration planning budget summary

Item	Water Resources Authority	U.S. Geological Survey	Consultants	Regional Science Research Institute	Institute for Environmental Studies	Total
Predictive model for Chester County				$ 6,450	$ 1,460	$ 7,910
Land use planning and intergovernmental coordination	$13,080			34,185	17,520	70,785
Property surveying		$ 5,500	$ 6,000[a]		6,450	11,950
Appraisal techniques and sample estimates			14,000			14,000
Drafting legal instruments			5,000[b]	5,000[b]	29,200	34,200
Hydrology and ecology		103,400			4,380	107,780
Attitude studies			19,000	2,580	4,380	25,960
Cost-benefit design		7,000		14,190	5,840	27,030
Administration	19,620				7,400	27,020
Publications	14,500					14,500
Miscellaneous	11,750			7,400	7,400	26,550
total	**$58,950**	**$115,900**	**$44,000**	**$64,805**	**$84,030**	**$367,685**

[a] Services by Chester County Planning Commission.
[b] Chester County and Water Resources Authority solicitors, $1,000; outside legal services, $4,000.

commitments sufficient to cover this period. At the same time we were seeking long-range planning research funds so that we could begin collection of data and make studies that would be needed if the plan were implemented. The budget revision, itemizing anticipated expenses and the basis for their estimation as well as individual budgets for each of the participating groups, is summarized in the table.

The $368,000 total was made up of grants of $240,000 from the Ford Foundation, $58,000 from the U.S. Geological Survey, $50,000 from the Pennsylvania Department of Forests and Waters, and $20,000 from Chester County. The Geological Survey was to receive the largest share of the funds because its work on the hydrology of the watershed required installation and manning of a sediment, flow, and quality monitoring system. Luna Leopold's hypotheses about the impact of urbanization on the hydrology of the basin required supporting data, and little existed elsewhere in the United States. The Survey's findings, combined with the measurements of the area, slope length, channel length, slope gradient, channel slope, and land use of each sub-basin of one square mile to be made by the planners, would establish a data base to which hydrologists and planners could return in the future to document accurately the effects of urbanization.

We agreed with Gordon Harrison that, if we received Public Health Service support for research items in the budget, the Ford Foundation would deduct an equal sum from its grant. We had requested Public Health Service funds for four areas of research: (1) determination of the comparative effectiveness of the proposed land use controls, (2) evaluation of the political response to the project, (3) measurement of the values which people place on the natural environment and clean streams, and (4) development of a comprehensive cost-benefit analysis.

The grant from the state was to go toward matching the Geological Survey's contribution, since the Survey could not commit its funds without matching amount. We were particularly happy about the state contribution, since Maurice Goddard wrote at that time that his department would also be willing to contribute to the second phase of the project, the acquisition of development rights. With the approval of the Ford Foundation grant in June of 1966, we were ready to work with Chester County and the Upper East Branch townships to develop the plan.

IV

the planners' honeymoon

JULY 1966 found us in a state of moderate euphoria. Planning funds were in hand, the Brandywine seemed an ideal location, and we had the nucleus of a fine staff. Difficult and challenging technical problems soon surfaced, but the honeymoon with the Brandywine continued unabated until early 1967, when the opposition organized. Our task was to get acquainted with the Upper East Branch: to determine what information would be needed, to set about getting it, to evaluate what we learned, and to develop the first draft of the Brandywine Plan. We knew that our task was enormous, given the time available, yet we all were optimistic that we could develop a plan whose goals would be compatible with those of the Brandywine residents and whose means of fulfillment would be acceptable to the Chester County commissioners.

This chapter describes the planning and decision process as we outlined it in 1966, then goes on to give a chronological account of what we actually did through February of 1967, when we published *The Brandywine: A Place for Man, A Place for Nature*, a brochure setting forth our objectives. Since each aspect of the planning process was related to all other phases, and since the entire planning process was tied closely to outside events in the community, a chronological narrative seems best, albeit confusing.

Projected timetables

There were two related timetables: one for developing the plan and one for public decision on the plan. Time, money, and responsibility were allocated for each. We recognized that, as of July 1966, when the Ford Foundation planning grant was approved, planning was out of phase with the most essential aspect of the decision process: public understanding. Some technical experts and, to a lesser extent, Chester County officials had been working with us to develop the initial proposal and, once we had selected the Upper East Branch as the planning site, to relate the proposal to that area. The municipal officials of the Upper East Branch townships had some familiarity with the proposal, having met with us during the winter and spring of 1966. Most residents, however, had never heard of it.

There were reasons for moving as we had from concept to specifics. Nevertheless, our failure to make up this early gap between planning and public involvement presented a serious handicap, one which never was overcome. That the concept came from outside the Upper East Branch watershed was undeniable. Further, there had been no crisis to awaken local residents to the need for any such plan. We had spent several years exploring the concept and had convinced ourselves that it was hydrologically, economically, and legally sound. Until we had done so we thought it premature to try to involve the people in the given area in a scheme which might prove technically impossible. Yet, ideally, the people of the area chosen should have been drawn in from the first stage of planning onward. More and earlier public involvement, even at the expense of hydrologic and economic accuracy, might have been the key to success—possibly the only key.

In our early concern for the technics of planning, we gave far too little thought to the political verities of American life. If we had a demonstrably "good" plan, good in its impact on water resources, good in its response to the expressed wishes of people for residential living and leisure activities, and good from the point of view of a broad public cost-benefit equation, surely some public agency legally empowered to do so would step forward to test it and to garner the data which would be needed to convince the general public. So we thought.

What we failed to comprehend was the depth and strength of the conviction that land is a private commodity. Nor had we grasped the mystical relationship between man and the land that later led a Brandywine resident to say, at a public meeting, "If a man's home is his castle, then his land is his fertility. To take away his rights in the land is nothing less than castration." When the Chester County commissioners later stated that their endorsement of the plan would be contingent on favorable recommendations from the township supervisors, and then when the supervisors of most of the townships turned over the decision to the people, we felt that the procedure agreed upon had been changed unfairly. We were faced with the prospect of winning over some thirteen hundred landowning families, while the municipal and county officials stood by and waited to follow their lead.

Instead of feeling deceived, we should have realized that it would have taken most exceptional public leadership to act in the face of such forcefully held private values. What we needed were public officials who were not only committed to the demonstration but who were also farsighted, elected to office for a long term, and far removed from the Upper East Branch area. Had we realized that this public leadership was crucial, our criteria for choice of a demonstration area would have been different. Without it, our only alternative was to reach the watershed landowners personally and individually. The possibility of doing so would have been greatly enhanced if we had worked with people in the Upper East Branch from the beginning, if we had limited ourselves to a much smaller sub-basin of the Upper East Branch, contrary to Luna's recommendations, or if we had selected a different watershed whose people had different, if atypical, attitudes toward land ownership. (This last possibility we had, of course, considered and rejected.)

The task we faced in the Upper East Branch was to develop a plan which would gain local backing while retaining enough demonstration characteristics to make it a valid land use experiment, deserving of public and private financial backing. From the planners' viewpoint, the demonstration objectives were of national significance. We all believed wholeheartedly that the Upper East Branch of the Brandywine would have a far better future, environmentally and economically, under the plan than under conventional development. However, as scientist-researchers, our principal interest in the Brandywine was as a national bellwether of better urban land use. For the Brandywiners, naturally, the priorities were different: their objectives were almost totally local, and the less experimentation involved the better they liked it. We hoped that our objectives and those of the landowners would come close enough to make the experiment successful. It was through the process of public decisionmaking that we sought consensus, to be reflected in the final version of the plan.

TIMETABLE FOR DECISION. Starting from July 1966, we had eighteen months to complete a plan and attract enough public support to carry it out. This period was satisfactory to Gordon Harrison of the Ford Foundation, to the three Chester County commissioners, to the Chester County Water Resources Authority, and to us, the five principals of the planning team. The time seemed short but adequate for the technical aspects of the plan; after all, for years several of us had been doing research that would assist us in developing the plan. The time for persuading the public to accept the plan was also very short. We had no prior work with the Upper East Branch people to match our prior planning research, and we were aware, although not fully, of the lag time between the introduction of ideas and their public acceptance.

Some county officials, and particularly Bob Struble, felt that even eighteen months was not enough time. On the other hand, the Ford Foundation, as the principal supporter of the project, was anxious to have a decision as soon as possible so that it could cut its losses if the project were not to proceed. We sympathized with both positions but acceded to Ford's, particularly as Gordon Harrison already had extended the completion date considerably. Bob Struble, attuned, over thirty years of experience, to the pace of change in Chester County, acquiesced reluctantly and doubtfully.

Bob was in charge of work directed toward the final public decision on the plan. We favored giving him and the Water Resources Authority this critical responsibility as a necessary first step toward local control of the plan and of decisions about it. Gordon Harrison, Bob Struble, and we agreed that receipt of and responsibility for the Ford funds should be divided between the Water Resources Authority and the University of Pennsylvania. The Water Resources Authority would have principal responsibility for work leading to a public decision and would receive funds directly from Ford for that purpose. The university would have responsibility for the planning funds and would share this work with the Regional Science Research Institute and the Geological Survey.

Once February of 1968 was fixed as the decision deadline, it was up to Bob Struble and the members of the board of the Water Resources Authority to decide what to do and when to do it. To a considerable extent, the Authority members left these decisions in Bob's hands. He was responsible for engaging field staff, for citizen education, for publicity, for committee organization, and for communication with local officials. The Water Resources Authority, on his advice and that of the county commissioners, had decided that our proposal could become their plan. Now it was Bob's task to bring the peoples' views to us and our views to the people so that the future plan would be our plan, the Authority's plan, *and* the people's plan.

Instinctively Bob set a slower pace than that dictated by the Ford deadline. A popular consensus, he thought, could be achieved only through a gradual, quiet education program for the general public. At that time we, and Gordon Harrison, still believed that the decision-makers were the county commissioners, not the landowners. Therefore, we looked to local leaders who would transmit information to and from the public. In 1966, when the timetable was agreed upon, none of us foresaw that not one of the three county commissioners who endorsed development of the plan would be in office when the time for a decision arrived. Bob Struble's intuitive approach to decisionmaking at the level of the individual closely matched the approach of the new Republican commissioners.

One unfortunate result of the difference in pace set by Bob Struble and the planners was that development of the plan continued to be ahead of public participation in planning. The timetable which we had proposed called for a number of steps to be undertaken as soon as possible and *simultaneously,* not consecutively. These steps were: (1) to find and hire a first-rate person to work for Bob Struble as fulltime project coordinator; (2) to publish and mail to all landowners a short, simple explanation of our goals and how we proposed to proceed; (3) to prepare and carry out a study of local attitudes toward the natural environment; and (4) to organize and launch three advisory committees—a coordinating committee of municipal and county officials or their nominees; a citizens' advisory committee of nominees of local organizations; and a technical advisory committee of those people who were most knowledgeable on some technical aspect of the venture. The project coordinator would call on landowners, organize small meetings of neighbors, do staff work for the three advisory committees, and speak to local groups, including clubs, granges, churches, P.T.A.s, and sportsmens' associations. The coordinator also would organize township-wide informational meetings; several of these would be held, one as soon as possible, one on completing a preliminary plan, and one on completing the final plan.

We planned several publications. In addition to the short initial description, we anticipated that the Water Resources Authority would publish the preliminary plan within one year of starting work and a revised, final plan at the close of the eighteen-month period. Other public information would include newspaper articles and radio and television interviews, as well as speaking engagements outside of the Upper East Branch when that seemed appropriate. The attitude study was to be prepared in the summer of 1966 and carried out in the fall, with the preliminary results to be available by winter of 1967 for use in the preliminary plan.

We thought that the coordinating committee should meet monthly so that there would be a frequent and regular exchange of ideas with the township and county advisors. The citizens committee might meet quarterly, or more often if it proved desirable. The technical advisory committee would be called together irregularly, as the planning staff found itself in need of advice. Reports to the county commissioners would be made whenever requested. Their decision on whether or not to seek the funds to carry out the plan was expected to be made shortly after publication of the final plan and its presentation at township public meetings.

By mutual agreement, Bob Struble turned some of these tasks back to us: we organized the meetings of the technical advisory committee, carried out the study of peoples' residential and environmental preferences, and handled publication of several of the Brandywine reports. Otherwise, Bob carried the major responsibility for organizing communication with the people of the Brandywine.

Tables IV–1 and IV–2 show the timetable for decisionmaking as we originally proposed it and it worked out in fact.

TIMETABLE FOR THE PLAN. The timetable for the three proposed publications established the dates for much of the planning work. The initial brochure, which was to be conceptual rather than specific, could be written with the technical information on hand by summer 1966. The preliminary plan, scheduled for spring of 1967, would require collection of a mass of detailed information about the watershed— peoples' preferences, land values, population growth and distribution, hydrology, and location of principal natural features, including swales, springs, and swamps. Analysis and preliminary synthesis of the data would be completed before specific proposals were developed. After people had responded to the proposals presented in the preliminary plan, the detailed work on implementing it would be done.

During mid-1966 the work was broken down into several components, and a budget, work description, allocation of responsibility, and approximate timetable were prepared for each component. Since the attitude study and intergovernmental coordination contributed both to planning and to the decision on the plan, they are shown in Tables IV–3-IV–5 as well as in the two preceding ones.

Several items were to be substantially completed before spring of 1967. A survey of people's attitudes toward the natural environment was to come first. We had already begun work on the effect of urbanization on water resources: our theories had to be fitted to the topography and hydrology of the basin and of the Pickering basin, the control area. Then we had to delineate the areas most significant for water resource protection and make recommendations for their use. We needed to know current population and development patterns as well as future prospects. Putting growth pressures and water resource needs together, we would come up with recommendations for land use controls.

Table IV–1. Proposed timetable

	July 1966	January 1967	July 1967	January 1968	February 1968
Project coordinator	●——————— continuous program of coordination and communication ———————●				
Attitude study	prepare questionnaire ●—— interviews ——●	●—— preliminary results ——● final results			
Publications	●—— brochure ——● ●—— preliminary plan ——●		final plan		
Township public meetings	●—— no. 1 ——●	●— no. 2 —●	●—— no. 3 ——●		
Coordinating committee	●———— quarterly meetings ———————●				
Technical advisory committee	●———— occasional meetings as needed ————●				
County commissioners	●———— occasional meetings as requested ————●			decision	

Table IV–2. Actual timetable

July 1966	January 1967	July 1967	January 1968	July 1968

———attitude study———

———3 technical advisory———
committee meetings

———Ken Wood working in the field———

———8 coordinating committee meetings———

———5 Brandywine Plan publications———

2 citizens
committee
meetings

———4 WRA-sponsored meetings———

———2 non-WRA public meetings———

plan rejected by county commissioners

Private property and the public interest

Between spring 1967 and January 1968 the agenda called for drafting of the land use controls, study of the governmental context in which they would be applied, research into methods of surveying property, studies of water supply and waste disposal systems for the development areas of the basin, obtaining sample appraisals to estimate the cost of the proposed land use controls, and development of a system for measuring the costs and benefits of the project. Much of this work could not be undertaken sooner because its content would depend heavily on the specific proposals of the plan. The final form of

Table IV –3. Organizational structure

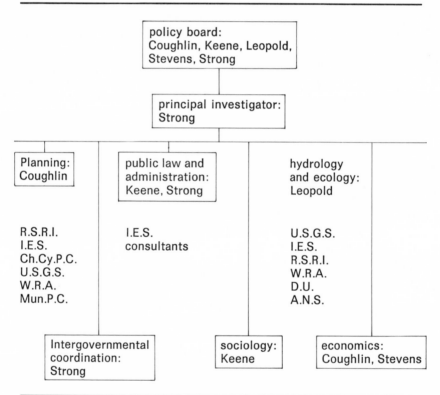

Note: abbreviations: R.S.R.I., Regional Science Research Institute; I.E.S., Institute for Environmental Studies; Ch.Cy.P.C., Chester County Planning Commission; U.S.G.S., U.S. Geological Survey; W.R.A., Water Resources Authority, Chester County; Mun. P.C., Municipal Planning Commission; D.U., Drexel University; A.N.S., Academy of Natural Sciences.

Table IV–4. Proposed allocation of planning work and budget

Job	Description	Primary responsibility	Estimate[a]	Timing
Intergovernmental coordination	communication with sponsors, participants, committees, and the community	Strong	$31,000	June 1965–January 1968
Attitude study	survey of residents and three control groups to determine environmental preferences and responses to land use controls	Keene, then Coughlin	26,000	July 1966–July 1967
Hydrology	development of proposals for preservation of present quantity and quality of water resources at target population; establishment of continuing monitor in basin and control area	Leopold	108,000	March 1966–September 1967
Land use planning	population projections; land characteristics, including development potential; mapping; real estate activity and land values; water resource area definitions; land use specifications	Coughlin	40,000	July 1966–October 1967
The law	determination of current land use controls and roles of different levels of government; determination of controls for carrying out the plan	Keene and Strong	34,000	September 1966–November 1967
Appraisal	calculation of total amount due landowners to carry out the plan; development of a system for calculating, property by property	Keene	14,000	June 1967–November 1967
Cost-benefit model	development of a model to describe in economic terms anticipated costs and benefits and their distribution, public and private	Stevens	26,000	April 1966–December 1967
Surveying	development of a simple, cheap, and legal means to use aerial photos to establish boundary lines for land subject to different controls	Leopold and Strong	12,000	August 1967–December 1967
Administration	coordination of development of plan and preparation of planning reports	Strong	7,000	December 1965–January 1967

[a] As a budget accompanying May 6, 1966, proposal to the Ford Foundation.

Table IV-5. Tentative planning timetable

	1966						1967											1968
	J	A	S	O	N	D	J	F	M	A	M	J	J	A	S	O	N	D	J

organization and conceptualization

brochure

hydrologic base

attitude study

local meetings

model design

develop plan alternatives

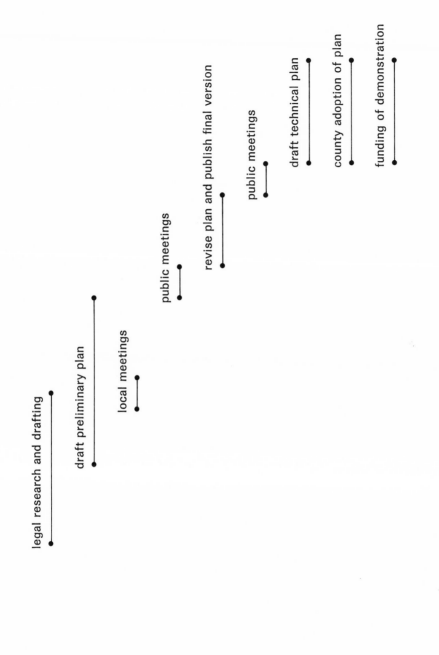

legal research and drafting

draft preliminary plan

local meetings

public meetings

revise plan and publish final version

public meetings

draft technical plan

county adoption of plan

funding of demonstration

these proposals, in turn, would not be determined until the public had had an opportunity to respond to the preliminary plan.

The work under way

The first months were the easiest. The lead time between the February 1966 preliminary approval of planning by the county commissioners and the July 1966 grant of funds by the Ford Foundation was used to begin finding staff, to parcel out assignments, and to prepare budgets. Now, with funds in hand, it was high time to get acquainted in the watershed and to plunge into specific planning tasks. As we became aware of the volume of work ahead and the data gaps and data collection problems, the pressure began to build up. On the public side, though, all was tranquil—too tranquil, in fact. It was difficult to find local people sufficiently interested to come to meetings and serve on committees.

The tone of the time was reflected in a December 1966 editorial in the *Daily Local News*. It said, in part: "What more commendable aims in a day when an ample supply of water is of prime importance and so-called 'developments' the source of considerable concern on the part of many areas over the country? . . . the experiment, if given the green light, will be followed with interest by other regions and not simply by our own county. This, at best, is a challenging project for the County Water Resources Authority."[1]

Throughout the winter of 1966–67 Ken Wood, the new project coordinator, got acquainted in the Brandywine and organized the coordinating committee. The field men of the Geological Survey started monitoring the Upper East Branch and the Pickering to learn about rainfall, flooding, sedimentation, water quality, and stream appearance. Bob Coughlin and his staff performed many tedious, time-consuming chores, such as preparing property maps, measuring hydrologic characteristics of thirty-one small sub-basins in the watershed, collecting and projecting population data, and starting to amass land sale and price information. John Keene looked at existing regulations of the townships, county, and state to get a sense of what was already being done to influence development and protect water resources. I gave further thought to land use controls which we might recommend, but, as our staff and jobs multiplied, I spent most of my time trying to keep everyone abreast of all that was going on.

Our first publication, *The Brandywine: A Place for Man, A Place for Nature*, was mailed to all watershed landowners in February of

1967, and caused scarcely a ripple—or so we thought. In fact we later learned that a few people began to organize against the proposal as soon as they finished reading the brochure. With careful, constant nurture the nucleus of an opposition would grow into the Chester County Freeholders and later would spawn the Regional Planning Commission of the Upper Brandywine. Soon people would be aroused, if ill-informed, and the honeymoon would end.

PLANNING STAFF. Several important people already were with us. Beatrice Solomon, who had worked with me for several years, took on the constantly expanding role of administrative assistant. Our office was the central point for exchange of information for our own staff and the staffs assigned to the project from the Water Resources Authority, the Regional Science Research Institute, and the Geological Survey. No one could have managed better the organization, staffing, and supervision of our office, the editing and production of an avalanche of memos, technical reports, and publications, and the daily load of inquiries, requests, and visits. Bea was helped by Laura Kessler, the principal project secretary for the Institute for Environmental Studies, who had also worked with me prior to the project. Her competence and responsibility were welcome assets.

Some graduate students in city and regional planning, law, or regional science worked on the initial proposal. More were added until at one point Bob, Ben, John, and I together must have been employing a dozen or so of them. Barlow Burke, a lawyer then attending planning school,[2] wrote some eighty legal memos for John and me. Dennis Sachs, a regional science student working for Bob and Ben, struggled in what seemed an unending effort to obtain Chester County land sales data. Mavra Iano, a planning student, was with us longest and handled every sort of task, from mapmaking to writing part of the plan. Some of the others will be introduced in the following pages.

The Geological Survey assigned people from its Harrisburg office to work with Luna and us. This arrangement worked well for the men whose duties were routine, such as building and monitoring stream gages. It was extremely unsatisfactory when innovation and initiative were called for. It was the outsider problem in a different guise. Luna arrived from Washington with his ideas and expected the local people to put a good young scientist to work refining the ideas and relating them to the Upper East Branch. It didn't happen. The scientist assigned was competent enough, but this assignment came on top of a full work load of his own choosing. By this time Luna had resigned as chief hydrologist of the Geological Survey and taken on the status of senior research hydrologist. While this change in position gave him time to pursue his personal research interests, it also meant that the lower echelons of the bureaucracy no longer were very responsive to his wishes. One man, hired by the Geological Survey for stream monitoring, did develop into a staff person of considerable value to all of us. In addition to his real interest in the hydrologic objectives of the project, John Troxell was a resident of the Pickering basin and a considerable help in picking up local reactions to our developing plan.

Bob Coughlin needed someone to be responsible for developing physiographic data for land use planning. This meant walking and driving about the watershed, finding out which spots always were boggy, how the forest cover had changed since the most recent maps, and where the loveliest views were. It meant making accurate maps of these observations, including all property lines. The work demanded someone meticulous and sensitive to natural values. We found such a person in Bob Myers, a young landscape architect and regional planner. We hired other people, skilled in planning law, demography, regional science, and programming, as the need arose.[3] Bob, Ben, John, and I were fortunate in our staff. Most of them were excited about the project and eager to be part of the planning team. They were bright, creative, and hard-working.

THE ATTITUDE STUDY. Our first step toward a plan and a decision about the plan was the attitude study. As soon as we were sure that funds were forthcoming, John and I began to list questions that we wanted answered. Before starting to shape the plan to the reality of the Upper East Branch, we needed to know what sort of environment the residents wanted. How highly did they value an attractive natural environment in choosing a place to live? How important to them was protection of the natural environment if it conflicted with preservation of their right to use the land as they pleased? The second was the crucial question.

By inquiring about residential preferences, leisure activities, and income levels, we hoped to learn whether a plan designed to protect water resources could also provide a living environment attractive to a major segment of the present population. The plan was to be presented to the people of the Upper East Branch but was actually designed to provide a place to live for a much larger future population, so that we also wanted to know how people currently living in more densely settled areas felt about the role of the natural environment in their lives. Therefore, our inquiry extended beyond the Upper East Branch and similar control areas to suburban Philadelphia and to long-established towns near the Brandywine.

We had another reason for putting the attitude study at the top of the work list. We wanted to interview the people of the Upper East Branch before they knew about the concepts of the plan so that the interviews would reflect people's attitudes uncolored by any specific proposal. Had it been adopted, we intended to carry out a second attitude study to compare responses, as influenced by the plan, to the initial responses. In fact, we did such a second survey in 1971[4] to see what more we could learn about reactions to the plan.

By September of 1966, John Keene and I had passed on our draft of the survey questionnaire to Mark Menchik,[5] an anthropologist-regional scientist then at the Regional Science Research Institute, for his emendations and for development of a coding procedure. He was to carry out most of the analysis of the survey data. With Mark, Bob Coughlin, and Ben Stevens we discussed sample size, survey areas, and the choice of a firm to carry out the interviews and keypunch the data. In addition to the Upper East Branch, we chose four survey sites within the metropolitan area: similar surrounding land in Chester County; another similar area located in Bucks County; the Chester County portion of suburban Philadelphia; and six Chester County towns, all beyond the Philadelphia suburban fringe (see map). An 11-percent sample of residential households was interviewed in the Upper East Branch and in the Bucks County area—165 and 109 households, respectively—while smaller samples were drawn from the other three areas, for a total of 457 households. The household was the basic sampling unit. When both male and female household heads were present, the interviewer selected one of them at random for the interview.

In October of 1966 the Water Resources Authority, on our recommendation, contracted with National Analysts, Inc., of Philadelphia to prepare the sampling design, carry out the interviews, and provide us with raw data. By December National Analysts had completed the interviews and had given us some preliminary data. I hired Jean Reid, a demographer, to work with Mark Menchik and Vartine Berberian, a programmer, to prepare tables and to analyze the data. They gave us enough information to guide us in our first round of public meetings and in preparing the preliminary plan. By July of 1967 Mark's initial formal report was finished.[6]

What did we learn, and how useful did it prove? We found that two-thirds of the people interviewed had been brought up in a rural area, most of them nearby or in their present homes; that over two-thirds worked nearby in Chester County; that over half were skilled or semi-skilled blue collar workers, while only 6 percent were farmers; that median income was $7,400 (just slightly in excess of the national median), with only 10 percent of families having an income of $15,000 or more; and that 70 percent owned their land.

In planning future land use, we wanted to know whether there would be a market for the large tracts of open land whose retention would be necessary to achieve the plan's objectives. Therefore, we asked people how large a property they currently owned and how large their ideal property would be. In the Brandywine, two acres was the median parcel size currently owned, although 24 percent of the people owned homes of eleven acres or more. Insofar as it can be said that there is a most desired, or "goal" parcel size for residential uses, it was estimated to be between four and five acres. While the median parcel size owned by the people in the other areas surveyed was one acre, the parcel size goal there was similar to that in the Brandywine. We concluded subsequently that, for hydrologic reasons, a maximum gross density of one dwelling unit per four acres should be permitted in woods and on steep slopes. The separate finding about people's preferences for residential lot sizes was encouraging corroboration for our opinion that there is a substantial market for properties this large.

The survey approached the question of the importance of the natural environment to people in several ways: by asking what factors influenced their choice of a place to live; by asking what they did with their leisure time; and by asking directly how important they judged the natural environment to be as part of their way of life. All of these were openended questions, subsequently coded into several categories, and more than one answer was often given. For that reason, total responses in these categories are higher than the numbers of people interviewed and total percentages exceed 100; for example, a total of 1,481 responses were received to the question about choice of a place to live.

These responses were tabulated in one of four general categories: natural environment; non-natural environment, such as neighbors or public services; accessibility; and characteristics of the particular house and lot. The people in the Upper East Branch placed far more emphasis on the natural environment in choosing a home than did people in the survey as a whole (see Table IV–6). Specific factors mentioned by

Table IV–6. Important factors in choosing a home

	Percent of people interviewed	
	Brandywine	Elsewhere
Natural environment	45	29
Non-natural environment	55	43
Accessibility	56	46
Characteristics of house and lot	63	71

Brandywine residents, in descending order of frequency, were house layout and equipment (37 percent), country-like character of the area (35 percent), accessibility (21 percent), desire to be near particular people (20 percent), school accessibility (18 percent), and desire not to be near too many people (17 percent). The natural environment in people's lives was categorized as providing tranquillity, privacy, and freedom (45 percent), offering a setting visually pleasing or interesting to study (70 percent), contributing to a good life (66 percent), permitting a particular enjoyable activity (30 percent), or other (3 percent). By far the most frequent response was enjoyment of birds, trees, animals, and other elements of nature. Answers to this question by Brandywine residents closely parallel those given by the rest of those interviewed.

Answers to the leisure time questions revealed that few people actively used the natural environment. Only 10 percent of the people in the Brandywine and 8 percent of those elsewhere described hiking, boating, fishing, or hunting as their most important weekend leisure activity. About an equal number engaged in active outdoor sports using man-made facilities, including tennis courts, swimming pools, and golf courses. The most popular leisure activities were visiting with friends and watching television. Comparing these answers to those about choice of a place to live, we concluded that most of the people who wish to live in a natural environment do so for the beauty and tranquillity provided, not for active recreational use of the rural land. This conclusion was compatible with our later recommendation to retain private ownership, without public access, of most of the land kept open to protect water resources. This would be cheaper than public ownership, would keep the land on the tax rolls, and would be more in keeping with prevailing attitudes toward government ownership of land. Through Marsh Creek State Park, partly located in the Upper East Branch, and Suplee Dam and lake, later renamed Struble

Dam in honor of Bob, the area would offer some public recreational opportunities for local people and for residents of more crowded communities. The remainder of the open land would provide the visual amenities and the sense of space and openness desired by residents and non-residents alike.

The most significant question asked was the following: "As you know, the suburbs are getting bigger and bigger. Because of this expansion, forests and farmland are developed for homes, stores, industries, and offices. Some people say that parts of the countryside, especially the most beautiful parts, should be kept the way they are for future generations to appreciate. Others feel that this land should be used in any way the landowners want. What do you think about it?" The answers to this difficult and complex question were coded in twenty-two specific categories subsumed under three general categories: preserve the countryside; preserve some countryside and provide for some development; allow landowners to do as they wish with their land. Many people gave answers which fell into more than one general category.

Table IV-7 compares Brandywine and suburban Chester County residents, shows the percentage of people giving answers falling in each of the three categories, and therefore totals over 100 percent. The suburbanites gave many more answers favoring preservation and far fewer answers favoring individual autonomy. This contrast in attitudes was borne out by our later experience; the Brandywine residents most similar to the suburbanites in income, education, jobs, and environmental preferences were the plan's strongest supporters.

The reasons most frequently given for preservation of the countryside were that it is beautiful, and that it is a natural heritage which, once lost, never can be replaced. People also stressed the desirability of preserving farmland, of keeping open space for recreation, and of preserving wildlife habitat. The dominant reason advanced on behalf of development was that each landowner should be able to do as he wished with his land. A secondary reason given was that development is needed to provide homes for an increasing population.

In the Brandywine, as in the other areas surveyed, there was a further notable distinction among the answers. Almost half of the Brandywine people and about two-thirds of the other people giving an answer or answers classed under "landowners should develop at will" also stated that it was important to preserve the countryside. However, less than a third of those in either group giving a "preserve the countryside" answer or answers also gave a "landowners should develop at

Table IV–7. Opinions about natural preservation and/or individual control

	Percent of people interviewed	
	Brandywine	Suburban Chester County
Preserve the countryside	72	84
Preserve some countryside; develop some	23	22
Landowners should develop at will	47	30

will" answer. Therefore, not only were the preservationists a larger group but they appeared more singleminded in intent. One can look at these answers in another, less auspicious way. If a substantial minority is wholly for individual control, one can predict a real conflict when the issue is squarely presented. Such a minority, if highly vocal, can succeed in halting programs requiring public action. As we were to learn soon enough, inaction can seem most attractive to public officials when faced with an organized opposition.

One final observation pertinent to our planning: many people said that they understood what planning, zoning, and conservation easements are, yet their answers revealed that in fact few did understand. For instance, while almost half said that they knew what conservation easements are, their answers showed that only about half of this group really did know. Further, only one-third of the Brandywine people answered correctly the question: "Does your township have zoning?" This gap between people's assumed and actual knowledge served as a warning of the difficulties that we would face in explaining one way, let alone a possible half dozen ways, of carrying out the plan.

The attitude survey yielded some highly useful, accurate information which gave us needed insights. It had a definite influence on our planning, and we would have done well to pay even more heed to the answers to the questions about preservation and/or individual control and about understanding of local land use controls.

THE TECHNICAL ADVISORY COMMITTEE. By summer of 1966, all of us knew that we faced a really tough job in trying to tie specific land use recommendations to our water resource objectives. Luna Leopold, who was as knowledgeable as anyone in the country, had a clear understanding of the relationship between different uses of the land and the resulting impact on water movement over and in the ground and in streams. However, he knew that there was little field data from which he could construct a detailed formula setting out which locations and which land types could support various forms of urbanization and which were so vulnerable as to make all development unwise. Also, Luna at that time had not studied the relationship between land use and water quality. Therefore, we set as an early priority the creation of a technical advisory committee largely composed of the best people we could find in such areas as sedimentation, stream biology, and sanitary engineering.

Bob Struble passed over to me the job of setting up this committee, since it was to work directly with the planning staff. Some of the fifteen members chosen also acted as consultants on some phase of the planning. Others worked for public agencies in the region and helped us informally from time to time. Still others contributed their expertise through committee meetings and in individual meetings. All were generous with their time and ideas. Their wisdom had a considerable influence on the plan's final form.

To give a sense of the qualifications and reputation of the committee members, here are their names and the positions then held by them: Norman Beamer, district chief, Water Resources Division, U.S. Geological Survey in Pennsylvania; John T. Carson, Jr., director, Division of Natural Resources, Bucks County Planning Commission; Maurice K. Goddard, secretary, Department of Forests and Waters, Commonwealth of Pennsylvania; Clayton Hoff, director, Forward Lands, Inc.; David B. Klotz, deputy director, Delaware Valley Regional Planning Commission; Joseph Langran, planning consultant for six of the eight Upper East Branch townships (East Brandywine, East Caln, Honey Brook, Upper Uwchlan, Uwchlan and Wallace townships); Clifford H. McConnell, chief engineer, Department of Forests and Waters, Commonwealth of Pennsylvania; John Munshower, executive secretary, Chester County Planning Commission; Ruth Patrick, chairman, Department of Limnology, Academy of Natural Sciences, Philadelphia; Walter M. Phillips, director, Penjerdel; Irwin Remson, professor of civil engineering, Drexel Institute of Technology; John Rex, chief of land acquisition, Department of Forests and Waters, Commonwealth of Pennsylvania; Gerald W. Root, soil conservationist, Soil Conservation Service, U.S. Department of Agriculture; W. Brinton Whitall, secretary, Delaware River Basin Commission; and M. Gordon Wolman, chairman, Geography Department, Johns Hopkins University. The technical advisory committee met several times as a group. In addition, almost all of the committee members met individually with us at various times to offer their advice on specific technical questions. For instance, Gordon Wolman made several trips to the Brandywine to advise us on the role of open space adjacent to streams—areas which we called stream buffers—in controlling erosion and sedimentation. We talked with him at length about how wide the stream buffers should be and what vegetation would be most effective in trapping eroding soils. Ruth Patrick, who generously included John Keene, Luna Leopold, and me in a short course on limnology, also was concerned about preserving stream buffers. Her main interest in them was in their role in keeping wastes from the stream. Walter Phillips drew on his knowledge as one of the principal creators of the Delaware River Basin Compact to suggest ways of involving county and local government in our proposal. All of these people were immensely helpful, and the staff relied heavily on their recommendations. They participated in some of the most difficult planning decisions: for instance, how much land must be kept open to maintain current water standards; which areas are most critical; and what is the best system for waste disposal.

The technical advisory committee fulfilled admirably our hopes for it. We needed, but did not try to create, a parallel committee with a comparable level of expertise to help the Water Resources Authority and us to establish an effective communication system and to achieve broad citizen participation in the planning process.

WATER RESOURCE MANAGEMENT. Put in simple terms, we were seeking to manage the water resources of the Upper East Branch to achieve a benefit-cost ratio for the watershed when developed which would favorably compare with the usual suburban development. The basic planning task which we set ourselves was to design a plan which would accommodate the projected future growth, and which also would (1) preserve the present desirable characteristics of the water resources of the Upper East Branch; (2) yield a basin-wide return from development at least as great as that from conventional development; (3) create a system by which all landowners could share in rising development values; and (4) provide greater individual satisfaction than that gained from conventional development. To assure maintenance of desirable water characteristics, it was necessary to plan the management of flow, quality, and water-related amenity for the projected population. From the start we set the constraint that the water supply for the future people of the Upper East Branch should come from within the watershed and that no wastes generated there should be exported for treatment. We all supported this as a planning principle but, until we had completed population projections and hydrologic measurements, we did not know whether the principle could be translated into practice.

Basing the plan on water resource management posed many new and intriguing planning problems. While these problems were of deep interest to us as planners, they are not the focus of this book and will only be mentioned here, with citations to other reports which discuss them more fully.

We needed a precise definition, and possibly a classification, of the areas most critical to stream health and stream appearance. Even if we could control use of land in these areas, there was still the question of whether locating most of the projected growth in the rest of the watershed could be done without impairing the stream regimen. We divided the hydrologic work into four parts and tackled three at once.

Setting up a system of monitoring stations in the Upper East Branch and adjacent Pickering basins was necessary to establish base line data about flow, sediment, and quality. This was needed for planning and for future comparisons should the plan be carried out. We hoped to be able to demonstrate differences in water infiltration, ground water levels, stream recharge rates, stream flow variability, and amounts of silt and wastes if one area was developed according to our plan and the other conventionally. The Geological Survey did this work, with the exception of biological monitoring. For that we engaged limnologist Ruth Patrick and her staff at the Academy of Natural Sciences in Philadelphia.[7]

A second assignment for the Geological Survey was to make an aerial photomosaic of the basin, on which we hoped to locate the flood plains. Later we intended to use this photomosaic to set up a system of open space boundary definitions for deed recording purposes. We wanted a cheaper, quicker substitute for metes and bounds surveys of the areas which we defined as critical to water resource protection. We wanted to experiment with a new method that would have wide utility elsewhere. Regrettably, the aerial photography was a dismal failure. Three flights failed to yield usable photos, and we had neither time nor money to try again.

The definition of critical areas could not await the compilation of data from the monitoring program. Luna already had a strong sense of priorities. To reinforce his judgment with some specific information about the Brandywine, he asked Bob Myers, our landscape architect-planner, to make a detailed series of measurements. The Upper East Branch was divided into sub-basins of approximately one square mile each. For each of these thirty-one sub-basins, Bob laboriously calculated exact area, average slope of stream channel in feet per foot, length of stream channel in miles, average slope length in miles, average slope gradient in feet per foot, drainage density in miles of stream per square mile of area drained, percentage of area in forest, and percentage of area in slopes of 10 percent or more. After converting average slope gradient to a percentage, Luna directed Bob to weight it by multiplying by ten, add it to the percentage of the sub-basin in slopes of 10 percent or more, and then compare the sub-basins. The steepest was four times steeper than the least steep. Luna sought to decide whether this variability was great enough to warrant defining the restrictions on use of critical areas in terms of the characteristics of a sub-basin; for instance, should we provide for more restrictive uses in sub-basins with higher slope characteristics? After studying the data he concluded that this was an unneeded degree of complexity for this watershed.

Luna was convinced that the land nearest to the stream was the most critical, the steep lands second in importance, and the forests third. However, how wide should a stream buffer be? Should the width vary with the area of the land drained, so that the bigger the stream the bigger the buffer? What about tree cover as a factor in limiting runoff and erosion? And, for these purposes, how do you define forests? All of these questions we took to our Technical Advisory Committee. Arthur Davis, of HUD, and Maurice Goddard, both foresters by training, went with us into the field to offer their advice. We measured, sampled, and calculated. Gradually, over many months, we combined technical judgments on water movement—runoff, percolation, and flow—with judgments of the most able people known to us in the field of water quality to reach precise definitions of the critical areas and of appropriate uses in those areas.

The last major hydrologic task was the design of water supply and waste disposal systems for the basin. This we delayed until Bob Coughlin had finished population projections and the Geological Survey had accumulated base line information about rainfall, runoff, soils, percolation rates, and stream flow variability.

The hydrologic work went on throughout our time in the Upper East Branch, and some of it still continues today. By late fall of 1966, when we issued the initial Brandywine publication, *The Brandywine: A Place for Man, A Place for Nature*, we were ready to state with some assurance that four areas were critical to water resource protection: flood plains and stream buffers should not be built upon, and steep slopes and forests should be protected from unlimited development. For other areas to be developed, we stressed avoidance of erosion, design of streets and storm sewers to slow runoff, and provision of adequate sewerage. We could be more specific in the spring.

THE PROJECT COORDINATOR. The role of project coordinator was possibly the most crucial one for the ultimate acceptance or rejection of the plan. Bob Struble's time already was overcommitted with his three jobs and particularly with the Marsh Creek project then under way. He could spend only twenty hours per month on the Upper East Branch project, so finding an assistant to take on most of the workload was vital. Although we had determined not to suggest any more candidates for the job, we did continue, through the summer and fall, to urge Bob to make a choice. Someone had to start getting acquainted with the people living in the Upper East Branch.

Bob had some difficulty finding suitable candidates. One man, who was then a Chester County official, turned it down because the Authority could guarantee only eighteen months' employment. We wanted and needed an experienced, highly qualified person for the toughest job in the project, yet we could offer a limited period of employment and a moderate salary. Any short-term demonstration project raises the question of how it is possible to attract a skilled person to such an assignment. Paying a salary that would compensate for the shortcomings of the job would help. The excitement of attempting something new is the major attraction, but if the job demands uprooting one's family and relinquishing a secure position, qualified candidates are likely to be few.

Not until October 1966 did Bob find and hire someone he thought suitable, Harold K. Wood, Jr., as project coordinator. Ken Wood had just finished his tour of duty as a naval officer. He had returned home to Chester County, a college graduate looking for his first civilian job. His family was well known in the county. What is more, they were close friends of Joe Munshower. Ken's father was a local lawyer, active in Republican politics, before being appointed a federal district judge; his brothers and cousins had stayed in the county, and Ken hoped to put down roots there as well. Someone suggested that he see Bob Struble; he did and was hired as soon as Bob checked with some board members of the Water Resources Authority and the Brandywine Valley Association.

Ken Wood brought to his role in the Brandywine youth, energy, a large measure of grit, and willingness to learn. He did not have any prior training or experience in water resource management, community planning, or public communication, nor did he know the Upper East Branch, since his family was from the southern portion of the county. Nevertheless, he plunged at once into what became a time-devouring, endlessly demanding job. He never stopped trying to do the best he knew how in a job that was far too big for one person. He was anxious to learn, receptive to others' ideas, and enormously patient and unyielding under pressure.

All of us—Bob Struble as well as the rest of us—grossly underestimated the amount of work involved in Ken's job. While we acknowledged that success of the project would turn upon our ability to reach people and to develop a plan acceptable to them, we thought that one person, with guidance from Bob Struble and technical assistance from us planners, could manage that task. Jumping from our originally proposed area of 2,000 acres to the 23,500 acres of the Upper East Branch meant that we now had to contact, in one way or another, a population of 4,200. The fact that none of us had ever engaged in an effort of this sort is little excuse for such a serious miscalculation.

Much later, Upper East Branch critics of the plan would place considerable blame on Ken Wood for its failure. He was, they alleged, an outsider who didn't fit in among them; he was rigid and aggressive. I think that these critics were mistaken as to their target, which was not Ken Wood but the planning proposals that he was espousing. He was the only staff person in contact with landowners on a daily basis, and it was his job to present the staffs' planning proposals to the people and to give us an accurate portrayal of the public response.

Ken's task was complicated by our lack of knowledge of community structure in the watershed. As noted above, we planners had made one serious error in assuming that the Brandywine Valley Association drew a representative number of its members and board from the Upper East Branch. These people, we thought, could provide us with an introduction to their community and could help bridge the gap between county and local concerns. In fact, we discovered that there were very few Brandywine Valley Association members residing in the Upper East Branch. What was worse, the organization had a widespread reputation there of being a snob group consisting primarily of du Pont executives living downstream. Our expectations of early contact with local leaders through the Brandywine Valley Association therefore proved illusory. We were also counting on the help of two board members of the Water Resources Authority who lived in the watershed. However, by the time Ken Wood set out to get acquainted, one man had sold his farm, moved elsewhere, and resigned from the Authority. The other was dead. Their loss was a serious handicap.

One of Ken's first and most tedious chores was compiling a list of all tracts of land in the watershed, showing location, size, name of owner, and owner's mailing address. Many people owned more than one tract; many people owned land in the basin but lived elsewhere. The county's tax maps and tax records were a basic source of this information. Ken and his secretary, Pat Moran, spent hours pulling this data together so that we could reach people—by mail, by a personal visit, and, later, with maps of their land as it would be affected by the plan.

At the same time, Ken began calling on people already identified as local leaders, including township supervisors, planning commission members, and ministers. He described the concept of the plan, asked for suggestions for membership on the proposed citizen's advisory committee, and, later, asked people to sponsor small local meetings so that he could reach a number of people at once. He began to get acquainted with county groups which would or could have a voice in the Brandywine proposals, such as the staff and members of the County Planning Commission, the board and members of the Soil and Water Conservation District, and the Board of Realtors. He also attended most of the planning staff meetings so that he would understand the proposals, including the reasons for technical decisions, and reported to us what the people he was talking with in the watershed and in the county were saying.

Bob Coughlin, Ben, John, and I thought that establishment of a coordinating committee and a citizens' advisory committee should be Ken's highest priority. All three committees were needed, but only the technical advisory committee fulfilled its intended role. The shortcomings of the other two committees contributed materially to the rejection of the plan.

THE COORDINATING COMMITTEE. The coordinating committee was conceived of as the principal advisory group to the Water Resources Authority on matters concerning the project. It was to be the primary means of communication between the Authority and the county and township officials. All county agencies whose work related to the plan and all township governments were represented on the committee, with each agency designating two people to serve. The three invited county agencies—the Planning Commission, the Soil and Water Conservation District, and the Park and Recreation Board—each named one of their board members and their staff director. Several of the eight townships named one supervisor and one planning commission member. Others named one or two people not serving in any other township capacity. Choice of these representatives was left to each township Board of Supervisors and proved critical to future relationships with the township. More intensive discussion with township supervisors at this point might have averted some serious future problems.

In several townships the choice of representatives handicapped planning from the start. Some committee members never attended a meeting; others came to only one or two. A few of the people appointed were conscientious and deeply interested in the plan but lacked effective means of communication in their townships. In only four of the eight townships did one or both representatives have an interest in the plan plus local clout.

The worst problem, though, was that of the people we omitted. Some community leaders were permanently antagonized because they were not appointed to the committee. It was important for the committee to start functioning early in the planning process, yet neither Ken nor Bob knew the townships well enough at that point to know who would or would not be influential and representative. Extended discussion with the supervisors about the plan and about the role of the committee at this time could have reduced, but would not have eliminated, the problem. Probably the best way to have built communication between the townships and the Water Resources Authority into the committee would have been to request that each township name to it one supervisor and one planning commission member.

The coordinating committee met first in October of 1966 and then seven more times until March of 1968, about half as frequently as the planning staff had proposed. There were only eight meetings because the more active members participated in other meetings held to discuss the plan—meetings called by some of the townships, public meetings sponsored by the Water Resources Authority, and the citizens' advisory committee meetings. Coordinating committee meetings were held in the evening, usually at the Glenmoore fire hall, with the planning staff and Water Resources Authority staff participating.

The role of the committee was described by Ken Wood in one of a series of articles on the project. Captioned "Local Participation Is Key to Brandywine Project," the article went on to say: "It is good to have the township coordinating committee for two reasons—first, ideas originate there and second, professional planners' schemes get a hearing at

Private property and the public interest

the grass roots level."[8] As with most committees, there was from the start a nucleus of people who were enthusiastic and prepared to give of their thoughts and time to develop an appropriate plan. Their suggestions were valuable and welcomed by the staff. There were others who attended meetings doggedly but said little. Then there were the rest, including about half of the township representatives and a couple of the county representatives, who took no part, coming to meetings rarely or never. While probably typical, this lack of participation was particularly unfortunate for the Brandywine Plan. The plan was innovative, and the new is always unsettling. Therefore, it was vital that each township's residents and officials should know what was being proposed and how to respond to any proposal.

THE CITIZENS' ADVISORY COMMITTEE. Although we urged Ken to organize the citizens' advisory committee at the same time as the coordinating committee, he did not do so. First, he did not know whom to invite to join, since the contacts we had depended upon had proven nonexistent. Second, Bob Struble was reluctant to establish this committee and advised Ken to wait. Members of the technical advisory committee with political experience stressed the need to get leading citizens involved in such a committee from the start, but Bob Struble wanted to wait until we had decided what the boundaries of the critical areas would be and what land uses would be allowed in them. John, Bob Coughlin, and I argued that going to a committee with a finished product was just what we were trying to avoid. Bob Struble had other reservations. He had hoped that the coordinating committee would serve as a link to and from the Upper East Branch people. He feared that a citizens' committee would be infiltrated by opponents of the plan who would dominate it and prevent it from functioning properly. He also feared that, just as with the coordinating committee, in the process of choosing members we would lose more than we would gain because too many not asked would be offended. The debate continued from October of 1966 until January of 1967, when Ken began a systematic effort to learn what organizations existed in the basin so that he could invite them to appoint representatives.

OUR FIRST PUBLICATION. We had hoped to introduce our goals to the people of the Upper East Branch by mailing them a short brochure early in the fall of 1966. We soon found this to be impossible; until Ken finished assembling the names and addresses of all landowners, we had no mailing list. As a stopgap, in November Ken and Bob wrote a short bulletin, mimeographed it, and sent it to township and county officials and to coordinating committee members. This was the first of six direct mailings of plan documents: two were sent only to public officials and committee members; the other four went to all landowners as well.

The brochure, *The Brandywine: A Place for Man, A Place for Nature,* was mailed to everyone in February 1967. It was twelve pages long, amply illustrated, with the text kept to a minimum. John and I did most of the writing, but everyone else had a hand in that, as well as in the design and layout. The brochure was published by the Water Resources Authority and carried on the second page introductory letters from the chairman of the county commissioners and the chairman of the Water Resources Authority asking for the ideas and help of the citizens of the Upper East Branch.

The brochure began by describing the problems that growth would bring to the watershed, stating planning objectives, and defining in general terms principles for guiding development. The next paragraphs were the ones which aroused and inflamed some of the residents and started them on their way to organizing an opposition. Because they express our thinking and because they were the grounds for our subsequent defeat, I quote them in full.

The plan will specify the restrictions necessary for each critical area to prevent inappropriate land uses. These restrictions would be in the form of agreements between individual landowners and the Water Resources Authority. For his part, the landowner would agree to limit development of the critical areas on his land. For its part, the Authority would agree to pay, by any one of several methods selected by the landowner, for the loss in fair market value caused by the restrictions. The land would stay on the tax rolls, assessed at its fair market value as subject to the restrictions. The County will bear none of the costs of maintaining the land and the public will have no access to it.

The landowner will enjoy continued private use of his land, will be able to sell it, or leave it to his children—always, of course, subject to the restrictions. No person now living within the basin will be forced to move from his home. No buildings will be torn down. Landowners will be paid to continue using their lands as they are now using them. For many, this is the way they intend to continue to use them anyway.

Most persons will probably want to continue to live in the basin after the restrictions are in force. The Water Resources Authority would simply purchase an agreement limiting land development from such an owner. Some landowners may not want to live in the restricted area or may be about to move away for personal reasons. The Authority would purchase the property of such an owner, place development restrictions on it and then put it on the market for private purchase. Other options might be suitable to other owners.

In any case, the Authority would hold its restrictions forever, so that all who live in the watershed, now and in the future, would be assured that the stream valley would be protected.

In order for such a result to be realized, all owners of land in the critical areas must cooperate. If one landowner insists on building on the flood plain when all others have agreed not to build there, it would be unfair to permit that one individual to jeopardize the protection of the Valley. To prevent this, it might be necessary for the Authority to use its powers of eminent domain. The Authority, of course, would pay fair value for the rights acquired.

The perpetual protection of the Upper East Branch will guarantee to the landowners a quality of water, scenery and general environment which could not be maintained by any other means. Instead of gradual deterioration, the Valley will continue to have those qualities desired by most of the present owners. As urban sprawl makes these qualities increasingly rare throughout the metropolitan area, the market value of land in the basin will rise. Until it does, owners will enjoy their land, the compensation paid them, and the low level of taxes reflecting the limitations on development. When values rise, taxes may also rise, but not as fast as if the land could be subdivided into building lots. Owners will continue to enjoy the land, the compensation, and the expectation of a greater return should they wish to sell the land.

All of us weighed these words carefully before putting them in print. We did not realize how utterly obnoxious the concept of sharing land ownership with government would be to many people, but we did know that including the words "eminent domain" was perilous. However, we believed emphatically that the plan could not succeed unless everyone participated, and we could not believe that everyone would participate voluntarily. Therefore, our choice, as we saw it, was either to remain discreetly silent in the brochure about how the plan might be carried out or to be candid from the start. We were unanimous in favoring candor even though uneasy about the outcome.

The brochure concluded by stating that a preliminary plan would be prepared, with the help of the coordinating committee and a citizens' advisory committee, reviewed with the townships, revised, and then submitted to the townships for approval, with the ultimate decision up to the Water Resources Authority and the county commissioners. The final words were a request for help from the residents in developing the plan.

Until late spring, when Harry Simms and other opponents surfaced, we had little response to the brochure. Few people followed the suggestion that they call Ken for information or to discuss the proposal. We were disappointed, yet we were also relieved that the statement about eminent domain apparently had not harmed our prospects. How wrong we were. Later, Ken was told that as soon as Harry Simms finished reading the brochure he was on the phone warning people of the danger and organizing an effort to stop the plan. He owned thirteen acres of flood plain and stream buffer land at Lyndell, in East Brandywine Township. Three points in the proposal outraged him: the fact that the rights to be acquired by the Water Resources Authority would be perpetual, that eminent domain was contemplated, and that the final decision would be made by the county, not the townships. These later proved the major points at issue.

Reprise: the first eight months

By the end of February 1967 we had a good and growing staff. Planning research was under way in the Upper East Branch. Through Ken and the coordinating committee we were beginning, though slowly, to get acquainted with the Brandywine residents. All of them had heard from us through the brochure, and, unknown to us, a nucleus of them had formed to fight our still nebulous plan.

Because we wished the brochure to be distributed before the first round of township public meetings, and because it had been delayed, we had yet to hold those meetings. The citizens' advisory committee had not been convened. Ken could not possibly shoulder all the tasks involved in organizing for public participation in planning. Because we had enough staff to carry on the technical side, the gap between the planning and the decision process began to widen.

Despite our difficulties and delays in reaching people, one tantalizing question remains. If we had said nothing about how the guiding principles might be carried out until the preliminary plan had been published, would this have given Ken sufficient lead time to find local leaders, involve them in planning, and establish a relationship of trust with them? If so, could this have changed the ultimate decision?

V

the opposition appears

FOLLOWING the release of *The Brandywine: A Place for Man, A Place For Nature*, we continued work much as before. We were in the midst of developing land definitions and land use specifications for the preliminary plan. We met with our technical advisors and with the coordinating committee to get their ideas. Ken organized the first meeting of the citizens' advisory committee and the first round of public meetings in the townships to make as many people as possible aware of our early thinking about the plan.

Meanwhile, Harry Simms and some of his neighbors in East Brandywine Township, outraged at the prospect of yet another government use of eminent domain, were busy organizing. Not until May 1, at the joint East and West Brandywine Townships public meeting, did we discover that a nucleus of aroused, fearful, and suspicious citizens had been formed. Soon the petition against the plan was posted on the door of Karl Bauss' greenhouse, Ken was threatened with physical violence, and escalation of fears began.

Then came a shock: the state purchased land, partly in the Upper East Branch, for a prison. This act further inflamed public antagonism to government intervention, and the prison dispute inexorably became entangled with the Brandywine Plan. Local politics, too, took an unanticipated turn, so that events seemed to be conspiring against us. When the preliminary plan reached people, in early summer of 1967, we were in deep trouble and we knew it.

Public communication

A program for reaching the Brandywine residents and hearing their ideas was high on our agenda. Identifying the landowners, setting up the coordinating committee, and mailing out the brochure had come first. Much more was to follow. We wrote and revised plans, developed and presented slide talks, made a movie, prepared newspaper articles, and appeared on radio and television. We held innumerable meetings, large and small, in fire houses and living rooms. We talked with hundreds of people individually.

The attitude study was designed, in part, to provide information which would help us to communicate with the public. We hoped to reach people through their community activities. The attitude study showed, however, that many of those who participated did so only nominally. Although 66 percent of the families surveyed belonged to one or more community organizations—churches, civic, social, or athletic groups—most were not very active. Of all heads of households, half said that they spent no time per month on any of these activities; 20 percent spent between one and four hours, often in the form of attendance at church services; and the rest were somewhat more active. In addition, many of these activities took place outside the watershed and involved people from many other areas, so that the organizations mentioned were not Brandywine-oriented. We concluded from this information that, while it was worth trying to contact people through existing community organizations, one could reach only a limited number in this way.

We asked people interviewed for the attitude study whether they thought they lived in a community and, if so, where the center of the community was located. We hoped to find several community foci. While people for the most part said that they lived in a community, they thought of its center as the nearest crossroad, usually with a gas station and country store, rather than the nearest town. There were no major community centers in the basin where people congregated.

We also asked about people's reading and leisure time preferences and learned that residents of the Brandywine were regular readers of national magazines. The most popular, *Readers Digest*, was read by 25 percent of families; several other magazines, including *Life, Look, Ladies Home Journal,* and farm journals, approached that figure. Most families did subscribe to a newspaper but, with half a dozen local papers and three Philadelphia papers serving the area, there was no single paper which almost everyone read. The West Chester *Daily Local News* had the widest distribution, followed by the *Philadelphia Evening Bulletin.* Television was the universal medium; in fact it was the favorite leisure time activity of 25 percent of the families. We assumed that many people listened to the local radio stations while getting breakfast or driving to and from work. We hoped that people would read the several direct mailings that we proposed.

Given the misunderstanding that developed later, it seems fair to conclude that our message was too complex. Further, we reached a limited national audience more readily and more clearly than we reached our principal audience, the people of the Upper East Branch. The efforts of the plan's opponents to confuse and alarm people certainly contributed to local communication difficulties. The decision we

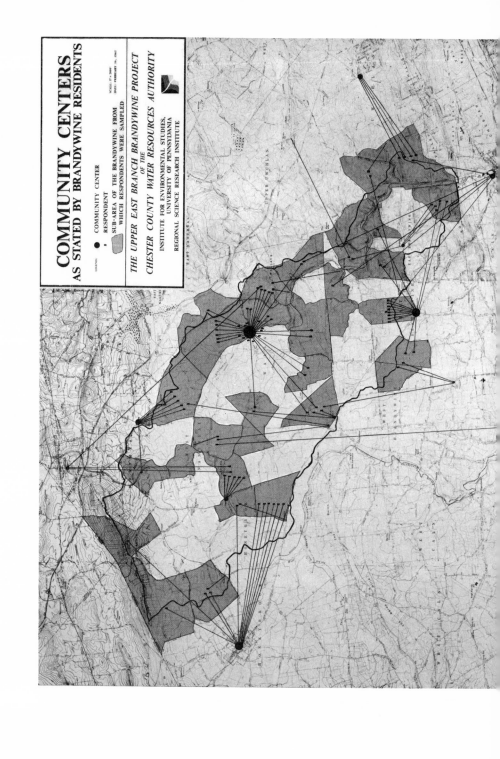

COMMUNITY CENTERS
AS STATED BY BRANDYWINE RESIDENTS

LEGEND:
● COMMUNITY CENTER
. RESPONDENT
SUB-AREA OF THE BRANDYWINE FROM
WHICH RESPONDENTS WERE SAMPLED

SCALE: 2" = 2000'
DATE: FEBRUARY 14, 1967

THE UPPER EAST BRANCH BRANDYWINE PROJECT
OF THE
CHESTER COUNTY WATER RESOURCES AUTHORITY

INSTITUTE FOR ENVIRONMENTAL STUDIES,
UNIVERSITY OF PENNSYLVANIA
REGIONAL SCIENCE RESEARCH INSTITUTE

sought from people was not based on a simple choice. In addition, we were seeking local participation throughout the planning period and so, in the early stages, we had no answers to many of the questions that people asked. This created an aura of uncertainty; yet had we waited until all of the planning work was done and then presented the people with a completed plan, there would have been no public participation. In sum, we tried to tell people too much. Our problem was that the plan *was* complex and embodied many new ideas.

THE PRESS. The most obvious means of reaching people was through the local press. We used it extensively and, in a different style, so did the opposition. Both of us sought to persuade, we by providing large doses of information and they by appeals to the emotions.

Very early, Ken introduced himself to the reporters for the dailies and weeklies read in the Upper East Branch. He then kept up his contact with many of them. The county newspapers gave ample news coverage to the plan. Reporters from two of the three county dailies, the *Daily Local News* and the *Coatesville Record*, and from the weekly *Honey Brook Herald* and *Downingtown Archive*, covered most public meetings. So many different reporters were assigned to cover meetings over the two-year period that some were not well informed about the proposals and the nature of the objections to them; for instance, seven different reporters covered the project for the *Daily Local News*. Nevertheless, their articles were fair and generally accurate. During the winter of 1967, Ken wrote a series of eight articles explaining the concepts of the plan and the decision process. The series was carried by the *Daily Local News* and the *Honey Brook Herald*. Dick Brown, local director for the Soil and Water Conservation District and a member of the coordinating committee, wrote additional articles for the *Daily Local News*.

Not until May did our opponents begin to use the press—taking ads, writing letters to the editor, and making statements to reporters. From then on, the Brandywine was one of the hottest local issues, regularly getting front-page attention.

THE BRANDYWINE VALLEY ASSOCIATION NEWSLETTER. Bob Struble proposed that we follow up the February brochure with a short and simple mailing in the form of questions and answers. Bob wrote this, in a very straightforward style, and included it in the March newsletter of the Brandywine Valley Association. The newsletter was mailed to all landowners in the Upper East Branch, in addition to the association members. This, and a subsequent endorsement of the plan by the Brandywine Valley Association board, were that organization's only contributions in support of the plan.

CONVENING THE CITIZENS' ADVISORY COMMITTEE. The planning staff envisioned the citizens' advisory committee as one more way of exchanging ideas with the community. The attitude study had proven what we had strongly suspected already: that there were no dominant communication links in the Upper East Branch. The diffuse press coverage has just been described, as has the scattered pattern of community organization and participation. This loosely woven, disaggregated way of living complicated the task of reaching people with ideas and getting their responses.

It was a diversified group of organizations which Ken contacted seeking members for the committee: women's civic and social clubs, granges, PTAs, coon hunters, rod and gun clubs, church men's clubs, and fox hunters. Most organizations agreed to name someone as a representative, but many never followed through. Some said that no one was interested in serving; some said that most of their members lived outside of the basin; a few churches said that the project was controversial and that they wished to avoid participating for that reason.

By March of 1967, six months after the coordinating committee had begun to meet and nine months after planning had begun in the Upper East Branch, the Water Resources Authority was ready to call the first meeting of the citizens' advisory committee. Many were invited; few came. Some who attended went away feeling that they were being told what was going to happen, instead of being asked for their involvement and ideas. So much had already been discussed with others and so many preliminary decisions had been made that this impression was not surprising. However, it was a mortal blow to our hopes for public participation through the citizens' advisory committee.

TOWNSHIP PUBLIC MEETINGS. The first round of township public meetings, in April and May, went better than the initial meeting of the citizens' advisory committee. In several townships the local members of the coordinating committee helped Ken organize and publicize the meetings and then one of them acted as chairman. We met three times with the coordinating committee between the February publication of the introductory brochure and the township public meetings. Once we invited the township supervisors to our meeting as well. This gave the committee members a reasonable feel for our proposals and gave us some sense of local thinking. During this period we worked out a more specific statement of our water resource objectives, defined precisely the areas most critical to water resource protection, and set forth tentative land use restrictions for the critical areas and for the remaining development areas.

Bob and Ken and most of the planning staff came to the first meeting, held in the Fairview Presbyterian Church in Wallace Township. About seventy-five Wallace residents were there. The supervisors, planning commission members, coordinating committee members, citizens' advisory committee members, and landowners whom Ken had already called on were somewhat acquainted with the planning proposals. Hus McIlvain, chairman of the Water Resources Authority board, chaired the meeting, and Bill Funk, chairman of the Wallace Township supervisors and a new appointee to the Authority, moderated the question period. Bob Struble and members of the planning staff described the concept, Luna told of the hydrologic rationale, and then we invited discussion. Most people sought more information, some of which was not yet available, and generally they seemed receptive to the concept. Only two people were openly hostile: one was a farmer who had fought, in vain, several gas pipeline and high tension lines easements across his land, taken by eminent domain. The other was a woman, Betty Templin, who had long battled against enactment of zoning in Wallace Township; she lost the battle with the January 1967 adoption of a zoning ordinance. Mrs. Templin now took on a new battle and soon became one of the most vocal opponents of the plan in Wallace Township. The press reports give an accurate picture of the tone of the meeting.

The panel emphasized that people in the area must want this project if it is to become a reality, and that it wouldn't be "forced down their throats." . . . Opponents of the project voiced their objections to "people from the outside telling us what we can or can't do with our property." . . . Opponents to the project seemed to be in the minority, however.[1] Reaction to the idea of keeping the area rural was generally favorable, though some in the audience had reservations about letting "outsiders" tell them what they should do with their land.[2]

The joint meeting for West Nantmeal and Honey Brook Townships closely followed the pattern of the Wallace meeting. About sixty people came. The one major concern expressed was that if the federal government contributed to the cost of the easements it might try to control use of the land.

On May 1 came the joint meeting for East and West Brandywine Townships. Harry Simms for the first time had an opportunity to identify himself publicly as the opposition spokesman and to issue a rallying cry against the proposal. A few weeks later, at the joint meeting for Uwchlan, Upper Uwchlan, and East Caln Townships, he again unleashed the rhetoric which was a feature of most subsequent Brandywine meetings. This is how the press reported it:

> The project would only go into effect, Struble said, if a majority of the voters or property owners or whatever system was selected agreed to the plan. . . . The most vociferous member of the opposition to the project was Harry Simms. In his prepared speech he felt the authority was making a "socialistic thrust" into the Brandywine Valley. Simms expressed the view that the authority denied the basic constitutional right of private property by invoking a writ of eminent domain and condemning the property of the minority who didn't agree with the project if it were passed. . . . [When Simms argued that] pollution could be prevented and open spaces preserved through voluntary individual sacrifice, a member of the audience hastened to point out it has been private initiative that has built industry which has in turn polluted our streams and built parking lots in the open space.[3]

In another press report, Simms is quoted as calling the project "blatantly socialistic," and stating that

> [W]e have boys fighting in Vietnam now to give the Vietnamese people the right to own unrestricted private property under a Democratic-Capitalistic system. What are we going to say . . . when we write to them?
> "Dictatorship is dictatorship," he declared. [Simms] said he has gathered about 160 signatures on a petition that reads: "We the undersigned do petition the township supervisors of East Brandywine Township, Alan McCausland, Charles Mentzer and Roy Nellius to protest the placing of any restriction by the public authorities into our titles, specifically the Chester County Water Resources Authority. . . . This restriction would abridge the sacred right of private property, creating a Socialistic precedent." William Bode replied: "It seems to me this is the antithesis of Socialism and Communism. I think this remains well within our constitution. . . . Pollution is physically, not literally, killing us." Bode drew the evening's only applause when he said "I think when someone throws out a word like 'Communism' then he wants you to stop thinking and get emotional."[4]

Local politics

The year 1967 was a local election year. While we were at work on the preliminary plan, local events were taking an unexpected turn. Harry

Simms was to find two political allies close to home, and the Brandywine was to become a hot issue in the campaign.

THE MAY PRIMARY. Pennsylvania counties are governed by three commissioners, all of whom stand for election simultaneously. Two commissioners are elected by the majority party and one by the minority party. Each party nominates two candidates; the victors are the top three votegetters of the four. In Chester County, where the Republicans outnumber the Democrats by about four to one, this means that two Republicans and one Democrat are elected to serve concurrent four-year terms.

The three incumbent commissioners had unanimously requested us to develop the plan for the Upper East Branch. We had considerable confidence in and respect for all three. Their presence had been a major factor in our choice of the Upper East Branch. Retirement of one of them and defeat of the other two at the polls was a severe blow.

Before the May primary C. Gilbert Hazlett announced that he would retire, having served three terms as chairman of the county commissioners. Widely known and much respected in Chester County, Hazlett had been a firm backer of the concepts proposed for the Brandywine, although he was undecided about the necessity for eminent domain. We had counted on his continued leadership.

Russell B. Jones was the second Republican commissioner, and in 1966 was president of the Brandywine Valley Association as well. He, too, was enthusiastic about the plan's land use proposals but was definitely skeptical about eminent domain. In June, as president of the Brandywine Valley Association, Jones announced his board's unanimous support of the plan, saying:

> We ask of those who disagree that they do so only after a full understanding of the facts. We must also ask them in complete sincerity if they have a better plan. . . . Zoning won't do it. History has proved that. Buying up the Brandywine Valley by some governmental agency isn't practical. We are strongly opposed to that. Leaving it alone won't save our valley. The East Branch concept of paying people not to build where they shouldn't holds out the only real hope.[5]

Jones anticipated being named by the Republican party executive committee to run to succeed Hazlett as chairman. Instead, the executive committee named its own chairman, Theodore S. A. Rubino. Jones declined the executive committee's offer of renomination to the second slot, and so the organization named J. Carl Empie, also a

Private property and the public interest

member of the party executive committee. There was a writein campaign for Jones in the primary, and he was quoted in the local press as saying: "If the people of Chester County prefer to select their own candidate rather than accept one handpicked by party officials, I would have no choice but to serve." He polled 9,600 votes to Empie's 27,000 and Rubino's 22,000. Rubino and Empie's campaign statement concerning the Brandywine Plan was "if the people are against it then the Commissioners will be against it."[6]

On the Democratic side, the incumbent, Leo McDermott, backed the Brandywine proposals unequivocally. He was renominated by the Democrats. As their second candidate, the Democrats nominated Louis Waldmann, an industrial management consultant and a resident of Wallace Township in the Upper East Branch. Since Rubino and Empie were certain of election, the contest for the third spot as county commissioner was between McDermott and Waldmann. The Brandywine Plan became one of their major points of contention. Waldmann's opposition to the plan was, in part, a consequence of his prior unsuccessful battle to keep eminent domain from being exercised in the Upper East Branch by the Philadelphia Electric Company. In 1962 he had been one of the organizers of the Chester County Conservation Committee and had served as its chairman in 1965 and 1966. The C.C.C.C. sought to change the route of a 500-kilovolt line so that it would not deface the Upper East Branch landscape, arguing that the line could be erected in an already existing right of way elsewhere. Chester County joined the C.C.C.C. in seeking relief from the courts, but the utility prevailed. By late 1966, Philadelphia Electric was scraping ground bare and building towers across the Brandywine countryside. In the spring, just as the Brandywine Plan was taking shape, the runoff from heavy rains carried with it a thick load of mud from the raw gash of the pipeline right of way. The Brandywine was an ugly brown for months. The eroded ground and the sediment-choked stream were a constant reminder of what the use of eminent domain by outsiders could do to the countryside.

The high tension line could not have been installed without use of eminent domain. Its construction left scars both in the minds of people and on the land. The local representative, Timothy Slack, introduced a bill in the state legislature which would have given the counties a measure of control over land acquisition by utilities for power lines and pipelines. The measure never was enacted. At about this time Albert M. Greenfield, Jr., another Upper East Branch resident who had witnessed the coming of the high tension lines and pipelines, took over as chairman of the Democratic party in Chester County. Greenfield was a Waldmann backer and became a Brandywine Plan opponent.

THE STATE PRISON. May of 1967 brought another threat to the serenity of the Upper East Branch and a hardening of opposition to eminent domain and government land acquisition. One day, with no advance warning, Chester Countians opened their newspapers to find headlines announcing that the state had bought land, partly in the Upper East Branch, for a state prison. The state did not use eminent domain; instead it engaged a prominent Philadelphia realtor to bid on its behalf for 533-acre Fuzzydele Farm when it was offered at public auction. At the time of the auction, no one realized that the state was the purchaser.

When the news broke, the local people were outraged. Fast on the heels of the announcement, the Citizens' League Against the State Penitentiary, the Northern Chester County Citizens Council, and the West Nantmeal Citizens Council were organized. Along with most local residents, Louis Waldmann was strongly opposed to having the prison built on this site. Leo McDermott disagreed. He thought that it would give the area an economic boost, provide jobs, and attract many new professionals, since the facility was to be a diagnostic center. Thus was born another campaign issue between McDermott and Waldmann.

Several people with a voice in the Brandywine Plan decision, including a township supervisor and Water Resources Authority member, told us that unless the prison was relocated they would not support the plan—that people were so upset over the prison that no public official would risk supporting another controversial proposal. Bob Struble did succeed in getting a commitment from the state to follow the principles of the Brandywine Plan in developing the prison site. This was the only intervention he and we thought appropriate, but it was not what the local politicians had in mind. Only if we could actually get rid of the prison would we have gained merit in their eyes.

To our relief, the issue soon was settled—solely on political grounds. This was one battle which the local people won. In July, Governor Shafer announced that the prison would be built elsewhere. The reason for this local triumph was that the governor was short of votes to pass his tax program. He traded the support of the Chester County legislative delegation on the tax program for his promise to abandon plans to locate the prison in Chester County. Representative Slack was hailed at a dinner at the Glenmoore fire hall as the architect of this victory. Although the prison threat was shortlived, its memory lingered on through the fall electoral campaign and at Brandywine Plan meetings. It was taken as further evidence that only local government could be trusted.

The preliminary plan

We listened to people at the April and May township public meetings, we sensed the gathering mood of negativism, fueled by the prison incursion, and then we wrote the land use recommendations of the preliminary plan. Our earlier thinking had been considerably modified. At the end of June 1967, a document entitled *Preliminary Plan and Program for the Upper East Branch of the Brandywine* was mailed to all landowners, along with two maps. One, on a scale of 1 inch to 1,380 feet (a scale used by the County Planning Commission), showed all of the critical areas, entitled the Water Resources Protection District, as well as all property lines within the basin. The same map was enlarged to a scale of 1 inch to 400 feet to show in detail the impact of the plan on each landowner's property. This map was cut into sections, and each landowner received a copy of the section or sections showing his property.

The preliminary plan was forty-nine pages long, typed single-space and interspersed with maps and graphs, unrelieved by photos. While the brochure had been attractive and easy to read but very general, the preliminary plan was thorough, solid, and, doubtless, intimidating except to the truly interested. It was written by Bob Coughlin, Ben, John, Luna, and me; the frustrating, difficult, and tedious job of preparing all of the maps was directed by Bob Myers. We had debated the desirability of preparing two preliminary plans, one a summary version of the other, and we also had debated the need for the 1:400 scale maps.

The desire to provide everyone with an opportunity to learn about his home environment, the prospects for change, and the bases for our recommendations, along with the recommendations themselves, we thought, outweighed the fact that the size and appearance of the document would deter many from reading it. I also think that the 1:400 scale maps were a mistake. We never heard that people found them particularly helpful. An enormous amount of time was spent in blowing them up from the base map, reproducing hundreds of copies, and then matching small sections of the maps with addresses so that each of the 1,400 landowners received all sections on which his property was shown. It took Bob Myers and several planning students a total of fifteen man-months to prepare those maps. It would have been far better to have devoted that time to meeting landowners at their homes and explaining to them, there on their property, how the plan would affect them. John and I did propose that some of the planners, with Ken, try to visit all large landowners during the summer, but others had different priorities. Our different sense of priorities was based on different perceptions of how much time we had in which to win acceptance for the plan. Bob Coughlin and Bob Struble wanted no fixed timetable and thought we should take as long as we thought necessary. John and I agreed in principle but did not think that this was an option open to us, as our conversations with Gordon Harrison had led us to believe that the Ford Foundation would insist on a definite commitment by early 1968. As a result, only Ken called on individual landowners.

The preliminary plan recommended that there be virtually no further development on the flood plains or on land extending three hundred feet back from either side of the stream network. Together the flood plain and stream buffer covered 26 percent of the Upper East Branch. The preliminary plan also recommended that development on slopes of 15 percent or more and in woods of at least ten contiguous acres be limited to a gross density of one dwelling unit per four acres.[7] These areas totaled 20 percent of the basin. We proposed some restriction on development in 46 percent of the basin. Development rights would be purchased by the Water Resources Authority, which would limit use of these areas in accord with the proposal.

The preliminary plan also stated that, in areas suitable for development, adequate water supply, sewage disposal, and erosion controls would be required. This was a recommendation which Bob Struble preferred to omit. It was not that he disagreed at all with its intent. However, he was worried at the extensiveness of our proposals for the Water Resources Protection District and thought that we should not add one more requirement that might prove the last straw to some people.

The recommendations already reflected accommodation to Upper East Branch preferences. Initially, Luna Leopold had recommended that, for hydrologic reasons, somewhere between 50 and 60 percent of the watershed undergo no further development and that all future growth be concentrated in the areas least critical to stream health.

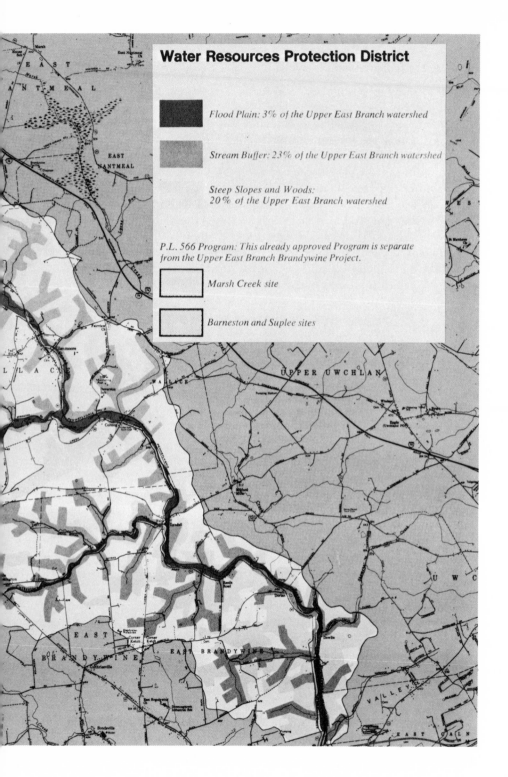

Water Resources Protection District

Flood Plain: 3% of the Upper East Branch watershed

Stream Buffer: 23% of the Upper East Branch watershed

Steep Slopes and Woods:
20% of the Upper East Branch watershed

P.L. 566 Program: This already approved Program is separate from the Upper East Branch Brandywine Project.

Marsh Creek site

Barneston and Suplee sites

Private property and the public interest

Very early we recognized, and Luna agreed, that a total development prohibition on half of the land would not be acceptable to the residents. He concluded that we could still meet our hydrologic goals by setting ten-acre lot minimums throughout the half of the basin determined most critical, and by superimposing on that restriction a total prohibition on development in the flood plains and stream buffers. Neither Bob Struble nor the coordinating committee thought that this provided enough development opportunity. Therefore we made our first compromise between hydrologic objectives and people's development desires. In the preliminary plan we retained the total prohibition on development in the flood plain (3 percent of the basin) but relaxed the requirements for all of the other critical areas and made provision for all hardship cases. As a result, everyone would be allowed to build at least one dwelling on land currently undeveloped.

In the stream buffer, no development would be allowed unless a propertyowner would thereby be denied all right to build on his land. In such a case the owner was to be allowed to build one house if his lot were less than four acres or one house per four acres, subject to specified setback, impervious coverage, and waste disposal regulations.

In the woods and on steep slopes a gross density of one dwelling unit per four acres was allowed, again subject to limitations on the amount of impervious area to be created. As in the stream buffer, people owning a tract of less than four acres almost wholly in woods and/or steep slopes were to be allowed to build one house.

Bob Struble never was happy with the three-hundred-foot setback from the streams. His concern was primarily with public acceptability, and he thought that we were including too much land in the critical areas. We planners, however, backed Luna's recommendations because our principal commitment was to a plan that would have a defensible hydrologic rationale. Throughout the planning period, there was an underlying tension between practicality and preservation of the underlying validity of the plan.

Another of our early responses to public sentiment was abandonment of proposals for cluster or planned unit development. The planning staff believed that one appropriate means of retaining parts of the critical areas in open space was through local zoning for cluster or planned unit development. Parts of a tract that were steep, wooded, or near a stream could be left open and the development clustered on more suitable land. The arguments of efficiency—lower costs of providing sewers, water, and other public services—and of better site design were not persuasive to many Brandywine residents. To them, cluster development meant cheaper housing and poorer people, which in turn meant that the present residents would have to provide more schools and pay higher taxes. They believed that large lot zoning, with lot area minimums between one and two and one-half acres, would be a shield against the "wrong" growth. It would allow enough development for landowners to reap a decent profit from development but not enough to bring in lots of new people.

Finding that any mention of clustering provoked a violently negative response, the staff regretfully abandoned such proposals. Nonetheless, its opponents continued to charge until the end that clustering would be one inevitable result of adopting the plan. One cannot help but wonder whether the response in the Brandywine to both planned unit development and easements or other development rights might have been different had the Pennsylvania Supreme Court decision[8] holding two-acre zoning unconstitutional occurred a few years earlier.

At one point we planners had seen the Brandywine Plan as offering a splendid opportunity to create a stream-related public recreation network. The abandoned railroad line running alongside the main stem could make an ideal hiking and riding trail linking the future Marsh Creek State Park and Barneston reservoir, and then heading toward the Fish Commission's forthcoming Struble Dam. Township parks could be sited along the streams. Camps, in addition to the existing scout camp on Indian Run, and private recreational development, like Mahlon Kurtz's well-managed fish hatchery and fishing ponds, could be encouraged. These ideas, too, soon were destined for oblivion.

It did not take long to learn how deep was the hostility to any form of public recreation. It would disturb the residents' privacy and quiet. There would be traffic, trash, and crime. Providing recreational opportunities would bring the city to the Brandywine, and almost everyone, supporters and opponents of the plan alike, was opposed to this. Therefore the only mention of recreation in the plan was for Barneston, Struble, and Marsh Creek, projects already approved by Chester County, despite the vocal opposition of many Brandywine residents, as part of the Soil Conservation Service watershed plan. It is not surprising, of course, that many people did link the Brandywine Plan with these other projects and criticized it for that reason.

Higher density for the critical areas and no planned unit development were the principal changes in land use recommendations made in the preliminary plan as a result of the public responses. The four-acre minimum for the woods and steep slopes and for hardship situations showed good promise of acceptability since, in the attitude survey, this was the lot size most often given as the preference of respondents.

There still was the amenity question. In the attitude study, many people had placed a high value on the natural appearance of the stream and its immediate surroundings. If we met the specifications suggested for water flow and water quality, would we also retain the desired natural characteristics of the stream valleys? Bob Myers and Ken took hundreds of photos, Bob worked on a scale model of the Upper East Branch, and members of the staff prepared maps to show which areas would be visible from the stream valleys. To our relief, these areas were almost entirely contained within the areas otherwise designated critical.

The preliminary plan devoted considerable space to the question of implementation. Landowners were told that they could choose among easements, compensable regulations, sale, sale subject to an interest for the seller's life or for a term of years, or some modification of these choices which suited their wishes. The possibility of a landowners' development corporation also was advanced. One of our premises was that implementation of the plan would bring about a rise in land values in the Upper East Branch greater than that which would occur without it. We believed that a guarantee that much of the land would remain permanently open would attract some people who wished to live on large tracts of open space and some people who wished to live on smaller properties with a view of open space. We were concerned with providing a means for all current landowners in the Upper East Branch to share in the anticipated rise in land values. Therefore, we suggested that those who owned land in the Water Resources Protection District and who would be paid by the Authority for development rights could invest the money they received in shares in a development corporation. The development corporation would invest in land suitable for development and, when the time was right, either sell the land or act as the developer. I had explored this idea before, while working in the Green Spring and in the Worthington Valleys in Baltimore County,[9] and it seemed a reasonable way to achieve an equitable distribution of the profits which urbanization would bring.[10]

Sample appraisals to provide an estimate of the total cost of the Brandywine program were scheduled for the summer of 1967, as were meetings with landowners to receive comments on the preliminary plan and preparation of the final plan. The fall was to be devoted to a series of public hearings and to township and county decisions on the plan.

Fears and threats

While we were back at the office completing the preliminary plan, the emotional temperature was rising in the Upper East Branch. May had brought the primary election, the state purchase of Fuzzydele Farm, and the second meeting of the citizens' advisory committee. That meeting was packed, mostly with non-members who came to allege that the committee was a front for the Water Resources Authority. Resentments that had been smoldering were now burning openly. One speaker alleged that I, as an author of the plan, was a Communist, a Socialist, and a dupe of the du Ponts. One rumor was that the du Pont company, located downstream in Delaware, was secretly backing the project in an effort to protect its water supply. Another allegation was that the federal government was going to tie up all the land of the Upper East Branch and then build a giant TVA-like reservoir and park—the park, of course, to be inundated every weekend with busloads of "Philadelphians" (a euphemism for blacks). (This fear had been expressed earlier about Marsh Creek.)

After this meeting the Water Resources Authority concluded that the citizens' advisory committee, with its believability tarnished, should be abandoned. At that juncture, the decision may have been the most realistic one possible. It might not have been so, however, had a substantial amount of staff time been invested earlier in the creating of a representative committee. During this period several people wrote angry letters to the press, denouncing the plan as a socialistic power play by government. However, one man, William T. Bode, wrote several letters to the papers in support of the plan. An excerpt from one letter follows:

I think it's time someone calls attention to the irrationality in the attitude and words of Mr. Kurt Wandel, Betty Templin and others about the Upper East Brandywine Project and the Marsh Creek Project. . . . [O]ne of the main problems, possibly the main problem, is that irrational charges tend to create such an emotional and unreasoning atmosphere that discussing facts becomes difficult or impossible.

In his letter to the Daily Local News of April 15, Mr. Wandel called the Upper East Brandywine Project a "strange plan" . . . a "socialistic plan." March 8 he wrote that the Marsh Creek Project is an "obvious hoax." Both he and Betty Templin (in her letter of April 18) hint at undisclosed mysticism motivating the Delaware River Basin Authority and other government officials involved. Discussing the "socialistic plan," Mr. Wandel says there is "much more to this than meets the eye and nobody wishes to be honest and tell the story in a straightforward manner." . . .

Private property and the public interest

The UEB Project has published a lucid booklet which has been distributed to citizens in the area. The booklet not only outlines the project step-by-step, it urges individuals with questions to discuss the study at any time with the project coordinator. . . . [R]egardless of what Mr. Wandel says the water in the streams is not "our own water." Chester County isn't a God-chosen vacuum with holy resources to be held at gun point from our socialist-communist neighbors in Delaware. . . .

Silence seems to condone. Because no one else has answered their charges, I'm writing this letter. . . . I live on 59.5 acres of land which will be affected by the Upper East Brandywine Project. Beyond that I have no connection with the project other than as a concerned citizen who believes that this really is "One World." . . . I don't think individual or group irrationality should be permitted to pervert either that debt or that responsibility.[11]

Three days later the *Daily Local News* carried another letter from Mr. Bode. An excerpt follows:

Let me describe the phone calls I received Wednesday night. During the evening three or four area residents called to thank me for having spoken out. At 10:30 p.m., however, I received a call from a man who identified himself as Mr. Chesterwaite. . . . Mr. Chesterwaite said he wanted to meet me. When I asked when and where, he said—and I quote him as I quoted Mr. Wandel—"Don't worry. We'll find you and get you. . . . We've been waiting for people like you to come out of the woodwork."[12]

The tone of the opposition in June 1967 is reflected in an ad placed by Harry Simms, reproduced here. Simms was a prolific writer and had a particularly choice command of language. Early in his campaign to defeat the plan, he wrote to McGeorge Bundy, president of the Ford Foundation, to object to Ford's support of the project. He sent a copy of the letter to the press:

Politically speaking this is a very conservative area. . . . As a group we feel that the private ownership of land and its management by the individual is guaranteed at the time of purchase by a clear title which admits no building restrictions. This, we feel, is a basic support built into the Keystone of a Capitalistic Democracy. To attack this keystone can only lead to further governmental infringement of the right of private ownership and in the long run could lead to the breaking down of our whole economic system. Perhaps, eventually even to the Nationalization of the automobile industry. . . . A number of these outraged citizens have already availed themselves of legal counsel which assures them of moving to the Supreme Court if necessary to secure their right to retain a title unrestricted by this Authority.[13]

Like Mr. Bode, several of us were convinced that the charges being broadcast should be publicly rebutted. Bob Struble and the Water

CITIZENS ALERT

All voters of Wallace, East Brandywine, West Brandywine, West Nantmeal, Upper Uwchlan, East Cain, Uwchlan and Honey Brook Townships

STOP THE LAND GRAB

Do you wish your land titles and those of your neighbors to be restricted eternally against any building? Do you wish "Big Daddy" government to perpetually restrict from 50% to 60% of the land area of entire township? Do you wish "Cluster-developments" and the tax-costly sewer-disposal plants that they will make necessary?

The Chester County Water Resources Authority has publicly advocated cluster developments as a suggestion to your township supervisors in order to implant this land-water grab.

In short, do you believe in the time honored rights of private ownership and land-management or do you wish a precedent to be established which gives the state the right to perpetually manage and restrict over half the land area in any township chosen? Do you believe in private ownership or state control, threatened with a writ of eminent domain?

Hundreds of voters have already chosen their political philosophy in East Brandywine Township by signing a petition which asks their elected township supervisors to resist this threat to the basic corner stone of American democracy. They have signed that they wish no title restrictions forced into their titles by the public authorities. If you wish to resist "Big Daddy" you may examine this petition at the green house of Mr. Karl Bauss, at Lyndell and go on record as one of the dwindling group of Americans who still feel that they can successfully manage their own affairs without the threat of their properties being seized by a writ of eminent domain.

There will be a similar petition for each township involved. Every voter, landowner or not, is urged to help prevent "Big Daddy's" fist from closing around our townships and dictating their management for all our future posterity.

This is the alert—The wrap-up of this grab is this November— Time is short—The issue is clean-cut. It is "Big Daddy" vs our individual rights.

Stand up and be counted, sign the petition to stop the land grab today at the greenhouse of Mr. Karl Bauss.

If you want Transportation or Information,
Call Mr. Harry Simms at WH 2-2792 weekends.

Group of Citizens Interested in Individual Rights.

Private property and the public interest

Resources Authority board disagreed, and the opponents of the Brandywine Plan gathered more and more frequent headlines with their allegations while we sat back and waited for the furor to abate. It never did.

With constant nurture the nucleus of an opposition would grow into the Chester County Freeholders and later would spawn the Regional Planning Commission of the Upper Brandywine. Soon people throughout the basin would be aroused, if ill-informed. Never again would there be a somnolent, poorly attended public meeting on the subject. With rumors spreading fast, we needed the preliminary plan to set out the proposal in explicit detail for all of the landowners to consider. We mailed it, and the honeymoon was over.

response and decision

THE PRELIMINARY PLAN told the people of the Brandywine whether their land would be affected and, if so, how. It was highly specific as to sites and restrictions on their use, and therefore we expected that it would evoke scores of questions. We were all a bit aghast at what the fall of 1967 held in store: much further technical work to undergird the plan; hearings and meetings to discuss the plan with all interested residents; the fall election campaign with the prospect of the plan as a major issue; decisions on the final version of the plan to be taken after evaluating reactions and events; and, finally, acceptance or rejection of it.

We were not the only ones to feel pressed. Despite our efforts, many people did not know that planning was under way in the Brandywine until the public meetings in the spring of 1967, while others had remained unaware of it until they received the preliminary plan. Therefore a deadline of January 1968 for a decision seemed unreasonable. Some people felt that they were being railroaded. Bob Struble hoped that the postponement of the deadline would allow things to cool down and improve the prospects for a favorable decision. With this in mind, in the summer and fall of 1967, first Ben and I, then Bob Struble appealed to Gordon Harrison for a six-month extension of the planning period to midsummer of 1968. At first he suggested that if we asked for a six-month funded extension it might destroy our prospects of receiving funds for carrying out the plan. However, in December he granted the six-month extension request, albeit reluctantly. Maurice Goddard volunteered an additional ten thousand dollars, and the Geological Survey continued its matching funds.

The time we gained helped us to work out a plan that was strong technically. It also was as close a match of people's environmental objectives with a practicable formula for achieving them as we could devise. Yet it was defeated. This chapter details the events of the final year of planning, leaving for later an exploration of what, if, and why.

Further planning

The technical planning job was little more than half-finished when the last words of the preliminary plan were written. Much of the basic data had been collected and the outlines of the plan had been limned, but considerable detailed analysis still remained to be done. Revisions would be needed after the public had had a chance to respond. The population projections were complete; now we needed to know whether the Upper East Branch watershed could supply that many people with water and handle their wastes without deterioration of water quality. We had proposed several legal techniques for regulating development areas and for controlling the use of land in the critical areas. Whichever of these proved most acceptable to the public had to be translated into easements, ordinances, and the like. Our hydrologic hypotheses were well advanced, but we needed data from the stream monitoring program to confirm them. Laborious searches of county records had yielded detailed information about the turnover rate and price of land. What was of consuming interest to Brandywine residents now was what this information meant in terms of the value of easements. All of this lay ahead, as did some hypothetical work on the prospective costs and benefits of the plan.

WATER SUPPLY AND SEWAGE DISPOSAL. In September of 1967, we contracted with Irwin Remson at Drexel University to tell us whether it would be possible to provide the projected population of 38,000 in the Upper East Branch with an adequate water supply, solely from the basin's water, and to cleanse their wastes so that the quality of water in the basin's streams and wells would not deteriorate. With Alexander Fungaroli and Robert Schoenberger of Drexel, Remson came up with explicit plans for location of water supply and waste disposal systems and cost estimates for all systems. Their work was a model of efficiency and clarity and was precisely the sort of innovative planning that we needed.

We provided quite detailed information about probable location, by sub-basin, of the future population, as well as about soils, geology, and precipitation. Using this, Remson and his colleagues designed a system which they calculated would cost $590 per capita, with total cost of water supply $8 million and sewerage $14.3 million. A stilling reservoir with nine days' storage capacity would be built on the mainstem. This reservoir would supply 14,000 people. The others would rely on groundwater, three-quarters of them from community wells and the rest, mostly living in the lightly settled critical areas, from onsite wells. Everyone living in the development areas would be tied in to one of four sewerage systems. The trunk lines of these systems would follow the ridges, rather than the stream valleys as is customary. This

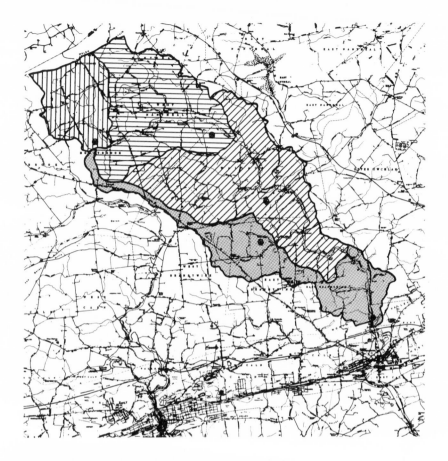

PROPOSED WATER AND SEWER DISTRICTS

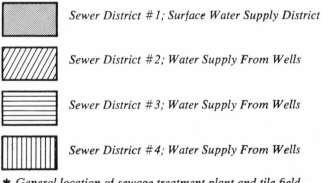

Sewer District #1; Surface Water Supply District

Sewer District #2; Water Supply From Wells

Sewer District #3; Water Supply From Wells

Sewer District #4; Water Supply From Wells

✱ General location of sewage treatment plant and tile field.

would avoid sedimentation of the streams during construction and subsequent exfiltration of wastes into the stream network. Also it would place the trunk lines in the heart of the development areas. After secondary treatment, including chemical coagulation to remove nitrates and phosphates, effluent from these systems would receive tertiary treatment by discharge to large (three to eight acres) tile fields, located at least fifteen hundred feet from any stream.[1] The construction costs of this water supply and waste disposal system were comparable to costs for conventional systems. The environmental benefits from properly designed recycling of the basin's water resources were substantial.

DEVELOPMENT REGULATIONS. Two sets of land use controls were needed, one for the critical areas and one for the development areas. We could not proceed with drafting the controls for the critical areas until we decided what types would be most acceptable to landowners.

However, John and I had no doubt about the needs for municipal regulation of the development areas to minimize erosion and runoff and to limit removal of trees during construction. John talked and corresponded with soil conservationists, reviewed many ordinances and regulations, and selected what he thought were the best provisions for inclusion in the plan. While no one objected to these recommendations for development regulations, no one responded to them with interest and enthusiasm. All attention was riveted on the key issues of development rights, eminent domain, and amount of compensation for land in the critical areas. The equally significant issue of management of development, including water supply, waste disposal, and erosion control, was peripheral to most people's concern. Power over property, not environmental protection, was their frame of reference.

DEVELOPMENT VALUE. Bob Coughlin and Ben Stevens gave the greatest attention to the conceptual problems of measurement and comparison of the costs and benefits of development under the Brandywine Plan with the costs and benefits of conventional development. Land values are one basis for this comparison. Therefore, it was essential to determine and record pre-plan land values so as to have a yardstick against which later values in the Upper East Branch and in the control area could be measured. This land value information also was vital for calculation of the value of development rights. We needed to know the rate and location of land sales in the Upper East Branch over recent years, as well as year-by-year changes in land values. Digging out this information from county records was tedious work for Bob Coughlin's staff. Since Chester County has yet to enter the age of the computer, there were no shortcuts.

Calculating values of development rights was a complex and challenging task. We took one large step toward simplification by deciding to estimate the value of easements only. We had suggested in the preliminary plan that landowners could choose whatever form of compensated land use control best suited them. However, it seemed probable that most would prefer an easement and that for purposes of an initial approximation, determination of easement value would suffice. This still left several complicating factors. First, there were several types of critical areas—flood plains, stream buffers, and woods and slopes—and under the plan each would be subject to different development limitations. For instance, there would be no development in flood plains, while there could be one dwelling per four acres in woods. An easement on woods adjoining an arterial road and in the path of growth would cost more than an identical easement on woods far from growth pressures because the former easement would cause a sharper drop in land value than the latter. Then too, parcel size and the amount of the parcel subject to the easement would influence the value of the easement.

We worked with three appraisers on this calculation of easement values. We approached the question analytically, the appraisers pragmatically from their long experience with the market for different types of land. While two of the appraisers were Chester Countians and thoroughly acquainted with the local market, neither they nor we had experience in appraising easements. This was a serious handicap and led to a delay which imperiled our credibility at public meetings. We sorely needed an appraiser with expertise in less than fee appraisals and had found such a person, a man with a national reputation. Unfortunately, local politics influenced the choice of the lead appraiser. The man chosen was sincerely dedicated to the goals of the Brandywine project but lacked the very special prior experience which we needed.

A question uppermost in the minds of Brandywine residents was what they would be paid for easements. A number rejected the very concept of market value, suggesting that everyone should receive the same price per acre regardless of current market value or appraised value of the easement. These were mostly people whose land had a low market value. Others thought that only annual payments, made perpetually and rising with the market, could approximate the actual worth of their development rights.

Disagreement over what constituted a fair method of computing

Private property and the public interest

value was compounded by delays in getting information from the appraisers. Several planning tasks took longer than anticipated. The delays in obtaining the appraisal figures were most damaging because they enabled critics to impugn the credibility of the Water Resources Authority and its planners, which they did often, and with relish. Since the amount of money to be offered was central to many people's decisions about the plan, and since this information was several months late, suspicions were aroused.

Bob Struble had an excellent idea. Pending receipt of the appraisers' report, he suggested that we take four or five local appraisers to a tract of land which included each type of critical area and describe the use restrictions for each, then request each appraiser to note on a card his estimate of loss in value to the critical areas resulting from the easement restrictions. This procedure would be repeated at several other sites and the individual estimates aggregated. This would have given us ball park figures to use at public meetings. The rest of us unwisely rejected Bob's idea. We thought that the more accurate figures would be available soon and that it would be better not to risk coming up with two sets of estimates that varied considerably. That would have been hard to explain to people and would have laid us open to charges of misrepresentation. As it turned out, we were accused of concealment and trickery instead.

Many landowners wanted to know exactly how much they would receive for an easement on their land before deciding to support the plan. From the landowner's viewpoint, this was an altogether reasonable demand. Yet a parcel-by-parcel appraisal would have cost tens of thousands of dollars. In addition, we did not know whether the plan would go forward, and even if we had had the funds for the appraisal such an expenditure seemed unjustified. Instead, we gave landowners some benchmarks. By providing a total estimate of easement value of all critical areas (some $3 million), by specifying the appraisers' bases for establishing the value of easements on different types of land, and by stating the range in value which they calculated for each type of restricted land, we thought that each landowner could roughly determine the price of his easement.

The appraisers, using Bob Coughlin's data on land sales for each township and for parcels of different sizes, gave their estimates of percentage of value added by proximity to urban growth and by road frontage and specified the range and average value for the fee value of each type of critical area. For flood plain land, the fee value ranged from $100 to $300 per acre, and the average was $250 per acre. The easement was calculated to be worth from 5 to 25 percent of the fee value, with an average of 10 percent. For stream buffers, woods, and steep slopes, the fee value ranged from $100 to $900 per acre, with an average of $600. Easement value was estimated to vary widely—from 10 to 90 percent of the fee value—with the average 50 percent. Easements for flood plains, stream buffers, woods, and steep slopes combined were calculated to be worth 48 percent of the total fee value. The fee value of these lands is lower than that of the remaining land in the watershed because wet or steep lands are less readily developable.

The complexities of fee and easement valuation are not easy to grasp, and we did not succeed in explaining them to the Brandywine landowners. Many people expected to be told that any easement, anywhere, is worth a specified number of dollars per acre. At the final round of public meetings, when we tried to explain how the easement values had been calculated and why all easements did not have the same value, some opponents were confirmed in their earlier suspicions that they weren't being given a straight answer. Yet if we had simplified our approach and offered to pay the average value to everyone—$25 per acre for all flood plain easements and $300 per acre for all other easements—those whose easements were worth more than the average would have been outraged.

The events of autumn

While we were completing the technical side of planning, three crucial events took place: the public response to the preliminary plan, the formal emergence of the Chester County Freeholders Association as a citizen organization to oppose the plan, and the November election of county commissioners. By the close of this period we were exploring alternatives to eminent domain, doubtful that we could transcend the deep and widespread opposition to it.

PUBLIC RESPONSE. The next group of Authority-sponsored public meetings was planned for the fall, after people had received and thought about the preliminary plan. By then, however, its opponents had stirred up considerable fear, animosity, and hostility to it. Also, it was election time, and the plan was a major issue. Bob Struble therefore decided to keep publicity to a minimum, dropped the second round of township public meetings, and in October announced that he was seeking an extension of the planning period.

Six meetings were held at this stage, but none was sponsored by the Water Resources Authority. One meeting, in East Brandywine, was organized by the opponents of the plan in that township. Two meetings in West Nantmeal Township were organized by the planning commission, the first so that township residents could discuss the plan among themselves and the second for discussion with the planning staff. One meeting, in East Caln, was organized by Ken Wood at the township's request. The other two meetings were held by Wallace and West Brandywine Townships.

At the West Brandywine meeting, the supervisors asked for a preliminary, informational vote from the forty-two people present. The vote took place at the end of the meeting, after Bob Struble had announced that the minimum lot size required in the woods and slopes districts had been reduced from ten acres to four acres and one supporter of the plan had told people that his mortgage company had assured him that it would lend money on properties subject to easements as proposed in the plan. Thirty-eight people voted: sixteen voted no, ten voted yes, and twelve said that they were still undecided.[2]

At the first West Nantmeal meeting the planning commission arranged a debate, with Donald G. Brownlow, the chairman, taking the negative side and James W. Cresmer, Jr., the positive. Fifty people heard Cresmer argue that the property would be more valuable open but express concern that the easements might not be permanent. Brownlow challenged the qualifications of the planners, and was quoted as saying of Wood, "I have more things against that man than you can shake a stick at. . . . The idea is good but not when in the hands of amateurs." One person at the meeting charged that the plan was being engineered by Du Pont for the benefit of industry.[3]

Two weeks later Bob Struble, Ken, John, and I were invited by the West Nantmeal Planning Commission to address their second meeting. Bob said that "eminent domain is a necessary part of government" and observed that most questions about the plan had arisen because easements were "a whole new concept." Among the comments from the residents were that Wilmington would get the clean water and the Upper East Branch only the pretty scenery and that "people want to get some appreciation in property values." Another person feared the "psychological nightmare" of government authority.[4]

Soon after these meetings, several letters strongly supportive of the plan were sent to the *Daily Local News*. Theodore and Elsie Baumgard, owners of a tree nursery in West Nantmeal, wrote: "That was an excellent group at the easement meeting. . . . It was informative, well planned and orderly. All power to the program."[5] Magnus Tornquist, a former member of the Honey Brook Township Planning Commission, said: "This 'open space' program deserves to be encouraged by all area residents and property owners. Let us keep Honey Brook the land of 'sweet waters' as its name implies and may we be a part of a worthy cause for the rest of America. . . . If we are to benefit from this project, we owe it to our conscience and our community to let our support be made known for a really good program before we lose it by default."[6] William Bode, writing of the East Brandywine meeting, again expressed his concern:

Someone described the meeting as "Democracy in Action." I guess I'd accept that view if everyone had declared honestly that they want to sell land at a profit, without restriction on use, regardless of the damage such sale or use does to the natural resources in the valley. . . . I speak out now because those honest words weren't spoken. Instead the charges of Communism and Socialism were hurled. . . . I'd like to see everyone be a little unselfish now for the sake of the future of the valley and of the county. I don't think eternal restrictions placed on our land will cost us as much as the rape of the valley will cost those who come after us.[7]

In sum, there was some strong support, but people were also confused and concerned. It had been stated that eminent domain would be used by the Water Resources Authority if landowners did not sell development rights voluntarily. People already felt threatened by government, with the gas lines, the high tension line, the Marsh Creek project, and the proposed prison, and many saw the Brandywine Plan as another government program to force people to use their land in a certain way. In actual fact, our approach was vastly different from that used in past public acquisitions. We were trying to involve local people in the planning process, we were entirely forthright about our recommendations, and the county commissioners had assured the township governments a decisive role in acceptance or rejection of the plan. Nevertheless, too many people did not trust the county government or the outside planners.

We turned to the coordinating committee for advice on the issue of eminent domain at a meeting in November. The group present that night split about evenly on the basic question. Some reported concern that the Water Resources Authority was moving too fast. A realtor said: "Tell these people what you are going to take and what you are going to pay."[8] While the discussion was thoughtful, the outcome was inconclusive. No alternatives were offered by those who recommended against eminent domain.

THE CHESTER COUNTY FREEHOLDERS ASSOCIATION. The group of people who had gotten together to fight the plan under the leadership of Harry Simms decided in the fall to establish a more formal organization and to try to broaden their base of support. A number of Brandywine residents active in organizing the Chester County Freeholders Association had had prior experience in the organization of such protests. Between 1962 and 1967 seven citizens' organizations were formed locally to oppose some form of outside intervention in county affairs. They died or became inactive once the fight was won or lost. Their leaders, however, were vigilant, ready to fight again when they perceived a new threat.

The purpose of the Chester County Freeholders Association was to lead the fight against the Brandywine Plan and, as part of this fight, to oppose passage in Harrisburg of a revised version of the open space legislation we had worked for in 1965 and earlier. Morris Jackson, the Freeholders' first president, had fought hard against the Marsh Creek reservoir. Harry Simms, first secretary and later president of the group, was the dominant voice and was by far the most active of its approximately fifty members. Representative Timothy Slack was the group's spokesman in the Pennsylvania legislature.

The organization at once plunged into the political fray, energetically backing Louis Waldmann in his campaign for county commissioner. On October 23, 1967, the Freeholders sponsored a meeting, attended by approximately two hundred people, at which the candidates for the post of county commissioner were asked to state their views on the plan. Harry Simms struck the mood of the meeting by observing that the federal government already owned 30 percent of of the land of the United States and warned that government had better "keep their hands off our private property." Reiterating a favorite theme, he forecast the beginning of socialism should the plan be adopted.[9] To this Bob Struble rejoined that the County Water Resources Authority was hardly the federal government, and that he had "never anticipated anyone getting excited about the plan one way or the other." Two of the four candidates spoke. Theodore Rubino, speaking for himself and his Republican runningmate, said. "When we're elected we will be responsive to the wishes of the people." Louis Waldmann said he was four-square against "eminent domain of any type."[10]

A few days later Morris Jackson announced that the Freeholders were preparing their own plan (which was never unveiled) and were endorsing Louis Waldmann. "Inasmuch as this organization stands opposed to easements and deed restrictions being forcibly imposed upon private property by any public authority and whereas Louis F. Waldmann has been the only candidate for office of Chester County Commissioner who has unequivocally publicly stated his stand against the forcible imposition of easements and deed restrictions . . . we hereby endorse him."[11]

THE ELECTION. Since it was inconceivable that either Republican candidate could lose, the race for the third county commissioner's seat was between Louis Waldmann and Leo McDermott. McDermott, as noted earlier, favored the Brandywine Plan and the Marsh Creek dam and had stated that locating a state prison in the county might be good for employment. In addition, as commissioner he had been active in bringing about active county participation in federal poverty programs and had supported public housing programs in the county.

Waldmann was vehemently against most of these programs or proposals and silent about the rest. He called eminent domain the crux of the Brandywine issue. "It's something politicans can't be fence-sitters on because it will eventually fall into the hands of the new county commissioners." The real question was not that of keeping the area in a natural state with clean streams, he said, but that of the unbridled use of eminent domain powers.[12] He was for "real conservation, not confiscation," and campaigned on the motto "Keep Local Government Strong." Waldmann backers urged people to split their tickets, voting for him and one of the two Republicans. Although the Republican party dissasociated itself from this move, it provided the margin of votes he needed to win. He received 19,918 votes, McDermott, 18,686.

The *Coatesville Record* summed up the Democratic side of the election as follows:

[I]t was election headquarters for the Chester County Democratic party, a minority party, and now a party turned in on itself. . . . Those in the plush room seemed more concerned that Leo McDermott, incumbent Democratic county commissioner win more votes than fellow Democrat Louis Waldmann than whether Democrats would gain more votes than Republicans. . . . Observers credited a letter sent out to Republicans urging a split vote for county commissioner—a vote for one Republican and the other for Waldmann —as leading a number of normally GOP voters to cast a vote for Waldmann. . . . "Ted (Rubino) and I are running about 1,000 to 1,500 votes behind the rest of the Republican ticket," Empie said at one point during the early morning hours. He blamed the split vote for the discrepancy.[13]

Prior to the election there were three commissioners interested in the plan and enthusiastic about finding a way to make it acceptable to the public. As of November 8, the only public statement made about the plan by two of the commissioners-elect was that they were ready to follow the people's wishes. The third already was committed to a course of public opposition.

As we became more and more aware of the tenuousness of our links with the people of the Upper East Branch, we discussed with Bob Struble the idea of engaging a public relations consultant. While we favored the idea, we recognized that such a step could arouse derision or suspicion among the Upper East Branch people. Bob was convinced that people would see this as evidence that the Water Resources Authority was out to sell the plan and therefore rejected the suggestion. We recognized the validity of his objection but regretted the loss of advice on the best ways to communicate with the Brandywine landowners.

PASSAGE OF THE EASEMENT LAW. The close of 1967 did bring one signal victory, for which John and I worked especially hard. The Pennsylvania legislature passed our bill, revised since 1965 to authorize counties as well as the state to acquire easements and other less than fee interests, by use of eminent domain, for water resource and other open space purposes. The Freeholders, with the aid of Representative Slack, did succeed in adding some amendments, but these did not impair the main purpose of the bill. With it enacted, any possible doubts about the legal authority to carry out the plan vanished.

As it became more and more apparent that the bill was likely to pass, the Freeholders intensified their efforts. Harry Simms reiterated his charge of socialism and matched this with the allegation that Bob Struble, under the pretense of seeking open space funds from the U.S. Department of Housing and Urban Development, was actually seeking development:

The membership of the Chester County Freeholders Association has been actively opposing the passage of State Senate Bill #253. . . . Bill #253 would empower the state . . . to place eternal building restrictions into private land titles by condemnation of the landowner's title, against his wishes, and by the use of force, via a writ of eminent domain. A farmer could be so restricted that his land might only be used for farming and not sold advantageously for private building. . . . Financial experts say that a whole new concept of mortgage equity and lending policy should have to be developed for the contractual transfer and transaction of jeopardized property. . . . Mr. Struble was politically inept enough to imagine that an uninformed rural area might be coerced into trading their time-honored rights of private ownership for a bold land-grab, thinly disguised under a very questionable veil of conservation. The validity of the authority's plea for conservation was exposed by such proposals by Mr. Struble and his group, as Cluster Development. . . . This whole idea is not conservation, it is conscription. It is not conservation; it is urban development, and that is just where Mr. Struble is asking for his funds, from H.U.D. . . . headed by Mr. Weaver. . . . The broad question is not one of open spaces, but actually our choice as to whether we remain a capitalistic democracy or embrace State Socialism.[14]

Not long after this, Simms took quite another tack in a letter to Robert C. Weaver, Secretary of HUD. Apparently adjusting to what he assumed to be Weaver's political philosophy, the plan was now not socialistic but neo-fascistic:

A very great many citizens when informed that H.U.D. was being contacted to fund this experiment in NEO-FASCISM, question the use of monies being paid to well-off landowners from funds commonly believed held to alleviate the very real economic suffering of a struggling minority group. . . . We hope that you, Mr. Weaver, will see through this thinly veiled power grab. That you will protect us against the first thrust of a forcible seizure of civil rights, which if allowed will create a precedent undermining the very bed-rock philosophy of our Democracy.[15]

The efforts of the Freeholders bore some fruit. Representative Slack did succeed in amending the bill to give the counties a veto power over state use of eminent domain. The press described Slack's report to the Freeholders as follows:

State Representative C. Timothy Slack of Coatesville last night told the Chester County Freeholders how, by a "bluff" [an old poker term, he explained] he was able to caponize House Bill 253. "Every time some genius comes up with a great idea," Slack said, "he wants to use Chester County for a guinea pig." Bill 253 reflected that policy, the firm-jawed legislator added. County members in caucus tried to hold back but, unable to do so because of "pressure groups," he bluffed: he asked to address the House and said he was writing an amendment to remove Chester County. Coughlin asked if he'd accept his original amendment giving county commissioners veto power and Slack said ok. Slack said that put the county in "excellent shape" since commissioners would control the easements.[16]

The bill then passed by votes of 29 to 9 in the Senate and 130 to 65 in the House.

A letter to the paper castigated Tim Slack for his stand, observing that he was serving the wishes of the fifty members of the Freeholders rather than those of the fifteen hundred members of the Brandywine Valley Association and the five hundred members of the Red Clay Valley Association. "As far as I can tell the only thing the Freeholders want done is to make sure no one can interfere with their right to exploit the countryside."[17] Speaking to the Chester County Board of Realtors, Slack and another Chester County representative, John Stauffer, explained their views. Slack said: "We battled right down the line" without getting "all that we wanted. We succeeded in taking eminent domain away from the state and giving it to the county commissioners. . . . We have at least knocked down the real fallacy of the thing." Stauffer added: "I have no quarrel with the Upper East Brandywine Plan as long as the owner chooses to voluntarily give up development rights to his ground, but we violate the rights of our people if the state can come in and condemn." Granting the state the right to condemn "goes beyond the sovereign rights of the people." Everett Hoopes, a prominent local realtor, defended the program, saying that easements would prevent construction of buildings "where there should be no buildings anyway" and noted that many people would be willing to pay more for properties adjacent to the open lands of the project.[18]

As it affected the Brandywine Plan, Representative Slack, the "caponizer," and the Freeholders saw a threat in the easement law where none existed. The plan did not propose that acquisition should be by the state; it was all to be local, through the county commissioners and the Water Resources Authority. Possibly because the prospect of state intervention roused such outrage, the opponents never tired of charging that it was a major element of the plan.

Eminent domain
renounced

Some Brandywine residents said that the planners and the Water Resources Authority failed to modify the plan to take the public criticism into account. The staff, however, felt otherwise. In fact, by the time we wrote the final version, some of us believed that such serious compromises had been made that the plan had little chance of being implemented. Some of the compromises were in types and densities of land use proposed; others were in the methods for carrying out the plan.

The only major public objection before which the planners did not give way was the issue of permanent easements. Many argued that the easements should be only for a limited period, such as ten years. If land values rose in the future, the critics wished to profit by this increase. If the restrictions were in force for only ten years, then everyone would be free at the end of that time to sell the land for development or to renew an easement at a price reflecting the increased land value.

While this is understandable from the individual landowner's viewpoint, to the planners it was a virtual guarantee that the plan would have only a ten-year life. Development pressure would be far greater in ten years, many people would be tempted to sell for development, and those who were not might want the public to bear a much larger share of the cost of keeping the land open for another ten years. Would the taxpayers be willing to pay more? And what would happen at the end of the next ten years? Soon no land would be covered by easements.

We suggested a ninety-nine-year term for the easements as a compromise, but the critics were looking for a profit within a short time. To them, ninety-nine years was forever; to us, it was a minimum. We also believed that short-term easements would be a waste of public funds. We were unwilling to try to raise money for this purpose, and in this the Water Resources Authority concurred. Since a ninety-nine-year easement seemed no more popular than a permanent easement, we retained the latter as part of the final plan.

Renunciation of eminent domain was the most difficult compromise for the planning staff to accept. In 1966, when we distributed *The Brandywine: A Place for Man; A Place for Nature*, we found that eminent domain was the most unappealing aspect of the plan. The more we learned of the bitter antagonism to eminent domain, growing out of the failure to defeat Marsh Creek dam and the utilities, the more clear our dilemma became. We could not conceive of a compromise that would be politically feasible and possible to fund. Also, a voluntary plan made our ability to prove our hydrologic and economic hypotheses doubtful.

For hydrologic purposes, the plan had to be carried out uniformly throughout the basin or one or more sub-basins, although the scale could be altered to a smaller basin, at some cost in results. Eminent domain, or at least the threat of it, was well-nigh essential to uniform application. If participation in the plan were voluntary, nonparticipants could develop their land in violation of the hydrologically imposed limitations and vitiate the efforts of the participants. Furthermore, those participating in the plan would be providing guaranteed open space benefits to the nonparticipants, causing a rise in their land values and further rewarding them for nonparticipation.

We hoped that, with time and discussion, enough people would understand the need for eminent domain to accept it as an essential part of the plan, but by early 1968 we realized that the plan would be rejected if we retained eminent domain. People did want the Brandywine to stay beautiful, but they saw no need for forcible government intervention to achieve this. Also, although development seemed remote, most people wanted to hang on to their ticket in the development sweepstakes. Antagonism to government, plus the desire to protect their investment, contributed to the public resistance to the methods proposed for implementing the plan. Few questioned the water management principles or the resultant recommendations for land use: it was eminent domain that was the sticking point.

Dropping eminent domain would raise another question—how to fund the plan. As noted earlier, the Water Resources Authority was unlikely to receive public or private money to carry out the plan unless it provided for eminent domain. The potential donors of funds for easement acquisition, including officials of the Ford Foundation, the Department of Housing and Urban Development open space land program, and the Commonwealth of Pennsylvania's two open space programs, had all made that clear. None of them could or would fund a program likely to raise the value of the land of a few people as a direct result of their grants. In each case, fear of public criticism outweighed the wish to see the demonstration take place. In principle they were right, but for an experiment in a new approach to land management a more venturesome spirit was required.

As we became more and more doubtful that eminent domain would be accepted, we turned to the local people for advice. Our November meeting with the coordinating committee, already mentioned, was the first of these discussions. Bob Struble talked to the county commissioners, and we met with the Water Resources Authority board and its solicitor and with officials of several townships, proposing a few methods short of eminent domain.

We sent out in advance of these meetings a short memorandum outlining alternatives to or modifications of eminent domain. The first alternative was that the easement program be voluntary but that it take effect only if certain conditions were met. We suggested that the Upper East Branch be divided into four sub-basins and that the Authority staff spend six months obtaining as many easement options as possible in one of these sub-basins. It would be agreed at the start that, unless owners of 75 percent of the Water Resources Protection District land in a sub-basin signed easement options during the six-month period, all options would expire and the plan would be abandoned for that sub-basin. We also suggested that, as an incentive, the Authority could offer owners a bonus over and above the appraised value of their easements if 100 percent of them agreed to participate.

We offered two choices if the 75 percent minimum were reached. The Authority could exercise its options, hoping that over time the remaining landowners would agree to sell easements, or the township governments could agree in advance with the Authority that, if owners of at least 75 percent of the critical areas agreed to sell easements voluntarily, the Authority would use eminent domain to obtain easements on the remaining land. Voluntary easements had one advantage over eminent domain. Eminent domain lacked flexibility. If we were to condemn easements, we would have had to apply the same rules throughout the watershed in order to treat everyone equally. However, there were properties whose topography would dictate taking more than three hundred feet—or less. Under voluntary easement acquisition, such flexibility would be possible. Not so with eminent domain.

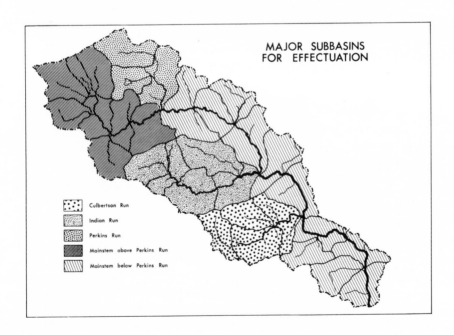

MAJOR SUBBASINS
FOR EFFECTUATION

Culbertson Run
Indian Run
Perkins Run
Mainstem above Perkins Run
Mainstem below Perkins Run

Private property and the public interest

The second alternative which we proposed in our memorandum was inverse condemnation. The townships would zone in accord with the plan recommendations for each type of critical area. At the same time, they would notify all landowners affected by the zoning that they had a limited period, perhaps six months, in which to claim that the township had in fact taken an easement from them for which they were owed compensation. A court would then determine whether the zoning was unreasonable and did constitute the taking of an easement and, if so, how much the landowner should be paid. The Authority would give money to the townships to pay for these easements, and the townships would transfer the easements to the Authority. Any landowner who did not file a claim within the specified period would be said to have accepted the fairness of the zoning. We warned that inverse condemnation had been used infrequently and presented several uncertainties—chief among them the number of claims which would be filed, the response of the courts, and the amount of money awarded.

The third alternative we proposed was for the townships to zone in accord with the plan and for the Authority to do nothing until a landowner sought a zoning change to develop in violation of it. At this time the Authority could either offer to buy easements at their value at the time of the proposed development or could condemn the easements. We stated that it would be exceedingly difficult to find money to fund this program because no one would be able to calculate in advance when or how much money would be needed.

Our fourth and fifth alternatives we listed but noted that we personally rejected them. A pollution charge might be imposed for violation of the plan, or easements might be rented for a renewable term of years. The former we found too complex, the latter unreasonably expensive to the public.

The only one of these options which evoked any enthusiasm among township officials was the wholly voluntary easement. Most of the county and township people with whom we talked understood the problems inherent in the voluntary easement. Many of them also saw the need for eminent domain, yet believed that the voluntary easement was the only approach which would be acceptable to the public. After lengthy debate among ourselves, we decided to recommend to the Authority the voluntary easement and an increase in the minimum amount of Water Resources Protection District land from 75 to 80 percent. There was one other choice under the voluntary easement proposal: the owner could sell the fee to the Authority, which would then resell the fee subject to an easement.

In February the East Brandywine township supervisors went on record as being opposed to eminent domain. Next, Louis Waldmann, who had received a final draft of the plan relying entirely on a voluntary approach, brought more pressure to bear by stating: "I have examined and read in detail the draft of their proposal and find it still relies heavily on the use of eminent domain powers to force mandatory deed restrictions on hundreds of Chester County landowners. This is not CONSERVATION. This is CONFISCATION."[19] Only the Philadelphia *Evening Bulletin* reporter followed this quotation with a statement that the draft had, in fact, eliminated eminent domain entirely in favor of voluntary easements.

In early April, the West Brandywine supervisors passed a resolution favoring the project and its goals but not eminent domain. A few days later the Uwchlan supervisors stated that they, too, were in favor of the objectives of the plan but opposed eminent domain.

On April 15, the Water Resources Authority, having carried the question over from its March meeting, formally voted to drop eminent domain and endorsed our proposal that it offer to contact all owners of critical areas in one of four sub-basins of the Upper East Branch to seek short-term easement options. Where the money for the options or the easements would come from no one knew. However, we had eliminated the major objection to the plan. No government would tell any landowner what to do. The choice to participate or not would rest with him, the ultimate democratization of the decision process. This approach also eliminated another objection, that not enough money would be offered landowners for their easements. Under a voluntary plan, each landowner would have an opportunity to accept or reject a specific offer.

Bob Struble was hopeful that, with the threat of coercion removed, almost everyone would participate voluntarily and that the few holdouts might be persuaded to participate by the weight of community opinion. He and Ken believed that enough landowners in the Indian Run sub-basin were in favor of the plan to make it quite likely that a voluntary approach would work there. Others of us were less sanguine but saw no alternative. This fundamental change in the plan did not have the hoped-for effect on public opinion. It did please some, but it in no way mollified the plan's opponents, even though eminent domain was the principal stated basis for their opposition.

West Nantmeal was one township which responded favorably. Donald Brownlow, chairman of the Planning Commission, said at this time that he thought that, after three to five years of a voluntary plan, people might even accept eminent domain. The supervisors and Planning Commission members wrote a joint letter to the Authority in unanimous support of voluntary easements,[20] but there was a catch. They demanded that the price per acre paid to all easement sellers should be the highest assessed price in the Upper East Branch. All property owners would receive the same amount per acre, whether they owned flood plain or woods, ten or a hundred acres, accessible or inaccessible land. Obviously, owners of lands of lower value liked the proposal while owners of lands of higher value totally rejected it.

The opponents of the plan simply ignored the change and continued to charge, right through the final public meetings, that the plan was obnoxious because it relied on eminent domain. Many people never understood that eminent domain had been dropped from the plan; others, voicing their distrust, said that the Authority, given any chance to launch the plan, would go back on its word not to use it; still others had an antipathy to government owning rights in private land—even rights voluntarily sold.

As we listened to the mounting clamor, we became more and more convinced that the plan would not be adopted. Knowing of John Carson's expanding water resources program in Bucks County, we wondered whether there was any chance that he and others in Bucks County would want, at this late date, to try to implement the plan. Carson expressed interest, suggested that the people at the Paunnacussing watershed might be receptive, and arranged for us to meet with several county and township officials. The initial soundings were encouraging. At this point we invited Gordon Harrison to meet Carson and to discuss the Ford Foundation's possible receptivity to a switch from the Brandywine to the Paunnacussing. After listening to Carson's assessment, Gordon said that he simply could not take the risk of authorizing a planning extension with the possibility of rejection still there. Further, he felt that the people of the Paunnacussing were too well off financially for Ford to put up funds for acquisition of development rights there. His response put an end to all hope of transferring the project elsewhere, and we returned to the task of preparing for the final meetings in the Upper East Branch.

Communication strategies: Ours and theirs

Through the winter and into the spring of 1968, we and our opponents, particularly the Freeholders, intensified our efforts to reach people. Though we tried to simplify our message, it was not easy. Both the reasons for the plan and the proposal itself were complex, and we were continually modifying it in response to public opinion. Its opponents did not face these problems. Their messages were simple and unchanging, although some were inconsistent with the facts, and their technique was constant reiteration. Both sides tried to reach as many people as possible individually and through the press, radio, and television.

By late spring, when the final round of public meetings began, most Upper East Branch residents had heard of the plan. What they had heard varied widely and what they believed ranged from acceptance of the Water Resources Authority statements at face value to conviction that the plan was a federal government plot to condemn all land in the watershed for a park, reservoir, and low-income housing project.

The problem of how best to communicate an understanding of a complex set of relationships and choices confronts every planning project. If the planner says too much, people become confused and irritated at the intricacy of the choices placed before them. If the planner oversimplifies, the choices offered are unreal and misleading. One approach which we took was to bring to the Upper East Branch individuals who had had relevant practical experiences elsewhere.

At a public meeting in January 1968, William H. Whyte, the prominent writer on open space, and Benjamin F. Mullen, chief of the Right of Way Division of the Wisconsin State Highway Commission, spoke to an audience of seventy-five about actual experience with conservation easements. Whyte urged their use, calling them "the middle way" between zoning and public ownership. Mullen reported on the acquisition of 1,300 scenic easements, 35 percent by eminent domain, to preserve the view along Great River Road bordering the Mississippi River. Some at the meeting objected that easements would mean co-ownership of land with government—in this case, with the Water Resources Authority. Others, however, expressed considerable interest in learning how easements had actually worked and what they were likely to be worth.

In March fifty people turned out to hear Clyde Stone, manager and engineer of Cheltenham Township in suburban Philadelphia, and Henry Folsom, a member of the county council in predominantly urban New Castle County, Delaware. Chester County Commissioners Rubino and Waldmann were among those attending the meeting. Both Stone and Folsom described the vast increase in flooding in their communities as a consequence of dense development and a major increase in impervious cover of the ground. Stone stated that his township was about to spend $7 million to correct flooding problems. Folsom said that the estimated cost of correcting flooding problems in New Castle County, caused by fifty years of inadequate planning in the Red and White Clay and Christina watersheds, was $11 million. Responding to a question from Harry Simms about eminent domain, Folsom said, "When the chips are down, you've got to use eminent domain for any government."[21]

On the day that the *Coatesville Record* carried a news article about this meeting, one of the reporters regularly assigned to Brandywine meetings offered the following wry recipe:

Sit in stiff chairs: Many experts on project
                      A Politician
                      100 outraged citizens
Add at intervals: Emotional outbursts (patriotic)
                      Slaps at "Big Daddy Government"
                      (Public utilities may be substituted.)
Stir in several crackpots, preferably ultra-conservatives, and allow to degenerate into a talk-fest.[22]

THE REGIONAL PLANNING COMMISSION. To Harry Simms and other freeholders, the prospect of eminent domain, at the county as well as at the state level, was the most fearsome and objectionable aspect of the planning proposals for the Upper East Branch. The Freeholders believed that all land use planning should be at the township level. William Ford, a member of the Freeholders executive committee, wrote the county commissioners to this effect in February of 1968. Not long after, an article in the local press described a Freeholders meeting attended by seventy-five people, and reported Ford's charges about the plans for the Brandywine: " 'There's no question about it; they are the beginning of a slow takeover.' Hinting that real estate interests are behind the plan, Ford said if the Brandywine proposal goes into effect, government sponsored developments will be built."[23]

Starting in February, the Freeholders began promoting the creation of an official regional planning commission for the eight townships of the Upper East Branch. As an official public agency, authorized by state law, the regional planning commission could vie with the Water Resources Authority and the quiescent County Planning Commission for the right and power to determine the plan and program for the Upper East Branch. Strategically, the move was a sound one. In each township members of the Freeholders contacted their supervisors and asked them to endorse such a commission. All the townships but East

Caln agreed, and on March 4, 1968, a preliminary meeting was held. Carl Maenak, chairman of the Wallace Township Planning Commission, was chosen chairman. William Funk, chairman of the Wallace Township Board of Supervisors and a member of the Water Resources Authority, said that the purpose of the commission should be to "accomplish locally the goals of the Upper East Branch Brandywine Project."[24]

The commission held its organizational meeting on April 16, 1968, the day on which the newspapers carried the announcement by the Water Resources Authority that eminent domain had been eliminated from the plan. At that meeting the new board of two members per township adopted its formal name—Regional Planning Commission of the Townships of the Upper Brandywine Watersheds. It also set forth its purposes:

1. to advise the townships about the Upper East Branch project;

2. to support local conservation and maintain the natural integrity of the Brandywine Valley;

3. to oppose eminent domain and publicize citizen views on this matter; and

4. to develop an alternative to the Brandywine Plan.

Since the Freeholders initiated creation of the commission, it is not surprising that a number of their more active members, including Harry Simms, William Ford, and Kurt Wandel, were appointed to the board.

By May, the new commission had published a formal statement of goals:

1. promotion of coordination and cooperation between the region's planning commissions and governing bodies;

2. the creation of a continuing planning program to meet the region's present and future needs and protect the equity of the residents in their properties;

3. to reinforce strong local government and continuous participation among the residents of the area in the planning of its future; and

4. to promote the conservation and preservation of all the natural resources of the region and particularly to guard and protect its watercourses.

All of these goals were fully compatible with the goals of the Brandywine Plan.

Later, during the final round of public meetings, the commission spokesmen would say as much and would argue that their objections were to the proposals for implementing the plan, not to its concepts.

THE MEDIA. During this period, while we were working on the final draft of the Brandywine Plan and the Regional Planning Commission was developing its goal proposals, all of us were stepping up our barrage of the public through the media and through personal contacts.

The local radio stations gave good news coverage to the plan. In addition, Bob Struble and Ken Wood each did a series of short programs for Chester County stations explaining the proposals. All of us and many of the Freeholders appeared from time to time on Philadelphia and Chester County interview shows. We appeared on an early morning television farm show, as did Harry Simms a week later. We never knew how many people we reached in this way, since no one ever mentioned hearing or seeing the programs. In 1967 and 1968 we were promoting a novel proposal for what seemed less than urgent problems. Since then the media have taken up environmental issues with a vengeance; the general public surely is far more aware of pollution, potential resource shortages, and the deterioration of the urban environment now than it was then. This change in awareness might mean that today there would be a more receptive public climate for the Brandywine proposals.

One newspaper, the Philadelphia *Evening Bulletin,* was acutely concerned with environmental questions. It supported the plan and carried several feature articles and favorable editorials on it. One article hailed the plan as a "National First":

A National First. BRANDYWINE EASEMENT PLAN SPLITS LANDOWNERS:
. . . Down in the rural village of Glenmoore, . . . a 70-year old woman shakes her head in disgust over the killing of hundreds of trout. Acid was spilled in the stream. "We feel terrible about the fish," she says. But in the next breath she condemns a proposed $2 million plan to preserve the stream.

"They're trying to take over too much," the woman says, referring to the Chester County Water Resources Authority in particular and government in general. Reactions such as these are threatening the first plan in the country to conserve water and land resources in an entire watershed.[25]

Although the news coverage was ample, none of the County newspapers took an editorial position during the course of the project. After the plan had been defeated, a planning staff member asked the editor of the *Daily Local News* why his paper had not taken a stand since its sole laudatory editorial back in 1966, but found him reluctant to discuss the matter.

Opponents of the plan took the initiative in use of the press. Through advertisements, letters to the editor, interviews, and news coverage of their meetings they kept hammering away. Commissioner Waldmann, for instance, received extensive coverage when he said that the Water Resources Authority "should not be negotiating ease-ments for this until the Upper East Branch plan is approved by this board of commissioners."[26] Although no easements had been or ever were negotiated under the plan, no Water Resources Authority spokesman responded to the allegation.

At Bob Struble's continued insistence, we limited our use of the press to presentations of the facts. Never did anyone connected with the Brandywine Plan respond to attacks in the press by opponents. In my opinion, both then and now, this was a major error. Bub Struble and Hus McIlvain, chairman of the Water Resources Authority, were deeply committed to "keeping their cool"—to being polite, calm, and rational at all times. They thought they and the staff should not respond to outrageous or ridiculous charges or to personal vilification. On one occasion, Hus said he didn't believe in "getting into a squirt-ing contest with a skunk." He and Bob believed that, in time, the more extreme critics would lose public credibility. We disagreed but accepted the decision of the Water Resources Authority.

Others did respond to many of the charges made in the press. Among them were Mr. and Mrs. Otto Spies, owners of a farm in Wallace Township, and Raymond Scott Maddux, a prominent realtor and resident of East Brandywine Township. In one letter, Mrs. Spies wrote:

Before making up their minds whether or not they want to avail themselves of the privilege of living in an area protected by the Brandywine Project, I wish all the residents of the area would ponder these words of Aldo Leopold: "Quit thinking about decent land-use as solely an economic problem. Ex-amine each question in terms of what is ethically and esthetically right as well as what is economically expedient. A thing is right when it tends to preserve the integrity, stability and beauty of the biotic community. It is wrong when it tends otherwise."[27]

Mr. Maddux directed his comments to several Simms letters of July 1968:

[Y]ou make your Chester County Freeholders Association sound like a venge-ful Mafia or Cosa Nostra group. Perhaps they can "buy and sell Mr. Wood financially and genealogically." . . . I question their ability to buy Mr. Wood intellectually. . . . Mr. Simms, you stress property rights. How about stressing property responsibility? [Maddux then noted that he was one of those participating in voluntary four-acre deed restrictions in East Brandywine.] There have been four sales under this restriction. I would challenge anyone to have gotten more money in any of these transactions had there been no deed restriction.[28]

MEETINGS. Our major means of communication continued to be personal visits and small meetings. Ken visited all the major landowners who were accessible and then wrote memos to the staff describing their reactions to the plan proposals. By summer of 1968, he had called on hundreds of people, returning two and three times when it seemed warranted. He had spoken at dozens of small meetings—at someone's home with several invited neighbors, at church groups, and at social clubs. More often than not, one or two of the planning staff joined him at these meetings. As the plan became controversial, it was sometimes difficult to arrange meetings. Some ministers and some landowners expressed their support but declined to sponsor meetings in order to avoid disagreement among friends and neighbors.

To back up Ken, some of the rest of us prepared slides to help explain the plan. Bob Struble was a past master of the slide talk; he could blend humor and anecdote with fact. He and we took hundreds of photographs of scenes in the Upper East Branch and, along with slides of key maps and graphs, developed presentations which showed the current condition of the watershed, the types of changes which were likely to occur, the impact of urbanization on water resources, and our proposals for averting these frequently harmful consequences. Bob and I each gave some twenty-five slide talks about the plan. He spoke mainly to Chester County civic and business groups, I to conservation and civic groups more removed from the basin but concerned with similar problems, such as the Water Resources Association of the Delaware River Basin and the National Audubon Society. Ken, John, and Bob Coughlin also used the slides extensively.

By the fall of 1967, when we were well aware that we had a communications problem, it occurred to us that a short movie might be an effective way of augumenting our slide talks. Through the Institute for Environmental Studies, John and I applied for a grant to make a movie from the Pennsylvania Department of Public Instruction under Title I of the Higher Education Act. Late in December our application was approved. Stuart Finley, Inc., with a series of excellent conservation films to its credit, was an obvious choice to tell the story. John and I had the script pretty well in mind, but by the time the money was available and we had chosen a filmmaker, it was midwinter. Our film would be far less attractive and persuasive if the footage had been shot then. Yet if we waited for spring the movie would not be shown to people in the Upper East Branch before the final decision on the plan was made. Six months had passed since we first discussed making a movie, and we now realized that the opposition in the Brandywine was to government intervention and that it was so deeply rooted that seeing a movie was unlikely to change many minds. With this in mind, we decided to wait for spring and to direct the movie to a wider audience, to residents of any area concerned with water resource planning for urbanizing areas. The Upper East Branch was the principal example, but we included others as well. The resulting twenty-two-minute movie, "Urban Sprawl," has been widely shown and won three prizes in documentary film competitions. It was well worth making for its educational value, but it was of no significance to our planning efforts in the Upper East Branch.

THE FINAL PLAN. The last publication sent to all landowners was the summary form of the final plan, titled *The Brandywine Plan*. It called for implementation only if owners of 80 percent of the affected land in a sub-watershed accepted offers from the Water Resources Authority to buy either easements or the fee to their land. It was brief—twenty-eight pages—handsome, simply written, and well illustrated. It was a Water Resources Authority publication but was written and designed almost entirely by the planning staff. It was submitted for review in draft form to the Water Resources Authority board as well as to the county commissioners, the township supervisors, and the members of the township planning commissions. The planning staff felt a commitment to the Ford Foundation to publish it and to hold the last round of public meetings within the six-month extension period granted by the Foundation.

This concern over the deadline was not shared by the Water Resources Authority. The board suggested that the Institute for Environmental Studies, rather than the Water Resources Authority, publish the final plan, since members of the board had not reviewed or commented on the plan during the several months that it was in draft form. However, the planning staff felt strongly that the summary form of the final plan should be issued under the aegis of the Water Resources Authority and agreed to a month's delay, during which the board assigned its vice-chairman, Harold Ladd, to review the draft with the staff.

This lack of review by the entire board was symptomatic of the noninvolvement of several board members with the plan. They were busy men, volunteering one evening a month, plus other occasional hours, to this activity as well as many hours a month to other civic enterprises. The involvement of the authority at Marsh Creek dam consumed all of the time which some members could commit to the Water Resources Authority. Only Harold Ladd, a retired Du Pont executive, attended our staff, committee, and public meetings and offered critical comment. He was an excellent example of the capable, knowledgeable citizen who, when retired, contributes much to the community as a volunteer.

The chairman, Hus McIlvain, had a double reason not to get involved too deeply: his business commitments as president of the Downington Paper Company were heavy, and he was already a target for bitter attack. Opponents of the Marsh Creek dam alleged that there was an improper connection between his positions as chairman of the Water Resources Authority and president of the biggest paper company in Downingtown, a future customer for the added water supply from the dam. Opponents of the Brandywine Plan regularly charged that the Water Resources Authority's sole interest in the plan was in keeping the stream clean for downstream industries, including Downingtown Paper and Du Pont. With four of the seven men on the board either current or former executives in industries relying on Brandywine water, such suspicions are not surprising.

Bob Struble relied on his board for guidance with the Brandywine Plan. The board left most choices to him, never disagreeing but never actively supporting him either. Since the plan was so controversial, this placed Bob in an exposed and difficult position, and it is small wonder that caution and compromise were his watchwords.

The summary publication, *The Brandywine Plan*, was a condensation of the detailed technical version, *The Plan and Program for the Brandywine*. The latter is over three hundred pages long and is filled with graphs, maps, and tables. Since the plan was a prototype study, the technical plan was designed to be useful to professional planners anywhere as well as to the people concerned with the Upper East Branch of Brandywine Creek. It provides a detailed exposition of the planning proposals and their underlying rationale. It was written by the planning staff and some of our consultants and published by the Institute for Environmental Studies, but not until October 1968, after the fate of the plan had been decided. In the spring of 1968, we concluded that our detailed technical findings were not going to influence public opinion, and we therefore postponed publication in order to complete our analysis of several Brandywine research studies. It was sent to about a hundred local and county officials, but most of the first printing of the fifteen hundred copies went to fill requests from planners outside the Brandywine, even from as far away as Africa and Australia.

The last round

Summer of 1968 was the time for popular decision on the Brandywine Plan. All landowners were sent the summary report in June. The next step was to be a public meeting in each township, then a decision by each board of supervisors, transmission of its decision to the county commissioners, and, finally, a decision by the county commissioners.

Even though the plan now called for voluntary implementation by each landowner, none of us would have gone ahead without a general climate of approval. How many favorable votes from the townships would be necessary for the county commissioners to decide in favor we did not know and the commissioners were not saying. Our hunch was that we needed a majority, or five, but it was only a hunch. We thought that we had a chance, but a slim one, for five yes votes.

Ken began to organize the final round of township public meetings in the spring of 1968. He had written and called the members of each board of supervisors to inquire how their township wished to arrive at a decision on the plan. He offered to mail postcards to landowners in the Upper East Branch basin or to provide a list of landowners if the supervisors wished to take a mail poll. Only West Brandywine took him up on this offer, and none of the township supervisors told their residents or the Water Resources Authority exactly how they intended to reach a decision.

Since the final version of the plan proposed that the Water Resources Authority select one of the four principal sub-basins in the watershed and seek options to purchase easements or the fee on a voluntary basis within it, the supervisors were being asked to endorse or reject future negotiation between individual landowners and the Water Resources Authority. Few, however, understood this proposal; fewer still believed that the Authority would not use eminent domain, regardless of what the plan said.

A DECISIVE SKIRMISH. After Ken had scheduled two township public meetings, in Honey Brook and West Brandywine, the Regional Planning Commission made two demands. The first was that the Water Resources Authority cease all activity in the watershed and, specifically, that Ken not make any further calls on landowners. Commissioner Louis Waldmann broadcast a similar demand to the press, saying: "We can no longer tolerate the tail wagging the dog situation."[29] This brought a response from Chairman Rubino, who was quoted by the *Daily Local News*: "I would question the motivation of the minority commissioner. Is it . . . a political gimmick? I can't see that any of the claims you make in the newspaper will hold water. . . . I think the WRA has done a wonderful job."[30]

The second demand was that the final round of public meetings be held under the auspices of the Regional Planning Commission, subject to its choice of rules of procedure. The planning staff protested vigorously to Bob Struble that this would destroy what modest chance there was for acceptance of the plan. Bob met with the board of the Water Resources Authority and they, in turn, asked Commissioner Rubino's advice. He told the press that the deletion of eminent domain from the final plan represented a true response to the wishes of the residents but, as to the procedure for the final meetings, "It is not our right to reverse the procedures and we do not intend, anyway, to use the influence of this office either for or against the project."[31] The Authority then decided to accede to the Regional Planning Commission demands in the hope that, by taking an agreeable and cooperative attitude, it might persuade the commission to reconsider its negative position. The Authority did conduct the meetings in Honey Brook and West Brandywine Townships which were already scheduled.

The Regional Planning Commission had attacked the Water Resources Authority for controlling the decision process, but all that the Authority had proposed was to hold a public hearing in each township, then leave it to the township supervisors to decide in whatever manner they chose. Further, since the final plan was voluntary, the townships were being asked only whether they favored the principles of the plan and endorsed contacting landowners on an individual basis. However, once again, what mattered was not fact but appearance.

Just as with the shift to the voluntary approach, this compromise gained the Authority no new supporters. In fact, Commissioner Waldmann reacted by saying, "You just can't dump the responsibility for the whole project on to the Regional Planning Commission," to which Commissioner Rubino responded that he was criticizing the Authority for doing just what the Regional Planning Commission had demanded.[32]

THE AUTHORITY'S TWO MEETINGS. On the day before the Honey Brook meeting, Commissioner Waldmann held a meeting to lambaste the

Brandywine Plan and the Marsh Creek project, lumping the two to-gether. Some forty people, many of them members of the Freeholders, turned up to criticize the Water Resources Authority for both the plan and the dam. Waldmann termed the latter "an utter disgrace." Among other comments from local residents were the following: "what can stop Goddard from enlarging his state park and taking the Brandywine Valley?"; water is to be "plundered" from the East Branch; and "we don't need another park."[33] The *Coatesville Record* observed that "most of the testimony was given by Harry Simms."[34]

The Honey Brook public meeting was held on June 13. Despite advance notice in several newspapers, the turnout was very small: the supervisors, some members of the Planning Commission, and several residents. Much of the township—29 percent or 7.2 square miles—lay within the watershed, but only 10 percent was affected by the plan. Being open, rolling farmland under little development pressure, the tracts of land were larger than in the downstream townships and thus fewer landowners would be involved.

Jim Umble, chairman of the Board of Supervisors, ran a quiet meeting. After Bob Struble's initial presentation, most of the time was spent clarifying some points on which people were uncertain. One resident objected to removal of eminent domain from the plan, stating that "eminent domain means equal protection," that people would hold out for more money in negotiating for easements, and that the change had weakened the plan.[35] He also said that there weren't so many people opposed to the plan, just a few loud talkers. Jim Umble said that people in Honey Brook did not seem worried about the plan but that he would ask around further before the supervisors made a decision.

The West Brandywine public meeting was held on June 19. It was a slightly larger gathering of about twenty-five people. The West Brandywine supervisors were the only ones to send out postcards to landowners, but at the time of the meeting few replies had been received. This meeting differed from the Honey Brook one in that there were two vocal and negative landowners present. One owned a sizeable farm at a very favorable crossroads location and, while protesting his desire to continue farming, angrily declared that no easements would keep him from selling. A man from the city, driving a big Cadillac, had just approached him, he said, and he knew his land was worth a lot more than he'd ever get from the Water Resources Authority. The other landowner echoed the first.

One strong supporter of the plan, a steelworkers' union official, opposed this reasoning and urged that people start thinking less selfishly and realize that what they were doing was destroying the Brandywine for people downstream. Other people asked questions, many somewhat diffidently. The supervisors were attacked for their failure to pass zoning measures early enough to keep out trailer parks. One supervisor acknowledged that they should have acted sooner, despite public opposition to zoning, but emphasized that changes due to lack of zoning should not be laid at the doorstep of the Brandywine Plan, as one man sought to do. With the exception of the protests of the two opponents, the meeting was a low-keyed one. The supervisors withheld a decision until the complete results of their mail poll were received.

THE REGIONAL PLANNING COMMISSION TAKES CHARGE. After this, the public meetings were run by the Regional Planning Commission. The first, on July 8, was a joint meeting for East Caln, Uwchlan, and Upper Uwchlan Townships. The results were inconclusive but not overly discouraging to us. Of the forty-five people who came, only eleven owned land in the area. Seven of these eleven people endorsed the principles of the plan, and four said that they were prepared to sell easements. Robert Worthington, of Uwchlan Township, speaking for the Regional Planning Commission, said that they were working on a comprehensive plan. "How can you get the same objectives in your comprehensive plan if you don't buy easements? Zoning is ineffective," one landowner said. "We hope to do something," Worthington replied.[36] An East Caln supervisor asked Worthington whether the Regional Planning Commission had any counter-proposal; Worthington replied that it did not as yet.[37] At about the same time, Carl Maenak was asked about the commission and was quoted as follows:

"The plan is too general. There's no guarantee the easements will not be handed over to another government agency or even a charitable organization. . . . We are not a negative fighting group. We've proposed an alternative, that a comprehensive plan for all the townships be prepared." All agree, Maenak said, with the basic plan: the need to keep streams clean, long-range planning for water and sewers, and strong regulations for subdivisions. Easements would upset local comprehensive plans, last forever, and have been bought at a fraction of the property's future value.[38]

An excerpt from one of Harry Simms' letters to the editor of the same period reads:

A new strategy was adopted in the top of the ninth inning by the All-Bureaucrats. They had been pitching an eminent domain spit-ball but when penalized by the referees they decided to use the newly developed "Voluntary Pitch." This is a tricky curve which will break when Slugger Goddard is successful in having the rules changed in the State Legislature to legalize the much despised eminent domain spit-ball. Slugger Goddard, who is really a Pro, and definitely Big League has his practiced eye far out in Left field (his favorite position) where there is a vast out-field beyond which lies 540,000 acres which he wishes to have under eternal restrictions by 1980.[39]

The East Brandywine Township meeting, described in Chapter I, was far different from the three preceding meetings and set the tone for what was to follow. The Wallace Township meeting took place on July 17 and the West Nantmeal meeting on July 19. We were sick at the tone of the East Brandywine meeting, and the next day I urged Bob Struble to take a more aggressive stance at the Wallace meeting. He disagreed, saying that he, Hus McIlvain, and several other Authority members believed that it was best to do a good job, keep calm, and let the results speak for themselves. He saw a ray of hope in the East Brandywine meeting because his secretary had heard two people saying that they had changed their minds and now favored the plan as a result of the tactics of its opponents.

On July 17 another prize Simms letter appeared; this time I was a joint target, with Maurice Goddard:

This proposal was pieced together in the secluded laboratories of the Department of Environmental Studies of the University of Pennsylvania under the wizardry of Dr. Anna Strong. She built this little left-sided Frankenstein and delivered it as a little pink kitten to Robert G. Struble. . . . A posse has been formed by the Chester County Freeholders Association and, joined by the voters, they are maneuvering a great big wooden stake which they hope to drive through Frankie's mechanical heart. . . . Frankie's real master, Dr. Maurice Goddard, Pennsylvania Department of Forests and Waters, has promised Frankie 540,000 acres of private land to be held under eternal restrictions by 1980. . . . Frankie's . . . big brothers are doing quite well in Soviet Russia and Communist China.[40]

The Wallace meeting was similar to the East Brandywine one, except that it was somewhat less bitter. The West Nantmeal meeting was quieter but rather negative.

One newspaper, summing up the last round of meetings, described the attitude of many people in these words: "I don't want any government body, any water authority, or anyone else for that matter, telling me how my land can be used now or in the future. These meetings have been stormy. Some have deteriorated into nothing but vituperative sessions by some of the opponents. No concrete plan as an alternative to that proposed by the Water Resources Authority is in existence."[41]

THE DECISION. Now all that remained was for the township supervisors and the county commissioners to reach their decisions. East Brandywine, of course, had made its decision on July 16.[42] Wallace also promptly voted no. On July 19 the supervisors passed a resolution directed to the township residents, as follows: "Be it resolved that the Board of Supervisors of Wallace Township, Chester County, Pennsylvania, does hereby reject the final proposal of the Upper East Branch Brandywine project recommended by the Chester County Water Resources Authority. Be it further resolved that we support the Regional Planning Commission in their charge to formulate regional comprehensive planning for the consideration of those Townships involved."[43]

East Caln was next to act. Its response was quite different. The letter from the chairman of its Board of Supervisors to Bob Struble said:

[W]e are in complete accord with the concepts of the plan and the course of action proposed by the Water Resources Authority. This is the position we took on the original plan and notified you by letter. While this Township has the least area involved, we feel that, since we are downstream from the remainder of the project area, we will probably suffer more than the other communities if the health of this stream is not preserved.

We had and still have no objection to the use of eminent domain in the project. If it can be done voluntarily so much the better, but it should be done.[44]

The other townships took formal action at their August meetings. West Nantmeal wrote as follows: "The West Nantmeal Township Board of Supervisors at their regular monthly meeting held Monday evening, August 12, 1968 at the West Nantmeal Municipal Building made and unanimously supported a resolution opposing the Upper East Branch Brandywine Project. In so doing, they represent the majority of West Nantmeal residents who oppose this project."[45] Upper Uwchlan sent a similarly brief, negative response: "At the regular monthly meeting of the Board of Supervisors of Upper Uwchlan Township held August 13, 1968, a motion was carried to turn down the 'final proposal of the Upper East Branch Brandywine Plan.' "[46]

When the Honey Brook supervisors met to vote on the plan, Carl Maenak appeared before them to urge a "no" vote. Several residents spoke in favor of the plan, and one noted the paradox that the Regional Planning Commission was rejecting what was "essentially a regional plan."[47] Two of the supervisors voted to endorse the plan on the understanding that eminent domain was excluded; the third supervisor abstained. The Honey Brook letter said: "After discussion at a regular township meeting held Thursday, August 1, 1968, the Board of Supervisors of Honey Brook Township voted approval of the Upper East Branch Brandywine Plan as recently submitted by the Chester County Water Resources Authority. The approval of this Plan by our Board is made with the express understanding that condemnation proceedings will not be used to implement the Plan."[48]

Uwchlan's letter was positive in tone and suggested that the Authority, in cooperation with the Regional Planning Commission, might yet come up with an acceptable plan.

The Supervisors of Uwchlan Township wish to take this opportunity to congratulate the Chester County Water Resources Authority for their hard and often thankless efforts to preserve the purity of the Upper East Branch of the Brandywine.

Although we can't recommend approval of the final plan as proposed, we do recommend that further efforts be undertaken by the Water Resources Authority to resolve the points of disagreement and to develop a workable plan. It is possible this could be achieved by working with the Regional Planning Commission.

The Supervisors of Uwchlan Township will continue to support the objectives of the Chester County Water Resources Authority.[49]

The West Brandywine supervisors voiced a similar hope:

We, Supervisors of West Brandywine Township, Chester County, Pennsylvania, upon careful study over approximately a period of two years and upon recommendation of the Regional Planning Committee of The Upper Brandywine Watersheds, hereby reject the Upper East Branch Brandywine Project presented by the Chester County Water Resources Authority in its present form.

Further, noting that the major landowners in the area are not in favor of the plan, nor are they satisfied as to the methods implemented in the plan, concerning easements, land restrictions, infringements on private lives, no assurance of tax relief, etc.

It is our hope and desire that the Chester County Water Resources Authority will work with representatives of The Regional Planning Committee, Upper Brandywine Watersheds toward development of a comprehensive plan that will be acceptable to the people of the area.[50]

It was the unanimous opinion of the planning staff that the West Brandywine decision was a close one. Two of the supervisors had shown a continuing and perceptive interest in the plan. They might well have found themselves able to endorse it had it not been for the unceasing pressure from its opponents in East Brandywine Township.

Two townships voted for the plan, with one including authorization for eminent domain. Two townships urged that work continue with the Regional Planning Commission to come up with an acceptable means of implementation. The remaining four townships gave a resounding no. With this tally before them, the Water Resources Authority board, on August 26, 1968, recommended to the county commissioners

1. that the Authority should initiate no voluntary purchase of easements;

2. that the Authority should continue to cooperate with the Regional Planning Commission;

3. that the initiative to develop a proposal for voluntary sale of easements should rest with interested citizens; and

4. that the research work of the Geological Survey should continue.

The Authority could have recommended that it be authorized to seek funds to carry out the voluntary easement plan in Honey Brook. That it did not is, I believe, a measure of the discouragement which we all shared.

The county commissioners accepted the Water Resources Authority recommendation on August 29. Chairman Rubino said that he had promised not to interfere: "If that's what the people in that area want —fine." Bob Struble, he noted, had taken a certain amount of abuse and criticism, but that was "democracy at work in this county." Bob Struble commented "Our error was trying to do too much too fast" and noted that a long-range educational program had been needed.[51]

Ken summed it all up succinctly in August of 1968, after the decisions were made, when he finally broke Bob Struble's rule against staff rebuttals of criticism. In a letter to the *Daily Local News* he took Harry Simms to task for accusing Bob Struble of "collaborating on a scheme to make money on land in the Upper East Branch watershed," for accusing Ken of "negotiating for a cluster-housing development in East Brandywine Township," and for charging that outside interests were behind the project. Ken concluded: "The real shame is not that Simms talked and wrote, but rather that people listened and read— and believed."[52]

The Philadelphia *Evening Bulletin* summed it up: "The experiment failed. More specifically, it resulted in a lovely plan that was rejected by local residents. . . . There were rumors of plans for low income public housing, or for forcible racial mixing."[53] The attitudes which emerged are common to many Americans, not just the residents of the Upper East Branch:

1. private ownership of land is a sacred right;
2. interference in an owner's use of his land is contrary to the intent of the Constitution;
3. eminent domain is wrong;
4. all profits from land development should inure to the land-owner;
5. government, except for local government, ignores the wishes of the people and is untrustworthy; and
6. big business is in league with government in derogation of the people's interests.

To its opponents, the Brandywine Plan was in outright conflict with these assumptions.

VII

same goals, other means

THE GOALS of the Brandywine Plan—protection of the water resources and the natural beauty of rural land while making room for development—are almost universally endorsed. The specifics—including the three-hundred-foot stream setbacks for development, the low density provisions for woods and steep slopes, and the water-related development regulations—likewise receive general support, in the Brandywine and elsewhere. The Brandywine Plan succeeded in taking one necessary step to specific land use proposals. At the next step, from land use proposals to implementation, we stumbled.

Our traditional American concept of land as a private commodity has made unacceptable to us many of the means commonly used in European countries to carry out land use plans.[1] We believe that each owner of land in the path of development is entitled to profit from it. The real issue of the Brandywine Plan boils down to this: how much, if any, of their chance for land speculation are people willing to forgo to achieve some other objective? In this, the Brandywine Plan differs not one whit from any other plan in which there is public intervention to alter the action of the marketplace. Each specific situation has many variables; among them are the attitude of the public toward the plan proposed, their perception of likely gain without the plan, and their personal circumstances.

The Brandywine Plan as we initially proposed it, including the use of eminent domain to acquire land from owners unwilling to sell easements or their whole property voluntarily, might well have been acceptable under other circumstances. However, in the Upper East Branch watershed in 1968, appreciation of the values of open space, water resource protection, and environmentally sound development, along with apprehension about conventional development, did not outweigh the fear of reduced profits and the reality of less control over their land by owners.

Alternatives to the plan

The Upper East Branch of Brandywine Creek was chosen because it was, in so many respects, a typical rural area lying in the path of urban development. Land values, jobs and incomes, and public awareness of the magnitude of impending change were typical of an area likely to see substantial development within a decade. Not typical, but of particular appeal to us, was the beauty of the Upper East Branch landscape and the sparkling clarity of its streams. We knew that the plan was new and complicated, and therefore demanded a considerable measure of faith from those asked to support it. Might we have altered the circumstances of people, place, and time to have had a better chance of success in carrying out the plan? If so, should we have done so?

THE PEOPLE. Our initial hunch was that the wealthy landowners— people who had had quite enough of the city and who had consciously sought out a choice spot in the country—would support the plan, easements, eminent domain, and all. While their land was an investment, most of them had sufficient other income so that speculation in land was not their prime objective. Its beauty, not its dollar value, was the prime measure of its worth to them. Furthermore, these people, as a result of past experience, were far more aware than others of the likely consequences of development for their way of life. In the main, we were right, but there were not enough of them in the Upper East Branch to be a significant force in the final decision.

Another group of people supported the plan for many of the same reasons. The Amish farmers love the land and wish to keep it as it is. They are struggling to sustain a life style unique in twentieth-century America. While the land is, for most of them, their only substantial material possession, its preservation as farmland is also their only chance to maintain a way of life. Development is a clear threat. Easement payment would have provided some gain from the land while assuring its continued use in accord with their wishes.

In fact, some of the wealthy people and some of the Amish farmers were critical of the Brandywine Plan because it did not preclude further development. This response was the key to our decision not to pick a watershed peopled predominantly by upper-middle and upper income landowners. It is not very difficult to keep the countryside unspoiled if there is no development; our goal was not only to have controls placed on use of the land but also to prove that, through them, it is possible to have a normal amount of development and to sustain a healthy natural environment.

Possibly this was hoping for too much. Possibly if we had persuaded some community that wished to exclude growth to adopt an easement program, its example would have provided enough useful information on the actual effects of such easements on land values and on the local tax base to convince communities like the Upper East Branch. At the time, it seemed the wrong approach—too roundabout and likely to end in the confusion of the planners' long-term goals of testing land use controls for effectiveness with the goals of the local community. Despite the outcome, I believe that we would all make this same choice again.

We also could have sought a watershed with only a few landowners. In fact, we knew of one such area of over fifteen thousand acres largely controlled by two families. I think we rejected this possibility much too hastily on the ground that it was atypical. Owners of such vast tracts necessarily view them as major investments. If their goals for the future use of their land paralleled those of the planners, working out the mechanics of the land use controls with them and their local governments would have been very simple, compared with an effort to deal with over four thousand individuals. Many, although not all, of the results we hoped for could have been attained. The information gleaned from such a first experiment could then have been used to predict the outcome of similar plans in more typical circumstances.

THE PLACES. A watershed of fifteen thousand acres with a few owners is an obvious rarity on the urban fringe. If having only a few owners with whom to plan would have been a great advantage, could we have substantially reduced the size of the watershed without destroying the demonstration value of the experiment? In 1964, as noted earlier, we thought that two thousand acres would be adequate in economic and legal terms. This figure was substantially revised to provide an area which Luna thought would be large enough to show the water resource consequences of carrying out the plan. Ignorant of the political complexities of attempting to plan for thirty-seven square miles, the rest of us agreed. This was our error, not his. An area closer to our original estimate of 2,000 acres would have been a far better choice. The reduction in the variety of hydrologic data that would be yielded by a small headwater basin would have been more than compensated for by the reduction in the time required for data collection and mapping, which would have freed us for contacting landowners and involving them in the project.

By this same reasoning, might government-owned land have been a suitable site? Public land presents a different mix of advantages and disadvantages. Initially the idea is very appealing. A unit of government can commit itself to an experiment of the sort proposed for the

Brandywine. Since the land is already publicly owned, there is no acquisition cost and it can be offered for sale subject to the conditions of the plan. Land in the flood plain, stream buffer, and woods and steep slope areas could be sold subject to appropriate easements. All other land could be sold subject to development restrictions covering sewerage, water supply, erosion control, maintenance of vegetation, etc. Part of the revenues from sales could be used to cover administrative and research costs; the remainder could be contributed to the local community to cover the costs of public services for the development areas.

It sounds attractive, but there are problems of location, law, and economics. We were looking for a watershed within the area of Philadelphia, where all but one of us lived and worked. In and around the Pennsylvania-New Jersey-Delaware metropolitan area there is little public ownership of large tracts of urban fringe land. The federal government holds or is acquiring a few large areas, such as McGuire Air Force Base in New Jersey and Tocks Island National Recreation Area in the Pocono Mountains of New Jersey and Pennsylvania. State ownership by New Jersey and Pennsylvania is more widespread, although still limited in areas prone to develop in the near future. Local government ownership is on a smaller scale than we needed. In the western part of the United States, finding an appropriate small publicly owned watershed would be simple. Not so in the East.

Further, since the federal and state lands within reach of Philadelphia were acquired for purposes specifically approved by the legislatures of the states involved, conversion to a different purpose —resource-based development—very likely would have required legislative sanction. For surplus public property, such as an abandoned military base, specific legislative approval might not have been necessary. However, in fact most of the public lands near Philadelphia were acquired and are used for parks and/or conservation. Land for these purposes was already in short supply. In 1966, before Congress passed any new communities legislation and New York passed its Urban Development Corporation law, the prospect of getting legislative approval for this type of demonstration on public lands needed for open space purposes was too remote to consider.

Last, for the experiment to yield useful data we needed to know the impact of public acquisition of development rights on market value. If the land already was in public ownership, there would be no base, or fee, value against which to measure its sale price under easements.

Private property and the public interest

THE TIMES. Times have changed since 1966. There is a new national awareness of environmental degradation and of urban blight which has spurred passage of much new legislation at all levels of government. Congress has vastly increased national spending for pollution control. Both Congress and the courts have demanded that increased weight be given to environmental values in deciding between development and resource protection. The Council on Environmental Quality has been created and given equal rank with the Council of Economic advisers. Congress has directed that the executive branch submit a biennial report on the nation's urban growth policy. Congress is considering a commitment to creation of a national land use policy. It also has set an objective of providing "a decent home and a suitable living environment for every American family"[2] by 1978. Meeting this target will require construction of twenty-six million homes, most of them in urban areas.

New York, with its Urban Development Corporation, was the first state to voice a similar commitment to meeting the growth needs of its communities and people. Other states are considering similar legislation. A number of states, Pennsylvania among them, have passed constitutional amendments establishing a basic policy of environmental protection. Most heavily urbanized states have restructured their cabinets so that management of all environmental resources is under one roof. New commitments, of intent and money, have proliferated to protect natural resources from unwise development and to begin to undo some of the havoc wreaked in years gone by. Coastal wetlands regulation from Maine to Maryland, control of beach access in Oregon and of strip mining in Pennsylvania, and lake and river shoreline setbacks in Wisconsin are but a few of the state measures recently enacted. The millennium surely is not at hand, but these laws are sound evidence of a new national awareness of the shortsightedness of past growth policies.

In this new climate of opinion, the concepts of the Brandywine Plan are far less startling than they seemed in 1966. Legislatures enacting the new environmental protection laws have been acutely aware of the possible need for compensation for loss of development rights. Under some state programs, such as the Wisconsin shoreline setbacks, there was a legislative assumption, since upheld by the Wisconsin courts, that the regulation is reasonable and that no compensation need be paid.[3] Under other programs, like the Wisconsin scenic highways program and the New York fishing rights program, the state has assumed from the start that compensation is necessary. Under still other programs, like those for many of the coastal wetlands, the state regulates the wetlands to prevent or restrict development.[4] Then it is up to the landowner to prove that the regulation is so unreasonable as to be a taking of property rights. If the court agrees with the landowner, the state can either pay for these property rights by condemning an easement or the fee or can lift the restrictions on the land altogether. Inverse condemnation was among the many alternatives we discussed and rejected for the Brandywine, but it warrants further thought. Under the changed circumstances prevailing today, many of these alternatives may now be acceptable to the public.

Alternative land use controls

The land use controls which we proposed for the development half of the Brandywine watershed caused little comment. While they were innovative and would have helped to assure development compatible with the land and water capabilities of the watershed, they were not threatening, and people gave them little consideration, focusing all of their attention on the easement proposals for the critical areas. Today, however, people in the Upper East Branch, like people in other urbanizing areas, recognize the need for development controls designed to protect natural resources. Measurement of the available water supply, planning for its use and reuse after removal of sewage, designs for location of wells and sewerage systems, and specifications for water withdrawal and for solid and liquid waste treatment all are essential precursors to sound development. So too are regulations governing cut-and-fill, dumping, and dredging; use of pesticides and fertilizers; prevention of erosion during and after development; and protection of existing amenities. Greater local recognition of the need for this sort of planning and regulation is one evident gain from the Brandywine Plan. The next chapter discusses some of the steps taken locally, partly in response to the ideas put forward in the plan.

Here we will look at some alternatives to the plan's proposals for the critical areas. Most of them were put forward by members of the planning staff. A few were suggested by others involved in the development of the plan, including two members of the Water Resources Authority. Two called for private action to carry out the plan; the rest relied on government initiative.

Many of these proposals could be used best in combination with one another, depending on individual circumstances and people's preferences, and in fact, we originally intended to offer a choice. However, when we realized how confusing it is for people to be presented with an array of choices, each subtly different from the others, we decided to describe only two possibilities to the public—voluntary sale of an easement on the critical areas or of the fee to the whole property. Given an atmosphere of trust, the best arrangement for each property owner could have been worked out from among a wide range of alternatives. As we said in our February 1968 memorandum, "There are advantages and disadvantages—political, financial, administrative, and legal—to all alternatives. . . . Possibly the townships' officials can propose other alternatives, which better suit the wishes of their constituents. The approach can vary from township to township, so long as the objectives of the Plan can be satisfied."

PRIVATE CONTROLS. The two private controls considered were restrictive covenants and a land development corporation. In either case, the local governments would approve the plan and then turn to private landowners to carry it out.

1. *Restrictive Covenants.* Restrictive covenants have a long history of use to prevent specified unwanted uses of land. They were already in effect in part of Culbertson Run, in the Upper East Branch, to limit the density of development to four acres per house. Several landowners, including one already a party to the Culbertson Run covenant, said that we should use them throughout the Upper East Branch. They believed that people would agree to restrictive covenants because they involved no government intervention and were entirely voluntary.

We rejected this approach for several reasons. Maybe people would have agreed to restrictive covenants for the woods and slopes, where limited development at a four-acre gross density would be permitted. However, 26 percent of the watershed was in flood plain and stream buffer, where almost no development would have been allowed, and it was hard to imagine that people voluntarily would sign away all development rights without a penny of compensation. What was more, we did not think that people should be asked to lose whatever development value their land had as the price of implementing the plan.

We had legal objections to restrictive covenants too. Only people who are parties to a covenant can enforce it. In the case of the Culbertson Run restrictive covenant, for instance, if one of the landowners who signed the covenant decided to build houses on half-acre lots, only the other landowners also bound by the terms of the covenant could legally enforce it. Neighbors living across from the proposed development would have no enforcement rights, nor would any local government. For a private agreement covering a small area, that is fair enough. For the whole Upper East Branch area, it would be important to have a public agency empowered to act to protect the public interest in management of water resources. If Chester County were a party to the covenants, then the county could go to court to enforce them. The same would be true of the townships. However, this would have eliminated one of the touted advantages of the restrictive covenants— that they could be entirely a private matter.

Another serious legal shortcoming from our point of view was that, sitting ten years from now, a court might very well find that a restrictive covenant, valid today, is no longer binding. Times and circumstances change. To avoid hardships and to meet new conditions, courts traditionally have used a degree of flexibility in deciding whether or not to continue to enforce a restrictive covenant. Given the use and nature of restrictive covenants, this judicial flexibility is highly desirable. However, the uncertainty that this introduces makes the restrictive covenant unsuitable for long-term restrictions on development. In fact, the restrictive covenant would be an invitation in years ahead to a developer to buy land so restricted and then go to court to try to get the covenant abrogated.

2. *Land Development Corporation.* As already mentioned, I was a consultant to the firm of Wallace-McHarg Associates[5] on "Plan for the Valleys," a plan for the Green Spring and Worthington Valleys of Baltimore County, Maryland. Wallace-McHarg's client was a private planning group, the Green Spring and Worthington Valley Planning Council, Inc. Many of the council's most active members were large landholders in the valleys. Therefore, as their planners, we were concerned with proposing ways for private landowners, as well as for the county government, to make the plan a reality. It was then that I conceived the idea of a landowners' private development corporation. The basic idea is simple enough. All of the landowners in a given area would be eligible to acquire shares in a private, locally managed enterprise charged with carrying out development and could have a voice in determining the character of that development. Whether the organization would be a corporation, a partnership, or some variant of these would turn upon such factors as the number of participants and their financial situation.[6]

The idea was well received by the Planning Council, but neither they nor I went further with it. My preliminary study revealed two serious problems that must be solved if the idea is to work. First, since the development of the corporation is wholly private, no one can be forced to join. If owners of the choicest properties, with the highest development potential, hold out, they may succeed in attracting the most profitable development to their land. This will reduce the money-making opportunities for the group's investors significantly. The second problem is closely related to the first. No method of valuing land as a basis for issuing shares or establishing interests in the development corporation will satisfy all landowners. If all land were the same, and had the same market value, there would be no problem. Of course, it is not all the same, and, on the urban fringe differences of topography and vegetation, accessibility and parcel size, all affect market value. Marshy land fifteen miles from an expressway interchange is worth but a small fraction of the value of well-drained pasture land a thousand feet from the interchange. This is obvious to everyone but the owner of the marshland. He doesn't want to hear that current market value for his land has built into it a discount rate which is an estimate of the years which are likely to elapse before development reaches him, nor does he accept the fact that his marsh would be more costly to build on than the pasture. If he is going to join a development corporation, he wants all land valued at a flat rate per acre. Naturally, the pasture owner disagrees vehemently and is tempted to be a holdout anyway, thinking that he can do better on his own.

There are partial solutions to these problems which may be adequate to get an organization launched. If a few big landowners in an area ripe for development together own enough prime land to bring in some profitable development, they may be able to set their own terms, attract further landowner-investors, and gradually expand the scope of the operation and the diversity of its holdings. Also, once they have some profits from development, they can negotiate for outright purchase of land from people unwilling to swap land for corporation shares or partnership interests.

Alternatively, a conservation group could create a non-profit development corporation. The Wissahickon Valley Watershed Association, in adjacent Montgomery County, Pennsylvania, is starting to do this, strengthened by an initial foundation grant of $500,000 to begin land acquisition. Their intention is to buy key pieces first, develop them in part, and then plow back the profits into further land acquisition, both for development and for protection of key open spaces.

It was our intention to work with people in the Upper East Branch who showed an interest in putting together a development corporation. We thought that this approach would appeal strongly to their preference for local, private management of development. I still believe that the idea would have worked had it not become a victim of the campaign to stop the implementation of the plan. In meeting after meeting, when Bob Struble and Ken suggested this approach as one way to carry out the plan, a few of the plan's opponents alleged that it was a thinly veiled scheme to allow Bob to profit from land speculation. They said to all who would listen that he had been buying up Brandywine land secretly and that the development corporation was to be controlled by him for the benefit of a few. Although the charge was without a shred of truth, it aroused enough suspicion to lead us, reluctantly, to abandon the development corporation as an alternative.

We had one chance which we failed to pursue. One of our opponents was a wealthy man in the real estate business who was also a major landowner in the Upper East Branch. He saw the potential for the development corporation and might have supported the plan on condition that he organize and control such a corporation. Maybe we should have explored this possibility further, but local circumstances deterred us. This man did not enjoy the confidence of a broad spectrum of the local people any more than we did: he was different—a commuter to Philadelphia, a leading Democrat on Republican turf, and a very rich land investor. We had hoped to spur organization of a cooperative enterprise and were fearful that control by a single, powerful individual would only engender more local opposition. While strong, solidly financed leadership was essential for the development corporation to succeed, it was our judgment that there were too many liabilities inherent in this particular combination of circumstances.

This type of dilemma arises repeatedly when one is trying to develop an action program which will gain popular support. Often a prompt decision must be made based on an intuitive judgment about local sensibilities. Once again, long-standing and widespread familiarity with the people of the Upper East Branch would have helped us make a more informed decision.

PUBLIC CONTROLS. The public controls which we or others proposed for the critical areas ran the gamut from traditional zoning to public purchase. They fell into three categories: regulation without compensation; a mix of some public control and some compensation; and complete public ownership with full compensation. Again, in our

Private property and the public interest

judgment, the best scheme was the one which offered the greatest opportunity for each individual to suit his particular needs.

1. *Regulation without Compensation.* Quite a few people suggested relying solely on large lot zoning, maybe with a minimum lot size of five acres. Though they did not always say so, many people felt that zoning always could be changed to suit changing desires for use of the land. One of the objections to easements was that they were permanent and did not give a landowner a chance to change his mind. We agreed with the feeling about large lot zoning—that it would be changed as soon as there was sufficient pressure for development. Either the township supervisors would rezone voluntarily or the landowner would get the courts to declare the zoning unconstitutional as a taking without just compensation. Our judgment was borne out when, in 1970, the Pennsylvania Supreme Court found unconstitutional two- and three-acre zoning in a nearby Chester County township, holding that "absent some extraordinary justification, a zoning ordinance with minimum lot sizes such as those in this case is completely unreasonable. . . . We once again reaffirm our past authority and refuse to allow the township to do precisely what we have never permitted—keep out people, rather than make community improvements."[7]

Others preferred to rely on large lot zoning because they had a personal stake in its success. Zoning had been enacted in several Upper East Branch townships only after years of battle between its proponents and others who saw it as one more socialist tool for a government takeover. In Wallace Township, this struggle went on for nine years, and zoning was only adopted shortly before we came on the scene. Quite naturally, those who had worked so hard for zoning resisted and resented our statements that it would not hold up in court as a means of keeping the critical areas open. They felt that we were undermining their years of work, and, in a sense, we were. We shared the common objective of protecting the natural resources of the area while meeting the inevitable demands for development, but we did not believe that large lot zoning could or should be used to keep land open. Since our goals were similar, it was particularly unfortunate that we failed to reach an agreement on land use controls with these people.

Cluster zoning or planned unit development zoning offers one excellent way of permitting appropriate development while also enforcing the planning principles for the critical areas. So long as a landowner holds a reasonable mix of development land and critical areas, he can propose a development scheme which concentrates the density permitted under prevailing zoning on the development land, leaving the critical area open in accord with the plan. Assuming that the prevailing zoning is not so restrictive as to be unconstitutional, this is fair to the landowner and carries out the plan without public compensation.

If the landowner has little or no land suitable for development, this will not work. There is a way out short of compensation. Gerald Lloyd proposes that landowners be allowed to buy and sell freely the right to build granted them under zoning. For instance, the owner of ten acres of critical area zoned for one-acre lots could sell the right to build ten houses to someone owning land suitable for development. This permits clustering even though many people own the land.[8] The idea is a promising one, but local attitudes foreclosed any approach that had an aura of clustering.

To the residents of the Upper East Branch, the whole advantage of large lot zoning was that it helped assure that newcomers would build houses expensive enough to yield enough tax monies to cover increased school costs. They thought that cluster development, described by some as "beehives," was sure to bring in cheaper houses, poorer people, and less tax revenue. This argument has been raised in most suburban communities where such zoning has been proposed. These fears have proven groundless in many places where cluster developments have been built, often because cluster attracts many tax-paying residents without school-age children. However, there is a very important point here. The school costs which accompany urban growth are huge, and they are borne in a disproportionate share by local residents through the real property tax. Redistributing the burden of this tax to a broader base would go a long way toward removing opposition to new residents of moderate income.

Flood plain zoning was one of the most acceptable proposals we could make. Development in the flood plain already was prohibited in four of the eight townships through their subdivision control ordinances. Extension of this prohibition to the other four townships seemed politically feasible. However, the legal status of flood plain zoning in Pennsylvania was uncertain. The only court decision was not binding on Chester County, having been handed down by the county-level court in neighboring Montgomery County. That decision threw out a township flood plain ordinance. Later, but not until 1969, the same court upheld a revised flood plain ordinance for the same township. Our judgment, in 1967 and 1968, was that flood plain zoning in the Upper East Branch was probably valid. Since appraisals showed only a nominal development value for the flood plains, we thought that a court would find that zoning did not constitute a taking. However, since the law was not clear, we included flood plains in the easement package and offered to pay compensation for their non-development instead of recommending zoning. This also was a small sweetener to encourage participation in the plan.

Requiring a setback from streams, as well as from lakes and ocean shores, may also be a valid use of regulatory powers on the ground of protecting public health. The basic question, yet to be settled by the courts of Pennsylvania, is how far is fair and under what circumstances. Wisconsin has enacted a statewide program which establishes a three-hundred-foot setback from navigable streams and a thousand-foot setback from lakes. Counties fix specific provisions under the umbrella of the state regulations. The Wisconsin Supreme Court has upheld as reasonable regulation the provisions of the Marinette County ordinance as applicable to wetlands.[9] These provisions allow forestry, hunting, and a few other activities as permitted uses and farming, dredge and fill, and several other activities as conditional uses.

Four of the Upper East Branch townships require stream setbacks. Two require a fifty-foot setback for all construction; two others require a hundred-foot setback. None has been challenged. Let us assume that the Pennsylvania courts would agree that a hundred-foot stream buffer is a reasonable zoning requirement. In the Upper East Branch, about one-third of the land within a hundred feet of the stream also lies in the fifty-year flood plain. Flood plain land, totaling 3 percent of the watershed, could be included in flood plain regulations. That would leave land equal to about 6 percent of the watershed to be regulated for open space uses as stream buffer. This is not at all bad for a start, particularly if combined with cluster and planned unit development zoning. Here, however, the possibilities for keeping the land open without paying something in return have about run out.

2. *Controls with Compensation.* There are many possible variations on the theme of compensated public control. Basically, the more compensation paid, the more control passes into public hands. This review will start with measures offering small compensation and small control and move toward those which pay more and exact more.

As has been stated above, the real property tax is a heavy burden, particularly on farmers who have little capital other than their land. One way to encourage continued farming is to offer the farmer a chance to promise to continue farming for a given number of years in return for a public guarantee that his land will be assessed at farm value during that period. This bargain does not cost the public much —the tax dollars forgone on the difference between farm and development value—but on the other hand it does not provide much control. Whenever the farmer gets a really tempting offer for his land, he can break his promise and pay whatever penalty the law specifies. This is exactly what farmers have done in New Jersey, California, and other states with preferential assessment legislation. The law we drafted provides for covenants between farmers and the counties, with a penalty provision for breaches. However, because the covenant is entirely optional and can be breached or terminated by payment of a penalty which is minimal compared with the probable sale price of farm land for development, we never envisioned this law as a real alternative for carrying out the plan. Instead, we saw it as a subsidiary, supportive control.

Another tax measure which could have very real impact is a state capital gains tax on land development such as that recently enacted by Vermont. Assuming that the tax is allocated to the various public agencies that provide sewers, schools, and other public services for new development, this is one way of shifting some of the burden from the old residents to the land seller and the developer, whose actions in changing the use of the land created the need for new services. The proceeds from the tax also could be used to pay for easements on the critical areas.

While this tax may achieve a somewhat fairer distribution of development burdens and benefits among landowners in an area, it exacerbates the problems of the people of low and moderate income who wish to settle there. If the developer must pay a substantial capital gains tax, he will try to recover as much of it as possible from higher prices on his houses. This will put the houses beyond the reach of even more people than they are at present. New development is costly. We have yet to face squarely the question of which of us should bear what share of that cost. We have yet to decide who should have a voice in requiring new development to be more efficient and better coordinated with available services. The newcomers to the suburbs, the old rural residents, and all the rest of us living in already settled areas may agree that the land specualtor who buys from the farmer and the developer who buys from the speculator are making a higher profit than we think reasonable. Even if we do agree on this and enact a new tax which pays for some of the new public services required, this will be but a partial answer to the question of how to provide "a decent home and suitable living environment for every American family." I, for one, believe that there is no answer short of a complete overhaul of the federal housing subsidy program so that all Americans have a fair choice of where to live. Clearly, that was not what we were about in the Brandywine.

Still another tax would be one akin to an effluent charge on municipal and industrial wastes dumped into rivers. The more you pollute, the higher the tax. In theory, uses of land counter to the plan would be taxed highly enough so that, taking the Upper East Branch as a whole, the objectives of the plan would not be violated. Some landowners would find it profitable to develop in the critical areas and pay the tax; the tax would have to be sufficient to cover the public cost of undoing the damage done by the development. Conceptually, such a land and water degradation tax is appealing. In practice, it would be enormously difficult to design an effective system of taxes to forestall damaging uses of land. People are still manipulating the effluent charge system in an attempt to control the character of liquid effluent from many discharge points into a single stream. The complex interaction of the land surface, groundwater, and streams of a basin is a far greater problem. Until there is more experience with the effluent tax, it is premature to say that it can be adapted successfully to control land development.

The next two alternatives offer the landowner the possibility of being paid for public controls, but only if he can show a loss resulting from the controls. Under compensable regulations, the public agency determines the market value of land and sets that as a floor. Next, regulations limiting or prohibiting development are passed. Finally, when the landowner sells he may claim public compensation if, and to the extent that, his sale price falls below the floor previously set, adjusted for inflation or deflation.[10]

Inverse condemnation is quite similar except that the courts, rather than the marketplace, are called upon to determine whether the regulations controlling development have caused a loss and, if so, whether the loss is so substantial as to constitute a taking. A recent Massachusetts case shows how inverse condemnation can operate. The state forbade certain marsh dredging. A landowner went ahead and dredged so that he could walk into the water to swim. The state told him to fill the marsh in again. He went to court and claimed that the state regulation was unreasonable and had caused a drop in the value of his property. The court disagreed with him and upheld the state.[11]

Both compensable regulations and inverse condemnation leave it to the landowner to show a loss. Where there is a valid question as to whether the regulation has actually caused a loss in land value, this is a very fair way of proceeding. Where the loss is obvious and significant, however, the public agency should establish the value of the interest it wishes to acquire, make an offer, and negotiate for acquisition of that interest.

Several types of easements may be appropriate under these circumstances. The easements would vary as to the land uses permitted. A basic easement for a marsh, for instance, could specify that no filling, dredging, paving, sewerage, or development would be allowed. The easement could be in force for a stated number of years, or it could be perpetual, with an option to buy such an easement whenever the landowner chose to sell his land. Of these, the perpetual easement would cost the most.

Several landowners had suggested that the easements be for one year only, renewable at a renegotiated price each year. The Commonwealth of Pennsylvania leases game lands on a similar basis, and local people were familiar with the practice. In the mid-1960s farmers were paid twenty-five cents per acre per year for a five-year lease permitting hunters on the land during the fall hunting season. For this purpose the lease system works well. The farmer gets a little added income at a time when his land is idle. The public has access to land for recreation. The state offers a fixed price, has no maintenance burden, and no land goes off the tax rolls. When the land is ripe for development, the farmer may drop out of the lease program and sell if he chooses. This last factor, though, is the principal reason why this approach would not work for the Brandywine Plan. We needed a scheme which would keep land open *when*, not merely *until*, development value had accrued, and one which would keep it open throughout the watershed, not on a crazy-quilt basis.

The easement option did become part of our final proposal. It would have been a short-term option, good only for the period we estimated the Water Resources Authority staff would need to contact all owners of critical areas in one of the four major sub-basins. Its purpose was to hold off development in the critical area while we were determining whether owners of 80 percent of that land were willing to sell easements at a price mutually agreeable to them and to the Water Resources Authority.

An indefinite right of first refusal to buy an easement at a fixed price was as attractive to the Water Resources Authority as it was unattractive to the landowners. Payment to the Authority would be deferred until an owner gave notice of an intent to sell. Then, depending on conditions, the Authority could decide whether or not to exercise its right to buy the easement. From the owner's viewpoint, the likelihood of the easement purchase would be omnipresent and would hamper sale negotiations, yet no one would have the right to compensation until the Authority had exercised its option. The courts might quite possibly hold his void as a restraint on sale. Therefore, we believed that this alternative was less desirable than many of the others considered.

A variant of this, which offers more to the landowner, is an indeterminate right to buy an easement whenever a landowner requests permission to develop contrary to the plan, with payment pegged at market value at the time of development. The risk here is that, if market value is very high when the owner wishes to develop, the public will be unable to raise enough money to pay for the easement.

PUBLIC OWNERSHIP WITH FULL COMPENSATION. The plan did provide for one sort of full public acquisition. If an owner wanted to sell the full title to his whole property, the Water Resources Authority would be committed to buy at market value. Then, however, it would be required to offer the land for resale, subject to an easement on the critical areas in accord with the plan. We planners, concerned with protecting the public investment in the land, would have preferred long-term leases by the Water Resources Authority rather than resale. However, we recognized that our views diverged sharply from those of most Brandywine residents and that we would be misguided to try to press for an acquisition and lease-back alternative.

This brings us to the last, the simplest, and the least popular alternative. We never considered it in the Upper East Branch, knowing that it would have been utterly unacceptable. This alternative is public acquisition, by eminent domain where necessary, followed by public long-term lease of all land in the development areas and in the critical areas for uses compatible with the plan adopted. This is the accepted way of urbanizing land in a number of countries of western Europe. A municipality, often with financial help from the national government, buys land well in advance of development, paying farm use value. It holds the land, leasing it back for farm use, until development is needed. Then, having planned where the development, with its accompanying transportation, communication, and utilities networks, will be located and what lands will be kept permanently open, development begins. The municipality builds the major part of the supporting networks and times the long-term leases of land for private development in accord with its plan. The profits from the leases repay part of the costs of land acquisition, construction of public facilities, and retention of open space. General tax revenues pay the rest. A look at the newly developed areas of Helsinki, Stockholm, or Rotterdam shows how this can be done economically and efficiently. What it takes is planning and a commitment of public money well ahead of development. It also takes a general belief that all people, rather than a limited few fortunate or clever enough to hold development land, should share in the fruits of development. In the Brandywine, such a proposal would have been too much, too soon.

VIII

epilogue

SEVEN YEARS have passed since the people of the Upper East Branch rejected the Brandywine Plan. What has changed in the Upper East Branch and its environs during that time? Can any of these changes be attributed to the influence of the plan? This chapter examines the Brandywine experience in three ways: first, as a few of us who had been deeply involved saw it shortly after rejection of the plan; second, in terms of measurable or perceived changes in the watershed over the past seven years; and third, as a precursor of changes in land use policies on the Philadelphia urban fringe.

An early retrospective

We devoted considerable thought during the summer and fall of 1968 to the exploration of what we had done wrong. We met together and talked. We exchanged memos. John and I hired Eleanor Winsor,[1] a friend knowledgeable about open space planning but unfamiliar with the Upper East Branch, to interview key supporters and opponents of the plan to find out why it had been rejected. A few people from the press came to interview us and to solicit names of opponents whom they might also interview before drawing their own conclusions. Almost everyone agreed that we had been overambitious in the scope, size, and timing of the project. Notions as to what might have succeeded varied with the perspective of the commentator.

LOCAL FEELINGS. The staff agreed that it would be helpful to us and to others curious about responses to the plan to hire someone sensitive to the issues, but with no prior involvement in the area or with the plan, to interview a few of the people who had played prominent roles. Using research funds from our Federal Water Quality Administration grant,[2] John and I prepared for Eleanor Winsor a list of the questions which most concerned us, and asked her to call on the people whom we thought had been most influential one way or another in affecting the outcome of the plan. John, Ken, and I picked forty people whom we recommended that she see—state, county, and township officials and people living in the watershed but holding no elective or appointive position. The list was split about equally between proponents

164

and opponents. Since everyone interviewed was assured that no remarks would be attributed to them, this summary must be general.

One can aggregate the interview notes in several ways, among them whether people were pro or con, whether they held a political position or not, and whether they lived in the Upper East Branch and would have been affected by the plan or not.

Eleanor's report focused on those people who lived in the area, some of whom would be directly affected by the plan. She made several general observations about them. As with most generalizations there were exceptions, yet certain attitudes and opinions were dominant enough to be noted. People not only did not identify with Philadelphia, its problems, and its growth but consciously rejected any such identification. One elderly farmer boasted that he had been to Philadelphia once as a child and had never seen any reason to return. Another resident—an affluent professional person—said, "I resent the idea that we need Marsh Creek here. Those metropolitan people have to go somewhere, but let them stay closer to the city. The people here have bought land to avoid the masses of people." A township official and one of the local opposition leaders said, "I don't want to be part of it [the metropolitan area] and don't see any reason why we should be."

Most emphasized that their ideal life style was to be unfettered by government or neighbors. One person summed it up: "Everybody leave everybody else alone." This preference was voiced by opponents and proponents, newcomers and long-time residents. They felt that, while some minimal services should be provided by local government, it should await a demand for such services and then respond rather than take the initiative.

These views are not conducive to development of strong local leadership. Therefore, it is not surprising that many people were unable to identify local leaders and that few who did agreed on who they were. When Eleanor asked who the most influential people in the Upper East Branch were, 40 percent of the respondents named a township supervisor or the supervisors as a group. A number of people—among them supervisors, planning commission members, and members of township political party committees—named themselves. Several of these individuals apparently were leaders without followers, since no one else named them. Only one person named someone in another township. One supervisor was named by four people, another by three. No one else was mentioned more than once or twice. One third of the people could not think of a single local leader, which is particularly notable because the people whom Eleanor interviewed were those whom we had identified as leaders.

When the residents were also asked to name organizations active in local or county affairs, their answers strongly suggest that they chose not to be active in civic or political groups. Three out of four people said either that there were no such groups or that they did not know of any. Four people mentioned the grange, and no other group was mentioned more than twice.

People interviewed who had settled in the Upper East Branch within the past ten to fifteen years split on whether they felt accepted. Those who did tended to be people who worked in the area and whose background was similar to that of the old residents.

Most wanted the natural amenities of the watershed to be preserved, and some wanted no further development. The goals of the plan were universally endorsed. Most saw local government as the proper or the only generally acceptable vehicle for achieving this goal. The question of how local government should act was where opinions differed. Most proponents thought that eminent domain was vital and that the plan was crippled without it. Most opponents said that the goals of the plan should be realized through local regulation, particularly zoning, yet many of these people also condoned zoning because of its flexibility and because of the possibility of rezoning if a landowner changed his mind.

There was general agreement on the grounds for opposition to the plan, although opinions differed as to whether those grounds were valid.

Eminent domain was number one on most people's lists. Many suggested that the timing of the plan was unfortunate because of the recent use of eminent domain for the Marsh Creek reservoir and for the pipelines and high tension lines. They thought that at another time, with more soft-pedaling, eminent domain might have been accepted. Others thought it unacceptable under any circumstances— even calling it unconstitutional, un-American, or communistic. It is surprising that one vocal opponent and member of the Freeholders said that, after the defeat, he had changed his mind about opposing the plan and about eminent domain. Most agreed that people never heard or else never believed that eminent domain had been dropped from the final version of the plan.

Probably second in the list of reasons cited for opposition was that the planners and the Water Resources Authority were outsiders. Both had bad local public relations. The Authority was soundly disliked because of Marsh Creek, and many people failed to distinguish that project from the Brandywine Plan. Bob Struble was suspect because he was the staff man for the Authority at Marsh Creek. Board members who worked for local industries needing Brandywine water also were suspect. As for Ken and the rest of us, in general the people who supported the plan thought highly of us but suggested that most residents would have responded better to a local person as principal spokesman for the plan. The opponents found much to criticize. Luna and those of us at the University of Pennsylvania were too academic or talked down to people or had long hair. Two women criticized the project for having a woman in a lead role. Ken was said to be too aggressive and didn't know local customs. He went to the front door. "He dressed too well to do the job right. People here like a fellow who's been shovelling manure for ten years." Whatever people thought of us, they agreed that we needed to have come to the Upper East Branch under the sponsorship of local leaders. However, few could identify individuals or groups in leadership roles, and most expressed the wish to be left to their own devices as far as use of their land was concerned. Therefore, without questioning the desirability of sponsorship by local leaders, one may ask how feasible it was.

Many people questioned whether, with the outsiders gone, local government could and would carry out the goals of the plan. Few, other than Planning Commission members interviewed, voiced hope for the Regional Planning Commission.

The time was too short, people said. With more time, they would have felt less fearful about the commitment they were being asked to make. Most did not feel any pressures from urbanization and did not believe anything would happen for another twenty years. They resented being hurried by our timetable.

Only a few people mentioned lack of local participation in planning as a reason for opposition. Those who did were opponents who were personally offended because they had been left out. They complained not of a general failure to bring local people into the planning process but of their own exclusion. One said, "They didn't listen to persons such as myself."

There was suspicion about the outside money to pay for the easements. Outside money implied outside control. Why did Ford or HUD want to spend money in the Brandywine? Wasn't there really some ulterior motive such as homes for blacks, a TVA-type reservoir, and/or benefits for du Pont? However, if it really was because the Upper East

Private property and the public interest

Branch was to be a guinea pig, that too sounded frightening and threatening.

Some people—a small but potent minority—really did not support the plan's objectives. Their interest lay in maximum profit from land sales. It was not politic to say this openly, so they voiced other reasons for opposition, usually the eminent domain and "outsider" issues.

There was a fair measure of agreement among all of the Brandywine residents interviewed that the above reasons were major causes of opposition. There was one other major reason: the concern aroused by the opponents of the plan. All agreed that the Freeholders, and Harry Simms in particular, had been extremely effective in bringing about its rejection. Most thought that many people had not read the plan but had formed their opinions based on what they heard, and that much of what they heard came from the Freeholders. Many of the people interviewed, including some opposed to the plan, condemned the Freeholders' tactics and thought that they had prevented a fair or reasoned consideration of its merits. Their tactics were said to have been intentionally deceitful, designed to breed fear and misunderstanding. One township official who was personally opposed to eminent domain called the Freeholders "an obnoxious bunch who went from meeting to meeting making trouble. They never gave people who favored the project a chance to speak out." Another township official called them "rabble-rousers." One farmer who opposed the plan because he wanted, eventually, to sell his large holdings for development, described the Freeholders as "a group of outs who want in." Some saw them as people using the plan to gain notoriety. Few, it seemed, thought well of the Freeholders, yet all agreed that other people listened to them and were persuaded by them.

Why didn't its proponents fight hard *for* the plan? Those interviewed uniformly described the group favoring it as being among the larger landowners, wealthier and better educated than their neighbors, but also relatively new to the Upper East Branch. This newness was cited as a handicap; people felt themselves to be outsiders, particularly if their jobs were elsewhere, lacked local contacts, and hesitated to assert themselves. Also, many were so offended by the vituperative, inflammatory language of the opponents of the plan that they shrank from verbal duels. They did not want to be drawn into a battle with the Freeholders and did not know how to organize in a way that would not precipitate such a struggle. Several said that they should have done more and should have been more vocal.

These, then, were the major reasons given by local people for failure of the plan. Avoidance of eminent domain, better public relations, and active sponsorship by local leaders were the principal means advocated for a successful, or at least more successful, approach.

The people holding public office had varying perspectives. Eleanor Winsor interviewed one state official, nine men working at the county level as elected or appointed officials or as county employees, and nine men holding township positions as supervisors, Planning Commission members, or members of a township political party committee. The Democrats candidly stated that they owed their political success to opposition to the plan. Both Democrats and Republicans had close ties to the Freeholders. Most Republican elected officials voiced personal support for the plan but said that they felt constrained to take a public posture of neutrality. Some said that this was to protect themselves politically, others that they believed it proper to reflect what they felt to be community opinion. No one suggested that his position carried a responsibility to take the initiative in promoting the plan if he believed in it. One township supervisor who thought it wrong to take a public stand said, "I think there is a great sincerity when people say they want the objectives of the Plan. The paradox is that they are not willing to take the initiative or endanger their self-interest." Another township official said, "The people don't understand communal responsibility toward the land for they are the lords of the land." This was what many residents said of themselves and of others and perhaps comes close to explaining why those holding political office did not exercise leadership.

THE STAFF. When we discussed the outcome among ourselves we concluded that there was not only an absence of strong leadership at the county and township levels, but also, as John Troxell put it, a need for exceptional leadership, since the plan was a radical one. While the land use objectives were conservative, the land use controls were not. In retrospect, we realized that we had been trying to get people to accept very considerable changes, whereas most politically acceptable changes are gradual and incremental. To people who had barely accepted zoning we were proposing a major invasion of their right to control the use of their land. Most simply were not persuaded that the circumstances required such drastic action.

This was an issue which Ken, John Keene, and I pondered. We recognized that most people are likely to become involved in a community enterprise only when aroused by what they see as a crisis. We were the crisis that enabled the Freeholders to mobilize. We, however, could produce no crisis to which our planning would be one response. A few years earlier the fight over the 500-kV line could have provided an entree to the community, but that fight was lost in the courts before we arrived, and the prison threat did not materialize until we were well along in our planning. Manipulating public concern about a particular event to achieve our ends would have required a degree of opportunism we apparently did not possess. Even when township officials told us that they would not back the plan unless we took action to get rid of the prison, we did not make condemnatory public statements or call state officials whom we knew because we thought that the prison probably would be economically beneficial to the area and would have few damaging social or environmental effects. The most we did was to offer to work with state officials to assure that the prison development would be in accord with the plan.

None of us knew how we could have stimulated widespread local interest in planning for the Upper East Branch in the absence of a real or artificially generated crisis. We did agree that, with more lead time, we could have done a far more effective job of finding a nucleus of local people genuinely concerned with planning for their area and that, working with them, we could have developed a plan which they would have seen as theirs, not ours. Even in that case, however, we doubted that such a group of local people could have persuaded their fellow citizens to take effective action to implement that plan. They would have stood a better chance than we did, but they too would have been confronted with the general lack of a sense of urgency and instinctive opposition to being told what to do.

John, Ken, Gordon Harrison, and I concluded that perhaps long-range land use decisions can only be made by an autocrat—a politician, a public agency, or a private entrepreneur (the Corps of Engineers, Robert Moses in his heyday, the New York Port Authority, and the Levitt Corporation, for example)—with enough power to make the decisions stick. Our approach had been intended as the antithesis to this.

Bob Coughlin, Ben, and I thought our approach might have succeeded if we had been less insistent on choosing an average population. Judging by those who were in favor of the Brandywine Plan, we suggested that had we picked a watershed with a larger number of relatively affluent people who had fled the city or suburbs seeking a beautiful natural environment, as well as a number of farmers who wished to continue farming, the population might have provided the margin of support that we needed. This guess was bolstered by a report from John Troxell. Several people had told him that they were keenly interested in the outcome of the plan. They said that they might well move to the Upper East Branch if it were adopted, since they wanted to settle in a place where their investment in open space and natural beauty would be protected.

All of us shared the view that thirty-seven square miles was much too much, and that our original two-thousand-acre area would have been better.

All of us also agreed that we had needed more time. The Ford Foundation had given us six extra months, but the extension had been granted grudgingly, and we felt keenly the intimation that, if we did not conclude the planning phase in the time agreed upon, there might be no funds for easement acquisition. Thus we pressed Bob Struble and Ken to move faster than they felt was right, and our pressure for a decision only heightened public anxiety. It is understandable that the grantor of funds for an experiment should want to cut its losses at some point and pull out, while the advocates of the experiment can be expected to think that more money and more time could bring success. We, however, felt that relaxation of this particular time pressure would have led to greater public receptivity.

We agreed that the Indian Run sub-basin might have been an appropriate initial choice in both size and composition of residents. Bob Struble believed then and still believes that we could have succeeded there.

We acknowledged that Ken had had an impossible task and that our accurate, detailed publications had not been of much help to him. Much more time spent working with fewer landowners and much less time spent on maps and hydrologic calculations would have been better. This is not to denigrate the hydrologic research. The knowledge gained about the influence of urbanization in the Brandywine on runoff, erosion, flooding, and drought[3] is of national significance and has been the foundation for much current planning. However, it won no friends for the plan. Almost everyone in the Upper East Branch assumed that the plan made hydrologic sense, but they were not interested in why it did. We committed so much of our staff time to helping Luna because the Geological Survey people either were uninterested in the project or could not give him what he needed, but it was a costly diversion of resources in terms of the plan, if not in a larger context.

A regrettably large sum of money went toward collection of data on land values, population growth, rate and location of land sales, and names and addresses of all landowners. Preparation of maps at the same scale to show property lines, parcel sizes and numbers, topography, roads, utilities, and the critical areas consumed vast amounts of time. The frustrations of dealing with different bases and scales and different systems of aggregating data are an old story to planners. Had the Brandywine Plan not been designed as a demonstration, so that this data base was as essential for the future as the hydrologic data, much of this work could have been omitted. For us, however, it was vital for later proof, or disproof, of our premises about development value. Staff costs for this type of work were far higher than estimated. At the Institute for Environmental Studies, for instance, at least half of the thirty-eight months of staff time spent on planning was devoted to this drudgery. At the Regional Science Research Institute, the percentage probably was higher. This meant budget cuts for other work, especially research on costs and benefits under the plan and development of new survey techniques.

The part of the planning program most severely under-budgeted was staff time for public communication. Even Ken had other chores, and no one else was paid to spend all—or even most—of the time contacting people. John, Bob Struble, Bob Coughlin, Ben, Luna, and I attended meetings, spoke to groups, wrote articles, talked to reporters, and spoke on the radio, but all together the time we spent in this way was only equivalent to that of approximately one and one-half people working full-time for two years. Twice that would not have been too much. Further, despite Bob Struble's valid concern, I think that we should have looked for advice to someone with professional competence in public relations.

I felt particularly at fault about our easement appraisals. The opposition attacked us again and again at public meetings because we did not have estimates of what would be offered for the easements. This part of the plan was months behind schedule, and intimations that we were concealing something took root. All of us knew that estimates of easement costs would be vital information, yet I did not insist on hiring the Philadelphia appraiser whom we knew could do the job and, what is more important, could stand up in public meetings and defend his appraisals effectively. Instead, I let myself be swayed by the political considerations of the Water Resources Authority.

Bob Coughlin, Ben, John, and I also wished that we had promoted the development corporation idea sooner and more effectively. It still seemed to us to offer the best way for people with land under easements to participate in profits from the future growth of the watershed. Because the local people would manage it, they would have a very strong voice in determining what sort of development took place.

All of us except Bob Struble thought that we should have responded more forcefully to the attacks of the opposition, but Bob had the backing of the key members of the Water Resources Authority board. Some of us thought that the Authority should have insisted on holding the final meetings. Bob Coughlin and Ben thought that we should have canceled those meetings—that, since the plan was voluntary, it was solely a matter between the Authority and each landowner, and that therefore the Authority could have moved directly to negotiations, property by property.

None of us knew how to find funds for a voluntary program, since Gordon Harrison had remained adamant that Ford would not contribute without eminent domain and the HUD officials had taken the same stand.

Bob Struble was the only one who was cheerful and optimistic. He wrote, in summer 1968, that "we broke new ground and much good will come of our endeavor." He hoped that, in time, people in the Upper East Branch or elsewhere in the country would decide that they wanted to carry out the plan and that, possibly with our help, they would find a way to do so. He was joined in his optimism by Harold Ladd, the Water Resources Authority vice-chairman, who was deeply interested in the plan. Ladd said that, if he could find one other Authority member who would try to put the plan across, he would tackle some area of the county and try to make it succeed.

THE PRESS. The local press offered no analysis of the reasons for the rejection of the plan. Once the meetings at which it was discussed were no longer front-page news, the plan vanished from the papers. Reporters from outside did come to talk to us and to the local people. The Philadelphia coverage was sympathetic to the plan. *Progressive Architecture* sent two reporters to interview a cross-section of Brandywine residents. Some of their impressions follow:

The reasons for the plan's rejection seem to lie in ingrained attitudes and values—a deep distrust of government, financial apprehensions, rejections of anything that seemed to threaten land values, and resistance to change. . . . A major source of defeat lies in the predominant personality characteristics of residents. About two-thirds were raised in rural areas where their worlds were essentially tangible, predictable, and stable. Since their property was a reliable element in their lives, anything that threatened that property attacked a central element of their personalities. Many saw the plan's proponents as a threatening power structure. They view change as a threat, not an opportunity, and those who accepted the inevitability of change preferred to deal with it personally, on their own terms, rather than as a group member with common objectives.

The typical opponent of the plan lives tightly bound by the moral commands of the Protestant ethic. They denounce anyone whom they consider lazy, communally oriented, free-thinking, or in any way "different." While they insist that they are not prejudiced, one of their major fears about the plan was that it might bring black Philadelphians into the area, either as residents of planned unit developments or as park users, although the plan did not include such development or parks.[4]

Science magazine also reported the defeat of the plan. Peter Thompson, in an article titled, "Brandywine Basin: Defeat of an Almost Perfect Plan," concluded:

So the WRA-IES [Water Resources Authority-Institute for Environmental Studies] Plan for the Brandywine is dead, and a plan based on local police power seems years in the offing; the time is right for the land speculation which always accompanies the change from rural to urban land use. If the time, money and effort spent on the Brandywine Plan was wasted on the Brandywine itself, the Plan is serving as a model for the development of watershed plans in other regions of Pennsylvania and the Northeast. Much of the work done by IES and its consultants can serve as base-line data for these other plans, which can thus be drawn up for a fraction of the cost of the Brandywine Plan. And perhaps the lesson in human relations which came out of the confrontation between "experts" and rural Americans is the most valuable piece of base-line data to emerge from the study.[5]

Several magazines and journals invited members of the planning staff to write articles analyzing our experiences. John and I wrote one for the *Journal of the American Institute of Planners,* Luna one for *Natural History.* Luna's article ended:

In the three years since the Brandywine Plan was voted down, great impetus has been given to the imperative need for environmental protection as a necessary ingredient in maintaining the quality of life. But even if the surge of public interest had begun earlier, the detailed problems faced by any new scheme for achieving rational land planning would have been the same. There is no substitute for local leadership in community action, in the collection and dissemination of relevant facts, and in grassroots organization. These take time. The terms of the financing for our planning effort did not permit us to take the time that, hindsight says, was required.

The protection of the environment is a lofty goal. Necessary as it seems in principle, it is in many respects diffuse and elusive. A society attains it indirectly by action or inaction on common and mundane matters, heavily influenced by custom, by monetary considerations, and by political forces. Experience on the Brandywine is a clear signal that the road to such a goal is long, steep, and rocky.[6]

In our article, John and I pointed out four principal requirements for success of plans like ours:

1. Sufficient time must be available to work out a program that is endorsed by a substantial number of residents. Two years was not long enough to do this in the Upper East Branch area.
2. Proponents must be willing and able to proceed with experiments on a fairly small scale so that some of the novelty of the program can be dispelled.
3. Objectives of the program should be modest, so as to allow more flexibility in working out a successful compromise of conflicting interests. The Brandywine Project, with its heavy baggage of legal, hydrological, financial and research goals, was probably overloaded.
4. Positive inducements should be available to balance restrictions perceived by residents. The development corporation concepts, though rejected in the Upper East Branch, appears to be one mechanism for making such inducements available.[7]

I have since revised my conclusion as to the third of these factors. Our proposal was not a modest one in its goals; it would have been a very different proposal if altered to be so. My current thoughts about implementation of a plan with such characteristics comprise the next chapter.

Five years later

In the five years between 1968 and 1973, there was little visible change in the Upper East Branch. There was, however, a considerable shift in the residents' perceptions of the character of the area and of the imminence of change. The pace of development nearby had quickened markedly, and land was changing hands at ever higher prices. The development we had predicted was nearly upon the residents. They did not like what they saw coming, but, for the most part, they still were not ready to work together to try to shape the future of the Brandywine: this was the conclusion of our second attitude survey, carried out in 1971, five years after the initial survey.

GROWTH. Chester County grew 77 percent in the decade 1960–1970, from 211,000 to 274,000, yet it remained the only county in the Philadelphia metropolitan area over 50 percent of whose municipalities were classified as rural. Subdivision is on the rise throughout the county. In 1969–1972, eighteen thousand subdivisions were recorded with the county. Richard Byler, a county planner, said in 1973: "Frightful economic and ecological problems . . . might come if the pattern of subdivision continues." The subdivision has occurred "in entirely the wrong places," away from areas planned for sewerage. "It seems to us that this is a very severe problem," said Byler, "way, way out of control"[8] In another interview in the summer of 1973, Byler noted that townships still feared that the county and the regional planning agency would usurp local powers: "Just ten years ago in Chester County, planning was looked upon as a form of Communism. People just did not want any part of the idea of restriction of lands, and they are not quite ready yet."[9]

From 1960 to 1970 the Upper East Branch townships grew faster than the county as a whole. The population almost doubled, rising from approximately 10,000 to approximately 19,000. While the rate of growth was rapid, the total amount was small, and Uwchlan Township accounted for much of it. Uwchlan was the fastest-growing township in the state, up 450 percent, from a population of 1,000 to one of 5,500. The part of Uwchlan where the growth occurred is just over the ridge from the Brandywine watershed, at the intersection of two major highways and near a Pennsylvania Turnpike interchange. A regional shopping center, industrial parks, apartment complexes, and strip commercial development were under way by 1970, and rapid growth continues today. Land at the heart of the Uwchlan development area now sells for $40,000 to $60,000 per acre.

The Downington area sewage disposal plant, designed to handle four million gallons of sewage per day, with a possible future expansion to twelve million gallons per day, opened in the summer of 1973. It will serve two of the Upper East Branch townships and several other municipalities. Its completion will be another spur to development. Thirty percent of the land in one of the townships is now held by absentee owners. Twenty-four percent of all parcels in Honey Brook Township traded hands in 1965.

Several tracts of 100 to 300 acres have been subdivided. A few trailer parks have been established. New housing consists of everything from mobile homes to $75,000 houses. One large planned unit development promises housing for low-income families, which is ironic in view of the charges that the plan would bring this about. Between 1968 and 1973, some Upper Branch townships—East Caln and Uwchlan in particular

—have taken steps to regulate development. Others, further from growth pressures, have altered their land use controls little or not at all.

THE REGIONAL PLANNING COMMISSION. Contrary to the expectations of many, the Regional Planning Commission remained in existence and, in 1972, completed and published a water resource protection plan.[10] It is its hope that many of the member townships will adapt its recommendations to their particular needs and adopt them. Seven of the eight Upper East Branch townships initially joined the Regional Planning Commission. East Caln did not. Subsequently, Uwchlan dropped out. Each township appoints two members who serve alternating two-year terms. Some of the original members remain, but the majority have been appointed since the rejection of the Brandywine Plan. Harry Simms continues to be a member and has served a term as chairman. It is interesting that through a political appointment he has also become an employee of Maurice Goddard in the Pennsylvania Department of Environmental Resources. As such, he has supported state parks, reservoirs, and many other activities of the "Big Daddy" government against which he campaigned so effectively in the Upper East Branch.

An early decision of the commission was to define as its planning area all land withing the seven municipalities, not just the watershed of the Upper East Branch. Some portions of the Upper West Branch of Brandywine Creek were included, and the organization adopted the name Upper Brandywine Watersheds Regional Planning Commission. Each township contributed $1,000 and the county contributed $1,800 to pay for the commission's plan. We gave our maps and data to the commission's planning consultant, Joe Langran, who said in his foreword to the published commission plan:

The fact that this [the Brandywine] Plan was not accepted by the residents is a matter of record, and this would be sufficient to state under normal circumstances. However, in spite of certain major features, the Plan accomplished three things which will prove more important with time. These achievements are:

1. It stirred up the residents to the point of realizing that *something* had to be done about protection of the Brandywine before it was too late;

2. As a result of "1" above, it sparked the establishment of a Regional Planning Commission, determined to come up with an alternate solution to the methods proposed in the Plan;

3. It provided a wealth of data not previously available to the residents,

Private property and the public interest

and the Institute of Environmental Studies graciously allowed the Commission to use that data, as well as all maps, charts, and even a model.

The fact that reaction *against* one effort stimulated another is not unique, for we often find that initial efforts serve a valuable purpose as a beginning. One cannot wonder if the Institute had not undertaken The Brandywine Plan, would there have been a Regional Planning Commission? History is replete with examples of people rising up in anger against what they feel is a "threat," and in counteracting it, they arrive at a solution which might never have been dreamed of. In short, there appears to have been sufficient time elapsed since the Plan was presented to safely say, "Thank you"! . . .

It must be made clear at the very outset that the data gathered and conclusions drawn by the Institute, with respect to the basic problem, are accepted as essentially sound and have been used as the starting point of this particular study. The difference is in the *method of achieving* the objectives, and *not* in the basic objectives themselves.

The Regional Planning Commission chose, in its plan, to elaborate upon that portion of the Brandywine Plan concerned with regulation of development practices—runoff and erosion control, flood control, and sewage disposal. The plan endorses our concept of maintaining an adequate water supply by collecting and treating wastes at small subregional plants, then discharging highly treated effluent to be reused. It rejects as politically unacceptable our recommendation that the treated effluent be sprayed on the ground, at a goodly distance from the stream, to soak into the earth and be further cleansed by the soil before reaching the stream.

Even though the commission did not endorse this approach to sewage disposal, it did co-sponsor a meeting with the Brandywine Valley Association and the Chester County Conservation District at which the "living filter" method was explained. The BVA already had created a sewage stabilization pond and spray irrigation system at a retirement community in southern Chester County, and thus it could speak from experience.

Partly as a result of that meeting, Honey Brook Township and Honey Brook Borough expressed serious interest in spray irrigation. They engaged an engineering firm to do a feasibility study and will ask the Regional Planning Commission for its comments when the study is complete. West Brandywine Township is negotiating with a developer of a 160-acre farm near the headwaters of Culbertson Run to keep half of the tract permanently open and to use spray irrigation. It is proposing that the developer sign deed restrictions which would include spray irrigation as one of the permitted uses of the open space.

The water quality standards recommended by the Regional Planning Commission are higher than those set by the state, and commission members have met with state officials to request that state standards be raised.

The boldest suggestion in the commission plan is that the seven townships create a regional sewer authority empowered to allocate effluent rights to the streams. As an alternative, each township might proceed separately but with a uniform approach. The rights could be bought and sold, permitting a developer to assemble enough rights for intensive use of his land.[11] The idea has much promise, and three townships have adopted effluent allocation ordinances.

The plan recommends that erosion caused by development be held on the site. This recommendation accords with an excellent new Pennsylvania law providing for state regulation of erosion from development.[12] The plan also recommends adoption of flood plain zoning for any area which would be flooded on the average of once in fifty years. Specifically proposed for consideration is the model ordinance which I prepared as part of a set of environmental regulations for The Tri-County Conservancy of the Brandywine. Most of the townships have adopted this ordinance. The commission suggested that the townships review the other ordinances drafted by John Keene and me for The Tri-County Conservancy and consider adopting some of them as well.

The philosophy underlying the Regional Planning Commission approach is stated clearly by Joe Langran:

How realistic are we in planning according to the desires of the present residents? Are we merely giving lip service to preserving the character in the Upper Brandywine Watershed? Does not the real answer lie in a moral judgment of what *should* be the future of this piece of real estate which we call the "Upper Brandywine Watershed," rather than attempting to find some magic formula which will please everyone?

. . . We must accept some limitations upon our freedom, through some forms of regulations, if we are to accomplish the Regional Planning Commission's objectives for the Watershed. In a basic sense, our problem is two-fold:

The *present residents* must be convinced that limitations on the use and ultimate disposition of their land are morally right; and,

Developers, either of subdivisions or of individual properties, must be made to conform to certain regulations, or their proposed improvements not permitted. This second problem will be easier than the first.

It seems obvious that alternative courses of action are available to the proponents of protecting the water resources, soils and natural environment of the Brandywine Watershed. One, to hold out for the most effective so-

Private property and the public interest

lution and accept that or nothing at all. Many of our finest accomplishments have resulted from a few strong-willed individuals having sufficient intestinal fortitude to hold out long enough, against all opposition, to achieve their original goal. The history of our Republic is replete with examples of this and today, long after the consequences have become known, we praise those few who stood firm.

The other approach, and one which is more the rule than the exception in planning, is to try another approach when it becomes evident that the first will not be acceptable. When time is of the essence, it is more practical to start with *some* of the desirable measures and accomplish a part of the desired objectives, at least. There is always the possibility that, once a measure of progress is evident, the merits of the most effective approach may be more generally accepted.

The enactment of local regulations in accord with the Regional Planning Commission recommendations is a positive step. To determine whether the debate over the Brandywine Plan has made the residents of the Upper East Branch townships more aware of the need to protect their natural environment *and* more willing to take action, we will see whether they move faster or farther than other similarly situated communities. The survival of the Regional Planning Commission and its transformation into an organization with positive ideas and recommendations is encouraging. Less encouraging were the results of our second attitude survey.

CHANGED ATTITUDES. A research grant which John and I received from the Environmental Protection Agency in 1971 made it possible for us to hire Judith Benedict and Cheryl Wasserman, graduate students from the University of Pennsylvania Department of City and Regional Planning, to carry out a second attitude survey in the Upper East Branch.[13] We hoped to learn how people perceived that their environment had changed between 1966 and 1971 and who had responded in what manner to the Brandywine Plan.

Judy and Cheryl spent the summer of 1971 interviewing half of the Upper East Branch residents who had been interviewed in the 1966 attitude survey.[14] John and I worked with Judy and Cheryl to develop a new questionnaire, using some of the more useful questions from the 1966 survey and adding others, many of them open-ended, to elicit what people knew and thought of the plan, what changes in the area they had noticed, and how they had responded to these changes.

In general, people felt that growth was underway; they found their immediate environment less satisfying than in 1966;[15] but few were prepared to involve themselves actively to try to shape future land use changes. A majority believed that local government, through zoning and other regulations, should and could control development and protect the environment.

As for the Brandywine Plan, only half of the landowners knew about it and had some understanding of what it had proposed. Of this group, those people who expressed an opinion were against the plan two to one, mostly because they believed that easements would unfairly restrict their right to do as they wished with their land.

There was widespread agreement that growth had steadily increased and would continue to do so because farmers were selling out to speculators or newcomers, either because farming was no longer profitable or because they received a good price for their land. Yet many people felt that the Brandywine Plan was unnecessary because the farmers near them were taking good care of the land and would never sell out. Thus people said that farmers were selling for development, yet when they talked of their own feelings about the plan and about their own immediate environment, they reached the conclusion that their neighbors would not sell. This was partly wishful thinking. Most people do not want further development: they are willing to accept a small amount as unavoidable but would be distressed if there were much development near them.[16] Therefore, so long as the farmers nearby don't sell for development, all is well.

Easements were objectionable to many because they would limit the future profit to be made from the land. The landowners who objected to them did not want to be financially damaged in any negotiations to sell property, yet they clung to the hope that their neighbors, similarly unimpeded by easements, would not want to sell for development.

We asked whether people thought that growth should be controlled and, if so, by whom and how. Almost everyone thought that growth should be controlled.[17] People differed as to whether this should be done by planning ahead or by tackling problems as they arise. A majority thought that local government was meeting the challenge of growth effectively, yet the specific examples given illustrated the inability of local government to resolve immediate problems and did not touch upon long-range growth problems. For instance, people complained of the failure of the townships to stop industries from dumping wastes in the Brandywine and to keep out mobile home parks.

When people were asked "what measures would you be willing to take to control growth?" zoning was far and away the most popular response. However, no one mentioned that the Pennsylvania courts have held two-acre zoning unconstitutional. The percentage of people endorsing various controls was as follows:

Control	Percentage
zoning	79
private covenants	34
easements	26
eminent domain	13
no action	11

The lack of enthusiasm for private covenants was explained in such phrases as, "here today, gone tomorrow" and "only cause trouble, don't hold up." One individual who favored covenants had turned to them after the plan had been rejected. He had persuaded several of his neighbors to join him in voluntarily placing deed restrictions on their land.

Only half of the people who said that, in the abstract, easements were a good idea were willing to see them used. Why is not clear. A few said that zoning had yet to be put to the test and that it would be better to try it first as a development control. Others recalled personal experiences with easements. One woman said, "AT&T came in and it would have been too costly to fight them. [They] ripped up my land, cut the electric wire, the cows and horses got loose. One cow fell in the ditch they had left. They didn't know better; all they were interested in was getting the line put down on the property."

Answers to questions about the Brandywine Plan itself showed the inadequacy of our efforts to reach people. All of the people interviewed in 1971 had lived in the watershed since 1966, and, even if they had not attended meetings or been visited by Ken, they at least had received the numerous mailings about the plan. These answers were quite discouraging.[18] The first question in this group was, "Who proposed the plan?" Half of the respondents had no idea. One-third were at least close: the Ford Foundation, F. Huston McIlvaine, Robert Struble, or, for a handful, the Water Resources Authority. The rest had a vague or totally wrong idea: du Pont, "some guy," "some committee," and so forth.

Next we asked what the plan had proposed. A narrow majority had somewhere between a limited and an excellent grasp of the goals and specific proposals of the plan. Only in Honey Brook, one of the two townships that voted in favor of the plan, did every person interviewed understand the proposals. Also most large landowners—those with the greatest stake in the plan—understood it reasonably well. Not surprisingly, most of those who understood the plan also were familiar with conservation easements. The rest either had never heard of it and or gave totally erroneous answers. Asked how the plan was to have been carried out, nearly half responded that easements were to have been used; most of the others had no idea.

Why did people think that others supported or opposed the plan? Why did they themselves support or oppose it? Those who had an opinion overwhelmingly agreed that supporters wanted to protect water resources and conserve open space. Opinions about reasons for opposition were diverse. In descending order of frequency they were: loss of full control of the land, distrust of those presenting the plan, distrust of outsiders, the unequal impact of the easements, and money reasons. Of this group of landowners, 22 percent supported the plan, 42 percent opposed it, 13 percent remained undecided, and 23 percent did not know enough about it to have an opinion. A majority of people in the following categories supported the plan: those not personally affected, those who owned less than two acres, those who thought easements were a good land use control, and those who had either a grade school or a college education.[19]

Answers to questions about the continuing impact of the plan were not much more encouraging. While half of those who knew about it thought that it had increased their awareness of the importance of protecting the natural environment, 85 percent said it had had no effect on their actions. Perhaps one could say that, if 15 percent did step up their activities to protect the natural environment as a result of the plan, this would be a significant outcome. We know of no basis for comparison.

Speculating on the results of their survey, Judy and Cheryl concluded that the development corporation concept might have been acceptable to Upper East Branch residents as a way of carrying out the goals of the plan:[20]

Although the development corporation of local landowners has been proposed but never tried in the United States, it could be an "out" to some of the problems encountered in attempting to gain acceptance for the plan, and suggests that, should the concepts of the Brandywine Plan be appropriate elsewhere, the development corporation should seriously be considered in conjunction with it. First, profits from the sale of any of the corporation's holdings are shared by all member landowners. This might have cooled the objections of those in the UEB who felt easements were selective, and therefore unfair in their restrictions. Because a development corporation controls the development rights to large areas of land and, therefore, the time and place of future development, profits realized from such a venture should probably at least equal, if not exceed, the profits to be gained from normal development.

Second, member landowners have direct control over the method, time, and place of development. This might have lessened the objections of all those who felt that the Brandywine Plan was forced upon them by outsiders and would not have been administered by persons they could trust. Furthermore the corporation is a more positive tool for guiding development than are easements alone. Easements can only prohibit building; a development corporation can specify where development should occur.

Third, if a development corporation bought the development rights to land, landowners would be left with property which would be taxed only according to the value of its present use. The corporation would pay the taxes on the value of the development rights. Since the holding costs of land are usually a heavy burden on large landowners, often forcing them to sell before their land reaches peak development value, the landowner will benefit from shifting the burden to the corporation.

Events nearby

Today there are a number of promising and innovative open space and water resource protection projects under way in the Philadelphia metropolitan area. Some of them, in part or in full, have drawn upon the work and ideas of the Brandywine Plan. The post-Brandywine projects have been concerned with collection of better information, enactment of new regulations, use of the tax relief law which I drafted and we worked for, and acquisition of development rights. Some of the efforts have been public, some private, and a few have been notable for an effort to bring about public and private cooperation. Happily, there are many projects which one could describe and laud. As illustrations, I have picked several with which I am familiar.

MONITORING. Brandywine Creek was the nation's most studied small stream when we picked it for our planning effort. It still is. Tom Hammer's thorough studies linking urban runoff to channel enlargement and changes in stream flow already have been mentioned. Another direct result of the Brandywine Plan has been the continued involvement of the Geological Survey in the Brandywine as well as in Chester County. Along with the Chester County Water Resources Authority, the survey has supported Bruce Lium, a limnologist who for several years has been monitoring stream biota throughout the county as a first step in linking waste discharges and stream health.

Several continuous water quality monitoring stations have been established by the survey with county support. Luna has continued to
advise Tom and Bruce on their work.

A new private organization has been established to protect the
environmental and cultural heritage of the Brandywine. Initially organized to fight industrial development near the stream, The Tri-
County Conservancy of the Brandywine, Inc., has developed two
vigorous, well-staffed programs. One centers around the new Brandywine River Museum and is particularly concerned with the art and
history of the area. The other focuses on the Brandywine itself and
encompasses hydrologic study, development of environmental protection ordinances, and acquisition of easements.

Ken Wood was the first director of The Tri-County Conservancy. He
was succeeded by John Troxell. Both did much to shape and launch
the environmental program. As a result of their experience in the
Upper East Branch project, they moved slowly and cautiously, spending much time establishing contact with township and county officials
to determine how the new organization might be of service.

Today the staff of the environmental program is cooperating with
the states of Pennsylvania and Delaware on an extensive monitoring
program for the Brandywine, covering flow, point discharges of wastes,
and water quality. The Conservancy staff has been working with a
dozen scientists from other institutions and agencies, focusing on the
development of a series of mathematical models which will describe
such effects as the impact of land use on water quality in the basin.
Luna, Ruth Patrick, and I served as technical advisors to this program.

REGULATIONS. Another major activity of The Tri-County Conservancy,
initiated by John Troxell, has been the development of a handbook of
model environmental protection ordinances.[21] John Keene and I
wrote the ordinances, an explanation of the need for them, and a
description of their legal status. They cover such matters as erosion
and sedimentation, flood plain use, planned unit development, solid
waste, noise, and pre-emption of all action of one level of government
by a higher one. Initially we met and worked with two townships on
the ordinances which they wanted, and we then derived a model from
these individually tailored ordinances. Later two local attorneys,
Sondra Slade and Fronefield Crawford, Jr., took over the job of township meetings, starting with the model ordinances and revising them as
they and the township officials thought appropriate. Frone Crawford,

incidentally, is from West Brandywine Township and serves as one of its representatives on the Regional Planning Commission.

The handbook, which now contains ten model ordinances, forms the basis of the Conservancy's ordinance program. Thomas Pierce, a planner in charge of the program, has been presenting the handbook to a number of townships and boroughs in Chester and Delaware counties and encouraging local municipalities to subscribe to an updating service. The service keeps the ordinances current with recent court decisions and pertinent changes in state legislation on an annual basis. In addition, new ordinances are developed and added to the handbook in response to the needs of townships subscribing to the program.

A considerable number of Chester and Delaware County townships have adopted one or more ordinances and have subscribed to the updating service. The Conservancy also has begun to cooperate with other nearby county planning commissions and with Pennsylvania state officials to bring about wider use of the ordinances.

John and I also worked with the Delaware River Basin Commission to see what further actions it might take to manage the water supply and water quality of the entire Delaware basin.[22] One recommendation which we made was that the Commission set standards for the use of all flood plain land within the basin. It has taken the first step toward establishing standards for use of flood plains and expects to move further in this direction in the near future.

Bob Coughlin, with much help from Tom Hammer and some help from me and others, has just finished a study for the City of Philadelphia and the Commonwealth of Pennsylvania which drew extensively on our Brandywine experience.[23] Part of Philadelphia's magnificent Fairmount Park lies along Wissahickon Creek. Near the park and within the Wissahickon watershed is a considerable amount of prime development land. We were to determine how urbanization of the various undeveloped parcels would affect the hydrology, ecology, and amenity of the Wissahickon portion of the park and to recommend how much development of what sort to allow in various locations and how to limit development through regulation.

TAXATION. Bucks County, under the leadership of John Carson, was the first to test the law authorizing owners of land used for farm, forest, water supply, or open space purposes to covenant with the county in which the land is located to continue the current use in return for an assurance that taxation would be based solely on the value of the land for that use. The county was at once challenged on the ground that the law was unconstitutional. The suit alleged that this was a form of preferential assessment in violation of the uniformity clause of the Pennsylvania constitution. The Common Pleas Court of Bucks County and the Commonwealth Court of Pennsylvania upheld the law. The Commonwealth Court said, in part:

Initially we must note that Act 515 would not appear to us to be a tax statute, and the uniformity clause, therefore, would not apply. . . . although the Act does provide that land restricted by a covenant shall be assessed at a value as so restricted, it does not directly impose any tax nor does it exempt any property from taxation. Even if Act 515 were a taxing statute, however, we do not believe that it would be violative of the uniformity clause of the Constitution. . . . Act 515 merely provides that a county may covenant that a tax assessment will reflect the fair market value of the land as restricted by the covenant.[24]

While the case was progressing through the courts, a constitutional amendment was passed authorizing preferential assessment of such lands. The legislature, in November of 1974, passed enabling legislation modeled after Act 515. Therefore, insofar as lower taxes are an incentive to keep land in open space uses, Pennsylvania landowners have that incentive available to them. Chester and Montgomery counties now are adopting regulations to enable landowners to apply for covenants.

Many people question the utility of this approach. A Ralph Nader task force has shown that in Connecticut, under a similar law, much of the land under covenant was soon developed. It was cheaper for developers to put the land in the covenant program and pay the back tax and the small penalty when ready to develop than to pay market value taxes every year. Although the Pennsylvania penalty is somewhat steeper than that in Connecticut, the same thing could well happen here. Bucks County has 2,200 properties, each consisting of fifty acres or more, already under covenant. The chairman of the Bucks County Commissioners recommended to a state legislative hearing that the compound interest penalty be raised to 10 percent from the current 5 percent,[25] but this recommendation was not adopted.

Several of the land use controls which we proposed initially for the Upper East Branch are now being tried. Easements have been acquired by gift, purchase, and eminent domain. Bucks County, several municipalities, and a few private organizations have purchased the fee title to land and then resold the land subject to easements limiting future use. Two private organizations are establishing development corporations to acquire land, develop a portion of it, and restrict the remainder to permanent open space uses.

BUCKS COUNTY. John Carson and Bucks County were the first to use the law (known as Act 442[26]) authorizing county and state acquisitions, by eminent domain or otherwise, of less than fee interests. Bucks County created the Neshaminy Water Resources Authority to implement the Bucks County portion of the joint Bucks County-Montgomery County-U.S. Soil Conservation Service program.[27] Bucks County floated an $8 million bond issue to cover land acquisition costs for ten dam and reservoir sites covering 5,132 acres. As of 1973, land acquisition is 98 percent complete, at an expenditure of about $14,184 million, averaging $2,760 per acre over all. Of this amount easements averaged $1,378 per acre; fee purchase averaged $2,973 per acre, or a ratio of easement to fee of 1:2.16. John Carson was put in charge of carrying out the project.

In 1970 John Keene and I asked Sondra Slade to make a detailed study of the Bucks County experience with acquisition of conservation and flooding easement for one of these project sites. Her report[28] provided much necessary information on problems of appraising and negotiating for easements. She gave great credit to John Carson and Bucks County for being willing to take the initiative to fund and carry out the program:

When it was decided that the Neshaminy Creek project was not to await the pleasure of the local governing bodies, a huge hurdle to its success was obliterated. On the other hand, those in charge of the project were canny enough to realize that all opposition by the municipalities could not be stemmed without a "sweetener." Recognizing that the chief concern of most local governing bodies is the tax rate and the loss of ratables, the county foresightedly undertook to pay all taxes—township, school district and even county taxes—on all properties acquired by it until such time as actual construction begins or, in the case of Act 442 lands, until they are sold, as is required by the Act, to private individuals. There has been, under these circumstances, no local governmental opposition to the program because there was no focus for municipal opposition.

There are three additional factors which have contributed greatly to the smooth and efficient operation of the program. First, unlike most and perhaps all other boards of county commissioners, the Bucks commissioners have taken an affirmative approach toward their problems and the suggested solutions for those problems. They have been at pains to find answers, not to reject them. They have recognized over the years that theirs is a pleasant, largely rural county with a good environment and they have and are willing to spend money to preserve that environment as the county becomes more populous. They have assembled an extremely competent group of planners and, when the decision was taken to establish a Neshaminy Water Resources Authority, appointed to it not those who represented special interest groups but five eminent Bucks Countians from varying walks of life who could have no conflict between their professional or business allegiances and their Authority membership. Secondly, as mentioned earlier, Bucks County committed a large sum of money to the program which gave it the great advantage of not having to be operated on a shoe string. And finally, the driving force behind the program has been an exceptional, man, John T. Carson, Jr., a biologist and Director of the Division of Natural Resources of the Bucks County Planning Commission, who is greatly admired not only by his own staff but by all who know him.

Two types of easement were acquired: a flooding easement for the land around the reservoir which is subject to occasional flooding and a conservation easement covering the remainder of the abutting properties. Impervious coverage in both areas is limited to 15 percent, and the amount of erosion permitted may not exceed three tons per acre per year. In addition, existing structures are to be removed from the flooding easement areas, and no new structures may be erected. Of course the area subject to the flooding easement will continue to be flooded on occasion.

Appraisal of the two types of easement proved difficult due to lack of precedent. However, after a difficult start the negotiators had considerable success in reaching voluntary agreement on easement prices. In a few cases, however, condemnation was necessary. In such instances, the fee to the whole parcel was condemned, and the land was resold subject to easement. As Sandy Slade concluded:

The single largest problem in conducting an easement acquisition program has, in the case of the Neshaminy project, proved to be the appraisal of easements. For the future, and until such time as there is more learning on the subject, the experience gleaned from the project may offer some guidelines if not solutions for appraisal problems in similar programs. Chief among these is that appraisals which are to form the basis for offers for the sale of easements must bear some reasonable relationship to the value of the property as a whole. Since the conservation easement is going to be impressed upon the entire parcel, its value, whether or not it—or the applicable zoning by itself— inhibits further development, cannot be said to be *de minimis*. Certainly, in the mind of the landowner, it is not *de minimis* and experience has shown that three percent or four percent or even in some cases ten percent valuations for conservation easements have resulted in demands for fee taking. The conservation easement when combined with a flooding easement should

Private property and the public interest

bear an even more substantial relationship to the value of the entire property since the flooding easement most assuredly does prevent further development even on a property which is not subdividable.

Finally, those appraising proposed land acquisitions must be so trained and instructed as to conduct their appraisals with a minimum of contact with and annoyance to the involved landowners. It is the appraiser's function only to form an estimate of value. It is the negotiator who must bargain.

The possibilities of planning and carrying through to completion a watershed program such as the Neshaminy project initially and ultimately depend upon an enlightened body politic and a highly competent staff intelligently and forcefully directed. These the Neshaminy program had in abundance. The body politic committed itself to the program; the staff is loyal, able and dedicated. The leadership is brilliant.

Land acquisition for this 161-acre reservoir site was completed in July 1971. It is ironic that, since this was the initial experiment with the new less than fee law, most owners in this site elected to sell in fee (thirteen properties, consisting of 151 acres, were acquired in fee at a cost of $655,337, or $4340 per acre including buildings). Those few who sold flood and conservation easements only (all of them small propertyowners with homes on their land) totaled six, covering 10 acres, at a cost of $20,641, or $2,064 per acre for the easements. Thus, the ratio of easement cost to fee purchase was 1:2.10.

Three of the properties which were bought in fee were resold after the flood and conservation easements were imposed. These three properties totaled 7.08 acres, of which 3.2 acres was in the flood area. Their fee cost was $102,577, including buildings. They were resold for a net price of $83,677. Thus, the easement cost was $2,670 per acre.

In December 1971, after imposing the easement restrictions and after a careful reappraisal of the value of the easements, the Authority offered another 15 acres of fee-purchased land for sale in whole or part by sealed bid. All bids were rejected, since they did not equal the appraised value. It is the consensus of Bucks County officials that the land be held for resale after the reservoir has been built, since the presence of a 10-acre permanent lake will enhance its value; and the uncertainty in the potential buyer's mind as to what he is getting will be dispelled.

A 1973 Bucks County Planning Commission report urged expanded use of easements to protect many types of natural resource areas, and particularly prime farm land.

THE TRI-COUNTY CONSERVANCY. The Tri-County Conservancy also has acquired some easements. As a private organization it has no power under Act 442. Its seven easements, covering 411 acres along Brandywine Creek, all have been donated by people committed to preserving the flood plain in an open, natural condition. The Conservancy hopes that other landowners will follow this lead and create a protected area from the junction of the east and west branches of the Brandywine south to Wilmington, where it would meet a city park. Since the easements have been donated to the Conservancy, the donors are entitled to claim a charitable deduction on their federal income tax equal to the value of their easements. The easement gifts made so far have come from wealthy landowners. For others, the tax advantage of a charitable deduction may be insufficient compensation. As the Conservancy staff approach people upstream, away from the area of large estates, they are finding that people are willing to sell, but not to donate, easements.

In September of 1973 the Conservancy announced its first land development project. It was instrumental in forming a limited partnership which then purchased a 192-acre estate overlooking the Brandywine Valley. The property is a historic one which was the scene of fighting during the Battle of the Brandywine in 1777. The Conservancy is planning cluster-type development compatible with preservation of the five historic structures located on the site and with protection of the amenity of the valley. It may continue to hold title to the land kept as open space. It is hoped that the development plan will serve as an environmental model which others will wish to emulate. Further, it is intended as the first acquisition in a long-range program. The Conservancy hopes to develop a mechanism through which it can purchase sizable tracts of land, define critical open space areas, and allow proper development on those portions of the tract suitable for habitation. Maintenance of the open space areas would be supported by those persons purchasing homes, since they would be the prime users of such open space.

PENNYPACK CREEK. A program of great potential significance is taking shape in part of the Pennypack Creek watershed. The Pennypack rises in Montgomery and Bucks counties and flows through Philadelphia to its junction with the Delaware River. Philadelphia land adjacent to the creek is part of the city park system. Beyond the park borders, the land is almost totally developed. In Montgomery and Bucks counties much of the watershed has been developed, with low- and medium-density housing predominant. There is one island of undeveloped land, mostly in a few large estates, which lies about midway between the headwaters of the Pennypack and its confluence with the Delaware. It is open for an unusual reason. The landowners came there early in the

Private property and the public interest

twentieth century to found a community centered on their church, the Swedenborgian Church of the New Jerusalem. Many members of the community prospered greatly and invested much of their wealth in the church, the church-run school system, and their homes. Few left the area, and what growth there was mainly represented the growth of the original families. Nearby development has touched the residents, particularly through the pollution of Pennypack Creek.

Recently, under the leadership of Feodor Pitcairn, a descendant of one of the founding families, the landowners have joined together to plan for the future of the area. Working in cooperation with the Pennypack Watershed Association and several consultants, they have devised a plan which provides for some growth while protecting those areas most sensitive ecologically. If the plan is implemented, some 1,600 acres would be kept in open space. The 700 acres adjacent to the stream would be managed by the Watershed Association as a public nature area. Another 600 acres would be leased to neighboring sewage treatment plants to be used as a "living filter" on which treated effluent would be sprayed. Executive campuses would be developed on a small portion of the land to provide some profit from the land and tax ratables to the municipalities. Cluster development would keep much of the remaining land in private open space, subject to some form of development rights.

It is proposed that the forty-six principal propertyowners form a corporation to manage use of the land in accord with the plan and to work with the appropriate private and public agencies—the Watershed Association, the three municipalities, Montgomery and Bucks counties, the Pennsylvania Department of Environmental Resources, and, in particular, the sewer authorities. The specifics governing the ownership of land, the tax implications of possible alternatives, and the distribution of profits have yet to be worked out. However, so far the landowners are strongly supportive of the concept.

Because the initiative and leadership are local, I think that there is real promise that the Pennypack Corridor Program will come to fruition. During my visits there as a consultant, I have found a sense of excitement and commitment which we, as outsiders, never succeeded in generating in the Upper East Branch. There are other advantages: the area is small, there are few propertyowners, people are bound together in a stable group by a common religious commitment, and, since most of the landowners are wealthy, return from the land is not an overriding consideration.

IX

conclusions

IT SHOULD BE apparent to those who have read this saga of planning that I still believe firmly in our goals but am convinced that we made major errors in attempting to implement them. The Brandywine experience can have a larger significance insofar as it may influence other planning efforts. These conclusions are hardly new ones, and to that extent we are at fault for not having learned from others before us. However, perhaps the relation of the conclusions to the specifics of our experience will make them more vivid and meaningful to others.

The nature of the goals

It is necessary but not sufficient to know what the goals of a plan are. It also is essential to characterize them: for instance, are they long-term or short-term, major or minor, complex or simple? This characterization is vital in selecting an appropriate client for the plan. The Brandywine Plan goals were to accommodate normal growth, protect the water resources, and preserve the natural amenities in an urbanizing watershed; and to compare the costs and benefits of the land use plan chosen with those of conventional development. Thus our goals were long-term, major, and complex.

We needed several years to develop and implement the plan. The land use controls would have been permanent and would have affected development over many decades. For demonstration purposes, at least a decade following implementation was required to monitor the watershed and the control watershed.

The major impact of the goals was in their reliance on increased government control of land use. We—accurately, I think—described the plan as conservative in its proposals for use of land. All of the development area could have been zoned in any manner preferred by the townships. The maximum gross density for the woods and steep slopes of four acres differed little from the existing zoning provisions. Much of the flood plain land already was barred from development under township setback regulations. However, if the land use proposals were conservative, the controls were revolutionary to the people of the Upper East Branch. Acceptance of them demanded a new view of the roles of the private landowner and government. One could hardly have picked a more fundamental issue.

193

No part of the Brandywine Plan was simple, and all its parts were interrelated. For water resource protection we were concerned with flooding, drought, ground water recharge, erosion, sedimentation, water supply, and waste disposal. Boundary definitions, hardship rules, and gross density limits represented attempts to achieve equity and flexibility within the framework of the planning goals. The offer of a choice among a variety of land use controls was influenced in part by a desire to suit each landowner, but also by our wish to learn which controls worked best under what circumstances. The comprehensive, comparative cost-benefit analysis which we had hoped to develop would have required data of great diversity and accuracy and a complex and novel model. The goals of the Brandywine Plan could not have been changed, but they should have exerted more of an influence on our choice of a client.

Choice of a client

Assuming that the planner has a set of goals and is seeking a client who will implement them, what are the key factors in choice of client? First, the client should share not only the planner's goals but their underlying rationale. It is far less desirable to have goals shared for divergent reasons. Equally important, the client must be able to implement the goals. Since power always is circumscribed, particularly by time and by other commitments, this suggests that the client must place the goals of the plan high on his list of priorities.

In selecting the Chester County Water Resources Authority as our client, we did consider these factors. However, I believe that we misjudged the Authority on all counts. Bob Struble and the county commissioners in office in 1965 did share our goals for future land use in the Brandywine. So did the members of the Water Resources Authority, though their level of interest ranged from tepid to keen. However, none of these persons was committed to our other major goal—a valid cost-benefit demonstration. There was absolutely no reason why they should have shared this goal and, in fact, it would have been extraordinary had they done so. County-level planning is concerned with short- and medium-term solutions to immediate local problems. We hoped for a demonstration that would have significance to urbanizing areas throughout the country for some years to come. The top officials in Pennsylvania and New Jersey and at the Delaware River Basin Commission did share this goal, which was more nearly compatible with state or regional concerns than with county, let alone municipal, concerns. John Carson in Bucks County also shared both of our goals, but the breadth of his interest was personal and could not be said to reflect the views of other county officials.

Our clients became, in fact, the residents of the Upper East Branch. Applying the test of shared goals, might we intentionally have chosen the residents of a watershed as our primary client, with the assumption that they, in turn, would involve government as a secondary client? The current planning under way in the Pennypack watershed suggests that this is a possibility, yet I suspect that it is uncommon. Even in the Pennypack the planning is by leading citizens and does not involve broad popular participation. Many people on the urban fringe wish to preserve natural amenities while recognizing that growth is inevitable, but few are ready to invest the time and thought to develop an acceptable plan for an area of any size. A crisis—the threat of a state park or a large-scale development—can rouse many, but only to repel the threat. Even then, sensitivity to the crisis declines rapidly with distance from the crisis area. Planning for a single-purpose limited objective, such as creation of the Brandywine River Museum, can engender public support and participation. Planning for something as diffuse, complex, and far-reaching as the future development of a watershed does not lend itself to widespread public participation.

There was a further, inevitable conflict between one of our goals and those of residents of an urban fringe watershed. Planning for normal future growth meant providing opportunities for people of various income levels to live in the watershed and enjoy the amenities preserved. If the present residents of a watershed are rich, they tend to want to preserve the watershed and block further growth. If they are less well off, they are inclined to want some development but only the kind which will attract top prices for their land and enhance the local tax base. Few now living in a lovely place want housing opportunities there for those less well off. A regional or state agency has a sufficiently diverse constituency to share our goal; a county agency may or may not. I find it less likely that the self-interest of the current residents of a watershed will coincide with the broader interest of providing for those who may live in the watershed in the future.

What about Honey Brook Township, which voted for the plan? I think that the local leaders and some of the large landowners did share our goals. Some were Amish farmers, some were gentry with a love of the land, and some were individuals of diverse backgrounds who shared these values. Had we concentrated our efforts in Honey Brook, it is possible that our goals and theirs might have been compatible

Private property and the public interest

enough for the plan to succeed. Because the population there is less mobile than in many other fringe townships, the local officials are more widely known and probably exercise more influence.

This brings us back to the question of power. Who had the power to carry out the Brandywine Plan? All levels of government which we considered as possible clients had the legal authority, but which had the political power? Clearly, neither the Chester County Water Resources Authority nor the commissioners, since they deferred to the townships, which, in turn, deferred to their residents. The Water Resources Authority had one project of much higher priority, Marsh Creek. Much political capital was being expended in the Upper East Branch area to make that dam come into being. There was little reserve left to draw upon for the Brandywine Plan. Further, from the Authority's perspective, Marsh Creek was necessary while the Brandywine Plan was only desirable.

I judge that the first set of county commissioners with whom we dealt placed a medium priority on the Brandywine Plan. They wanted to know what political support it was likely to cost them, and they were willing to lose some for its sake. Their Republican successors gave it a very low priority; if people wanted it, they could have it. Since the Democratic commissioner owed his election in part to opposition to the plan, he had an obvious stake in its defeat. We should have been more aware of the political currents in the county prior to making our choice and should have foreseen the change in power at least as a possibility.

Would the Delaware River Basin Commission have had the power to act? Surely not, unless requested to do so by a county or municipality. Despite its compatible goals, the plan would not have been worth enough to the Commission for it to risk exercising power in a novel way. As a regional agency with teeth, it already had enough enemies and was moving cautiously and gradually in asserting its authority. Using eminent domain to acquire development rights contrary to local wishes would have exposed it to too much fire.

What about the states? Pennsylvania would have assigned a high priority to implementing the plan but would have been crippled politically without county and township support. The statewide township associations are a potent force in the state legislature, which, of course, controls departmental appropriations. In New Jersey, state government is stronger and has a more activist history. Past state programs to acquire open space and current programs to protect wetlands and flood plains and to manage solid waste disposal lend support to the notion that New Jersey might have had the power as well as the will to act with or without local endorsement.

Bucks County, too, might have had the muscle to go ahead without township approval. It was first in Pennsylvania to acquire easements under the open space law and to implement the tax covenant law, good evidence of political priorities and power at the county level. So, too, is the county's initiative in implementing a county-wide solid waste disposal plan and in approving a large bond issue for the small watershed program. Bucks County government is competent and confident.

To reinforce my earlier conclusion, without a powerful, committed client who shares his goals, the planner has no chance of seeing those goals realized. Even then, unforeseeable and unpredictable events may so alter the political climate that action becomes impossible.

The climate for change

We have been discussing a plan which seeks to bring about major change of a complex sort. Early implementation may be critical because, with delay, the opportunity to act may be foreclosed by rising costs and/or alternative land use decisions. Therefore, a gradual and piecemeal approach is unlikely to suffice.

How is it possible to predict people's receptivity to a proposal for major change? Certainly it will turn on how they see the change—as good, bad, or neither. However, even where the change is viewed positively, the status quo is always attractive. People don't like change. It can be argued that where stable, rigid living patterns have been fractured by change, new ideas are easier to introduce. It can also be argued that rapid changes may outpace people's capacity to absorb them and so may engender feelings of apprehension and instability.

Unless or until people lose hope of being able to influence the course of change, they may fight fiercely against it. At a time when many individuals feel that they have lost control of the events which shape their lives, the power to determine the future pattern of local land use seems still to be within their grasp. More often than not, this is but an illusion, but it regularly causes people to band together to fight land use changes. The victories gained often are Pyrrhic ones.

It is possible that major changes in land use policy and land use controls may be most acceptable at a time when people can see that the magnitude of forthcoming growth has brought the adequacy of past policies into question but before that growth has brought a surfeit of change. In this sense, the Brandywine Plan was premature. Our attitude studies showed that in 1966 people felt little development pressure and that in 1971 they felt some pressure but still believed that conventional land use controls could regulate growth to their satisfaction. Our perception of the nearness of change was not shared by the Upper East Branch residents, and we did not succeed in altering their perceptions. Yet the plan could not possibly have been implemented had urbanization been much more advanced in the Upper East Branch. Land costs would have been prohibitive, and the ability to protect water resources would have been impaired.

Some major changes may never be viewed as good by the residents of an area. In such cases perhaps the most that can be hoped for is that they will be accepted as the least worst of a number of alternatives. For this to occur, the other alternatives must appear as real threats. If they do not, and if there is strong local opposition to the change, the public agency seeking to act must have adequate support from its constituents outside the area. This situation is most likely where the impact and benefits of the change are widely distributed. The failure of the Upper East Branch residents to stop the utilities' high voltage line and gas pipeline is an illustration. Thus a regional housing plan or a regional parks plan has a better chance of success than a plan for a single housing or park project.

Given these observations, an experiment such as the Brandywine Plan is particularly difficult to carry through. Its benefits are hard for the public to grasp. It disrupts the status quo and asks people to live with some uncertainty. It must go forward before people have recognized the need for change and have evaluated alternatives. All of these handicaps lead me to reiterate that the commitment of the client to the plan and the political strength of the client are far and away the most critical factors determining its success or failure. As I have said before, we should have given this one factor as much weight as the sum of all others in choosing a site.

What we planners did was also critical. There is no doubt we focused on the technical credibility of the plan to the detriment of adequate communication with the Upper East Branch residents. We all agreed that the area was too big and the time too short. However, even if we had limited the plan to Indian Run, we would have needed more staff in the field. We wanted people to give up a basic value. For this to occur, they needed to understand clearly the rationale behind the plan. They also needed to know us and the Water Resources Authority well enough to trust us. Had such trust existed, our opponents would not have found such fertile soil for their rumors. We *were* technocrats from outside, as they charged. Our lives, our future expectations of income, and our sense of personal control were *not* affected by the plan. Theirs were, and we owed them more than they received.

The technical quality of the plan was important, particularly since it was intended as a prototype. Establishing base line hydrologic data was essential. So were good appraisals. However, much of the detailed and costly work that went into accurate boundary maps, sub-basin measurements, and land value records could have been postponed until implementation of the plan was assured. With those funds we could have hired qualified field staff to work with Ken.

Choosing an area whose population was somewhat skewed in favor of our proposals would, in one sense, have diminished the value of the plan as a prototype. However, if this change materially increased the chances for implementing the plan, I think that it would have been justified. The information gathered from an actual demonstration has greater value than that from a pristine but rejected plan.

The development corporation was a good idea. Its principal merits were assuring everyone of a chance to share in the gains from future development and placing land management in local hands. We should have introduced the idea sooner and promoted it more vigorously.

Our continued insistence on eminent domain was crippling. Were we right, or was there a better alternative? My present view is that we judged correctly the importance of implementing the plan consistently throughout a watershed but that we clearly misjudged the depth of opposition to eminent domain. With a smaller planning area, a somewhat different population mix, more contact with residents, and more time, our chances of winning extensive support for eminent domain would have improved. Never could one anticipate universal support. However, with substantial support, one could expect that the public agency involved would go ahead, using eminent domain where necessary.

Once we had accepted the futility of winning wide support for eminent domain in the Upper East Branch, we had several choices: to quit at once, to try a voluntary scheme, or to go somewhere else and start over, applying the lessons already learned. We wanted to try the last two. Bob Struble and Ken wanted to try to sign up owners of 80 percent of the Indian Run critical area. The rest of us also wanted to make a parallel effort to see whether the people of the Paunnacussing would endorse the plan with eminent domain. However, lack of money stopped us before we learned whether either would work.

At Indian Run the risk was that, on achieving 80 percent participa-

Private property and the public interest

tion and buying easements, owners of nonparticipating land would develop it, profiting at the expense of the participating owners and destroying the demonstration potential of the watershed. In the Paunnacussing, there was the risk that the plan might not be implemented, even though the area was small, more people were predisposed to accept its premises, and the political leadership behind it was outstanding. In either event, the public and private agencies investing money in the plan would find their judgment questioned. Ford already had invested generously and was unwilling to gamble on further ventures. HUD was waiting to make a commitment until success was assured. Foundation officials and government leaders call for innovation, yet seldom are they prepared to take the risks which that entails. We were fortunate in having had as much foundation, federal, and state support as we did, yet I cannot help but wish that our backers had stayed with us until we determined whether the Indian Run or Paunnacussing alternatives would work.

From this one might conclude that to generate support, one should be right the first time around. This is as unlikely in planning as in the rest of the activities of life.

notes

NOTES FOR CHAPTER II

1. Royal Commission on the Geographical Distribution of the Industrial Population, *Report and Evidence* (London: His Majesty's Stationery Office, 1940); Expert Committee on Compensation and Betterment, *Final Report*, Cmd. 6389 (London: His Majesty's Stationery Office, 1942). Together these reports laid the foundation for Great Britain's many postwar experiments with government intervention to redistribute gains and losses in the private land market.

2. As set forth in the Town and Country Planning Act of 1947.

3. Land Commission (Dissolution) Act 1971, c. 18.

4. See Ann Louise Strong, *Planned Urban Environments: Sweden, Finland, Israel, The Netherlands, France* (Baltimore: Johns Hopkins Press, 1972), for discussion of the differing approaches in Sweden, Finland, Israel, The Netherlands, and France.

5. Abrams was an authority on housing and planning. He served as a consultant to the United Nations and other international organizations.

6. William H. Whyte drafted a conservation program for the state of Connecticut, wrote the proposal later enacted by the Johnson administration as the Urban Beautification Program, and published several highly influential books, including *Cluster Development*, *The Organization Man*, and *The Last Landscape*.

7. William Matuszeski, "Less Than Fee Acquisition for Open Space: Its Effect on Land Value" (Philadelphia, Pa.: Institute for Environmental Studies, University of Pennsylvania, 1968).

8. Until his death, Jacob Beuscher was professor of law at the University of Wisconsin.

9. Professor of law at Washington University, St. Louis.

10. Griggs v. Allegheny County, 369 U.S. 84, 82 S.Ct. 531, 7 L.Ed. 2d 585 (1962).

11. Professors of law at the University of Pennsylvania Law School and Rutgers University Law School, respectively.

12. For detailed explanations of the compensable regulations proposal, see Jan Krasnowiecki and Ann Louise Strong, "Compensable Regulations for Open Space: A Means of Controlling Open Space," *Journal of the American Institute of Planners* 29 (1963), and Jan Krasnowiecki and James C. N. Paul, "The Preservation of Open Space in Metropolitan Areas," *University of Pennsylvania Law Review* 110 (1961): 179-237.

13. Formerly he was secretary of Forests and Waters. This department then became part of the new Department of Environmental Resources.

14. See Ann Louise Strong, "Incentives and Controls for Open Space," in *Metropolitan Open Space and Natural Process*, ed. David A. Wallace (Philadelphia, Pa.: University of Pennsylvania Press, 1970), for a further discussion of this idea.

15. *Open Space for Urban America* (Washington, D.C.: Department of Housing and Urban Development, 1965).

16. See, for instance, Kamrowski v. Wisconsin, 31 Wis. 2d 256, 142 N.W. 2d 793 (1966) (scenic easements); Cheney v. Village II at New Hope, 429 Pa. 626, 241 A2d 81 (1968) (cluster); Griggs case, cited in n. 10 above (inverse condemnation); Kansas City v. Kindle, 446 S.W. 2d 807 (Mo. 1969) (compensatory zoning).

17. Bob Coughlin holds an M.C.P. degree from M.I.T. and a Ph.D. degree from the University of Pennsylvania. Before joining the Regional Science Research Institute he was chief of comprehensive planning for the Philadelphia City Plan-

ning Commission. Ben Stevens received both his M.C.P. and Ph.D. degrees from M.I.T. Regional planning and economics has been his area of specialization.

18. Ann Louise Strong, "A Time To Experiment," *National Civic Review* 54 (1965), adapted from a speech at the Municipal League's annual conference in 1964.

19. Professor of city planning at the University of Pennsylvania.

20. Wallace is a planning consultant with Wallace McHarg Roberts and Todd, Philadelphia. See Ann Louise Strong and William Grigsby, "Plan for the Valleys" (Philadelphia, Pa.: Wallace-McHarg Associates, 1964).

21. See Strong, "Incentives and Controls for Open Space."

22. Strong, "A Time To Experiment."

NOTES FOR CHAPTER III

1. J.D., Harvard Law School, M.C.P., University of Pennsylvania, and now associate professor of city and regional planning, University of Pennsylvania.

2. J.D., Harvard Law School, and now a senior attorney at the Council on Environmental Quality.

3. See William Matuszeski, "Less Than Fee Acquisition for Open Space: Its Effect on Land Values" (Philadelphia, Pa.: Institute for Environmental Studies, University of Pennsylvania, 1968). See the report for specific findings.

4. Luna B. Leopold holds a B.S. in civil engineering from the University of Wisconsin, a M.S. in physics and meteorology from the University of California at Los Angeles, and a Ph.D. in geology from Harvard. He is currently professor of geology and geophysics at the University of California at Berkeley.

5. Later research by Bob Coughlin and others at the Regional Science Research Institute showed strong preferences among a diverse group of people for the same views that we found beautiful. See chs. 5 and 6 in Robert E. Coughlin and Thomas R. Hammer, *Stream Quality Preservation through Planned Urban Development*, EPA–R5–73–019 (Washington, D.C.: U.S. Government Printing Office, 1973).

6. Dated August 18, 1965.

7. Paul Van Wegen was later appointed U.S. commissioner for the Delaware River Basin Commission.

8. Reported in *Philadelphia Inquirer*, January 14, 1971.

9. Now Congressman Coughlin.

10. 16 P.S. 11941 et seq.

11. Memorandum from Vernon D. Northrop, U.S. commissioner, dated June 2, 1966.

12. Now director of the Water Resources Authority.

13. *Sunday Bulletin*, May 1, 1966.

14. *Daily Local News*, April 19, 1966.

15. Letter dated May 10, 1966.

NOTES FOR CHAPTER IV

1. December 13, 1966.

2. Now professor of law at American University.

3. Among them were Mavra Iano, Stephen Bayly, D. Barlow Burke, Jr., Carolyn Ganschow, Anita Holland-Moritz, Dennis Sachs, and L. Scott Seaman.

4. Judith Benedict and Cheryl Wasserman, *The Brandywine—Five Years After* (Philadelphia, Pa.: Institute for Environmental Studies, University of Pennsylvania, 1971).

5. Assistant professor of geology, University of Wisconsin.

6. See Mark D. Menchik, "Brandywine Residents and Their Attitudes toward the